'Beautifully written and full of p
will lead you into and through t
invite you to reflect on its rel
prepared to be surprised and excited, even amid the challenging times through which we are living.'

Prof. Craig Bartholomew, author and Biblical scholar

'Andrew Ollerton sketches out a remarkably accessible roadmap for those who want to trace the big story that Scripture tells. For the believer, seeker, sceptic or just-plain-confused, this is an essential guide to understanding how the Bible continues to speak to modern life today.'

Justin Brierley, Unbelievable? show host,
Premier Christian Radio

'For over 40 years, I have been reading, studying and teaching the Bible and I can attest to you, from my own experience and the experiences of thousands of others, that there is no book in the world like the Bible. After reading, *The Bible: A Story That Makes Sense of Life*, I think you'll agree.'

Brian Brodersen, Director, Creation Fest UK and
Senior Pastor, Calvary Chapel (California)

'Full of examples and stories, this book provokes the reader to discover more of the Bible for themselves. It will be great as a devotional or small group resource for people hoping to encounter God again in our time.'

Deirdre Brower-Latz, Principal of Nazarene Theological
College, University of Manchester

'Practical, accessible and inspiring. This wonderful book highlights the relevance, power and necessity of the greatest book ever to the lives of all people.'

Gavin Calver, CEO, Evangelical Alliance

'Andrew Ollerton's *The Bible: A Story That Makes Sense of Life* stands out like a luminous gem. This is an expertly written and user-friendly guide to the book of all books. Andrew brings his gifts as a scholar and pastor to bear and has produced an amazing resource which is in-depth and illuminating but also practical and applied.'

Greg Downes, Director of Ministerial Training and Dean of the Wesley Centre, Wycliffe Hall, University of Oxford

'Andrew Ollerton's guided tour of the world's bestselling book will help both seasoned readers and those new to the Bible encounter the God who is able to meet our deep desires for meaning, freedom, peace, love, community and home.'

Peter Dray, Head of Creative Evangelism, UCCF: The Christian Unions

'Dr Ollerton not only opens up an accessible way to make sense of this complex, powerful book, but he also distils from it a lively, attractive account of Christian essentials, punctuated by vivid personal anecdotes.'

Prof. David F. Ford, Emeritus Regius Professor of Divinity, University of Cambridge

'Andrew offers us not just keys to understanding the Bible but also skilfully makes sense of our own purpose within the beautiful narrative. The wildest most wonderful thing any generation whispers to the next is that we are written into God's story – this book celebrates and embraces this essential truth.'

Rachel Gardner, Director of Youthscape and author of *The Girl Deconstruction Project*

'Honest, revealing insight into the bestselling book of all time.'

Bear Grylls, adventurer and Chief Scout

‘A stimulating and accessible survey of history’s most influential book.’

Tom Holland, historian and author of *Dominion*

‘Ollerton is a master communicator, and here he manages to make something so vast so relatable. A very human, accessible read that will open your eyes and cause you to open your Bible.’

Paul Kerensa, comedy writer and stand-up comedian

‘This is a masterpiece. Andrew Ollerton takes the complexities and intricacies of the Bible and arranges them in an accessible and engaging way. Punctuated with great stories, carefully chosen metaphors, humour and insight, *The Bible: A Story That Makes Sense of Life* masterfully pulls together the threads of the greatest story ever known.’

Phil Knox, Evangelical Alliance

‘A really helpful guide for those wanting to understand the world’s most influential book.’

Elizabeth Oldfield, Director of Theos

‘This very well-written, widely researched work conveys Andrew’s great love for the Bible and his desire that we might know its divine author and his great plan for our lives. This excellent resource will be a blessing to many.’

Dave Smith, Senior Pastor, KingsGate Church (Peterborough)

‘For many of us, the Bible feels inaccessible or outdated. This book brings it to life in a way that makes sense. Andrew explores the world of the Bible and relates it brilliantly to our contemporary lives today. Personal and profound; informative and practical. If you want to experience the Bible as a rich source of guidance and hope, this book is for you.’

Simon Thomas, former Sky Sports and Blue Peter presenter

'Like the very best of tour guides, Andrew Ollerton leads us through the Bible's plotline in a highly informative, compelling, and entertaining way. This book will enhance your experience of the Bible, no matter who you are or where you're at on your journey.'

Paul Woolley, CEO London Institute for Contemporary Christianity

'Every now and again, a book comes along which makes such overriding sense and joins up so many figurative dots that you can hardly put it down. Few people succeed in expounding and communicating the complex spiritual truths of the Bible with such clarity and ease as Andrew Ollerton.'

Siân Wyn Rees, Director, Evangelical Alliance (Wales)

'In this compelling book Andrew unlocks the big themes of life by exploring the Bible with a rare combination of passion and expertise. If you want to understand the story of your life, I can think of no better place to start than in the pages of this book.'

Pete Wynter, Director, HTB Leadership College London

'Andrew Ollerton brings the Bible to life in ways that make it highly accessible and show its relevance to our daily lives. He skilfully disarms our modern confusion by revealing, in striking and simple terms, what the Bible meant to its original audience and how surprisingly up-to-date this ancient text really is.'

Paul Williams, CEO, British and Foreign Bible Society

# THE BIBLE

## A Story That Makes Sense of Life

# THE BIBLE

## A Story That Makes Sense of Life

ANDREW OLLERTON

First published in Great Britain in 2020 by Hodder & Stoughton
An Hachette UK company

1


Diagrams by Neal Manning
Maps by Rosie Collins

Paul's Missionary Journeys, Jerusalem and the Time of Jesus and Abraham's Journey Copyright © British and Foreign Bible Society. Used by permission



A CIP catalogue record for this title is available from the British Library

Trade Paperback ISBN 978 1 529 32700 7
eBook ISBN 978 1 529 32702 1

Typeset in Ehrhardt by Hewer Text UK Ltd, Edinburgh
Printed and bound in Great Britain by Clays Ltd, Elcograf S.p.A.

Hodder & Stoughton policy is to use papers that are natural, renewable and recyclable products and made from wood grown in sustainable forests. The logging and manufacturing processes are expected to conform to the environmental regulations of the country of origin.

Hodder & Stoughton Ltd
Carmelite House
50 Victoria Embankment
London EC4Y 0DZ

www.hodderfaith.com

# Contents

# Acknowledgements

I am deeply grateful to so many who have invested in this book. The team at Hodder have been so helpful and enthusiastic. In particular my editor, Joanna, for her patience and expertise along the way. I've been humbled by the attention friends gave to earlier versions of this book. John, Tom, Betty, Galia, Howard, Steve, Joseff, Liz, Chris – thank you for reading and commenting so thoroughly. In addition, I am grateful for Bible Society's support of this project. Particular thanks to Paul Woolley who encouraged the book from start to finish. Finally, I owe so much to my family. Whenever I emerged from another stint of writing, they replenished my energy with love and laughter and cheered me on all the way. Lastly, to my mother – thank you for reading the 'good book' to me when I was young and living it out ever since.

# Prologue

I wonder why you've picked up this book? Maybe you were intrigued by the front cover? Perhaps you're looking to understand the Bible better? Maybe life is tough right now and you are searching for answers? Or perhaps you just love a good story and the idea that the Bible might be just that is intriguing?

For people of all ages, stories are captivating. Neurologists have scanned the human brain to see what happens when we become invested in a compelling tale – whether a film, a novel or a story told in the flesh. Powerful chemicals are released to enhance our imagination. The same hormone that bonds mother and child helps develop empathy with fictional characters and the 'pleasure-drug', dopamine, is released when we celebrate a happy ending. When was the last time you felt moved by a story?

> I HAD ALWAYS FELT LIFE FIRST AS A STORY: AND IF THERE IS A STORY THERE IS A STORYTELLER.[1]
>
> *G. K. Chesterton, philosopher and author (1874–1936)*

Every Friday night I face the daunting task of making up another tale about 'Davey the Dragon' for my children. Each time I begin with the same opening line: 'There was once a young dragon called Davey. He was a kind dragon with a big heart and a small brain . . .' Most episodes involve Davey being shot at by a farmer for stealing sheep. Even when a different narrative unfolds, it has the same basic plotline: Davey goes off with his friends, disobeys his parents, and gets into trouble, before a lucky escape. The moral of the story? Always listen to your parents! But despite the predictable plotlines, every Friday without fail my kids insist: 'We want a Davey!' or as my youngest son chants, 'Make up a Davey!'

The power of a story lies in its correspondence with our lives. We humans are living, breathing plotlines, played out between birth and death. In the face of so much pain and tragedy, we need to know that life is heading somewhere and we are part of something bigger. In order to make sense of life, we need to inhabit a narrative that gives meaning. That's why Davey the Dragon resonates with our kids. As I tell the story, their vivid imaginations enter Davey's world. Whether it's fact or fiction becomes irrelevant at this point. The story has a deeper resonance.

This book isn't primarily about whether the Bible is fact or fiction. It's about whether it resonates, whether it makes sense at the deepest level. Can it still scratch our contemporary itches and answer real-life questions? This gets to the heart of my journey with the Bible: having previously dismissed it as an old-fashioned moral code, I have come to see it differently. Like the spectacles I wear on the end of my nose, the Bible provides a lens through which to see the world and make sense of life's experiences – the good, the bad and the ugly. So now I don't just read the Bible, I see myself through it. As J. R. R. Tolkien concluded, the Bible is a 'story of a larger kind', an archetypal plotline.[2] That's why even its ancient history remains relevant. We are not Israel enslaved in Egypt, but the Israelites' quest for freedom mirrors our own. We are not with Jesus on the shores of Lake Galilee, but our need for a messiah is just as real. In our modern age, perhaps we need the Bible's grand narrative and ancient wisdom more than ever?

> To be rooted is perhaps the most important and least recognised need of the human soul.[3]
>
> *Simone Weil, French philosopher and political activist*

I developed this book during a global crisis. The first few chapters were written BC (Before Coronavirus). The final sections were penned during lockdown, as our world faced unprecedented levels of disruption. At times, it felt like the film set of an apocalyptic movie that served to remind us of our fragility. Human beings cannot control the world as masters of our own fate. We are vulnerable creatures, prone to anxiety in the face of our mortality. To live with peace we need to be anchored to a larger plotline. To live with confidence, we need a hope that even death cannot snatch away.

> Don't underestimate the power of the words of the Bible. So often they have been light to a dark path for me and strength to a failing body.[4]
>
> *Bear Grylls, adventurer*

This is precisely why many people are revisiting the Bible. It claims to make sense of who we are and the experiences we have, from holding the tiny hand of a newborn to holding the dying hand of a loved one. At this point you may be thinking: *But isn't the Bible a dusty religious text, a relic from a bygone era? How can it make sense of my life today?* This book is an invitation to explore these questions. So, come with me on a journey through the storyline of the Bible and decide for yourself whether it's still relevant.

> NOW LET ME AT THE TRUTH WHICH WILL REFRESH MY BROKEN MIND.[5]
>
> *Mumford & Sons, British folk rock band*

The book begins with a short section called *Introducing the Bible* that sets the scene. Then we move through the plotline of the Bible in six parts, from our *Origins* (Part 1) to our future *Hope* (Part 6). Each is based on a major episode in the Bible that connects with our human needs and desires. After a short introduction to the theme, each part consists of seven mini-chapters that take ten to fifteen minutes to read. At the end of each mini-chapter there is a recommended Bible passage and a 'reflect' exercise that provides some breathing space and a moment for self-awareness. So you could try reading a mini-chapter each day, along with the recommended Bible passage and 'reflect' exercise. Or why not share the journey with others in a group?

In summary, this book will enable two things at once:

- *We will make sense of the Bible*
  The Bible is big and complex. But when we see the big picture, we grasp how the whole story fits together. By the end you will be able to navigate the Bible's plotline confidently.

- *The Bible will make sense of us*
  Each chapter explores the Bible as part of our human story, considering the relevance of its ancient wisdom and drawing down resources that help us live well today.

SCRIPTURE IS LIKE A RIVER, BROAD AND DEEP, SHALLOW ENOUGH HERE FOR THE LAMB TO GO WADING, BUT DEEP ENOUGH THERE FOR THE ELEPHANT TO SWIM.[6]

*Gregory the Great, Bishop of Rome (c. 540–604)*

Finally, the Bible is open for everyone to explore, whatever your age or experience. Imagine it like a watering hole or an oasis in the wilderness. Recently, my family and I went to Kenya and enjoyed some magical days on safari. Early one morning we made our way to a viewing point overlooking a small lake. As we watched, animals quietly emerged from all directions to lap up the water. Some were understandably cautious and stayed near the edges; others strode nonchalantly into the deep. The diversity was incredible. For a few moments, the animal kingdom laid aside its differences to drink from a lifegiving source. The Bible is like a divine watering hole. It's a source of guidance, wisdom and hope for our human race; a refreshing oasis where people from all walks of life can quench their thirst. You may already feel quite confident; why not wade in deeper? You may feel cautious. But you don't need to know it all to make your way to the edge. The only qualification is desire. As Jesus himself said: 'Let anyone who is thirsty come to me and drink' (John 7:37).

Andrew Ollerton
June 2020

# How to navigate the Bible

The Bible is a strange book. Finding your way round it can feel challenging. The individual books are made up of chapters and verses. To locate a particular book (for example, Genesis), try the Table of Contents at the front. Bible references locate a specific passage by referring to chapter and verse numbers: for instance, Genesis 1:3 means chapter one and verse three. In this book we will mainly quote from the New International Version of the Bible, which is a modern translation of the whole Bible. Where I have wanted to highlight particular words or phrases, I have used italic text.

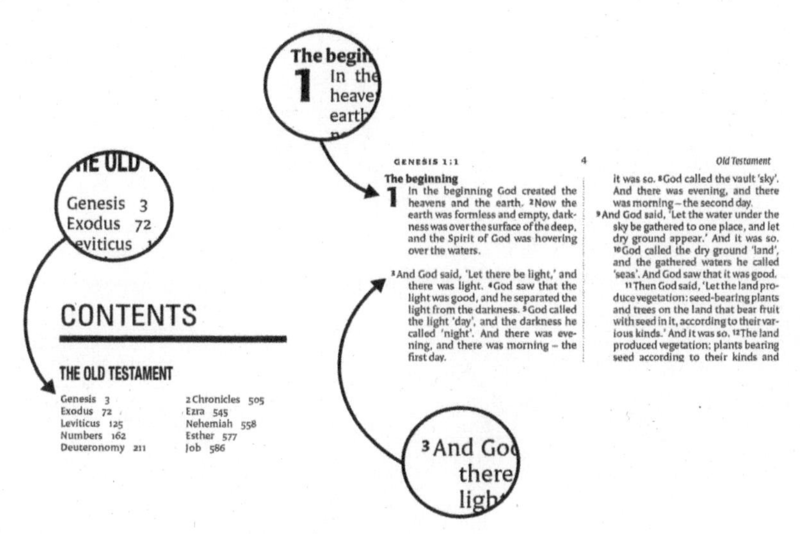

# INTRODUCING THE BIBLE

The French philosopher Voltaire (1694–1778) famously declared: 'A hundred years from my death the Bible will be a museum piece.' As it turned out, Voltaire's old home in Paris became a distribution centre for Bibles in order to feed growing demand across the French-speaking world. In China, during the twentieth century the Bible was outlawed by the Communist Party and copies were confiscated by the Red Guards. In spite of this, demand for the Bible continued to grow and a Chinese printing press (Amity) recently celebrated the milestone of printing 200 million copies.[1] What is it about the Bible? It just won't go away. No book has been burned, banned or debated more vigorously over the centuries. Nevertheless, it continues to dominate bestseller lists year on year.[2] The Bible has many critics but no rivals.

I met with some leaders recently from across the Middle East. One of them spoke movingly about their work with refugees. In the midst of an unfolding tragedy, he recalled the scene when a shipment of clothing arrived. The aid workers laid out neat piles according to size, then as an afterthought they put a stack of Bibles in Arabic and Farsi next to the clothes. When the warehouse opened and word got round the camp, there was a stampede, not for the clothes but for the Bibles. Despite living in rags and having nothing, the refugees knew that when the bottom falls out of life, it's the Bible you need.

In the United Kingdom, we live in a secular culture. We are more likely to run away from the Bible than stampede towards it. However, if you listen carefully, the Bible still keeps surfacing. My car broke down recently and a kind mechanic towed me home. En route he asked me what I did for a living and I explained that I researched and presented the world's bestselling book. I spent the next few minutes persuading him that I did not work for J. K. Rowling nor the publisher of *Fifty Shades of Grey*. Eventually, he let his guard down and admitted that he had recently tried reading the Bible himself. Why? Because his younger brother was in prison and there in the confines of his cell he'd opened up the world's bestseller and discovered a depth and force that catapulted his life in a new direction. My companion remained suspicious but as we journeyed home he plucked up the courage and asked: *So what exactly is the Bible?*

Great question. I wonder what answer you would give? We probably all have preconceived ideas about the Bible based on cultural stereotypes or personal experiences. Maybe you had it pushed at you growing up? Or perhaps you've witnessed the Bible being used negatively, with verses quoted to justify harmful behaviour? This chapter invites us to lay aside past experiences and to reimagine the Bible on its own terms. When human hands take hold of a hard copy or turn on a Bible app, what are we engaging with?

> WHY DOES THIS HUGE, SPRAWLING, TACTLESS BOOK, SIT THERE INSCRUTABLY IN THE MIDDLE OF OUR CULTURAL HERITAGE . . . FRUSTRATING ALL OUR EFFORTS TO WALK AROUND IT?[3]
>
> *Northrop Fry, Canadian literary critic*

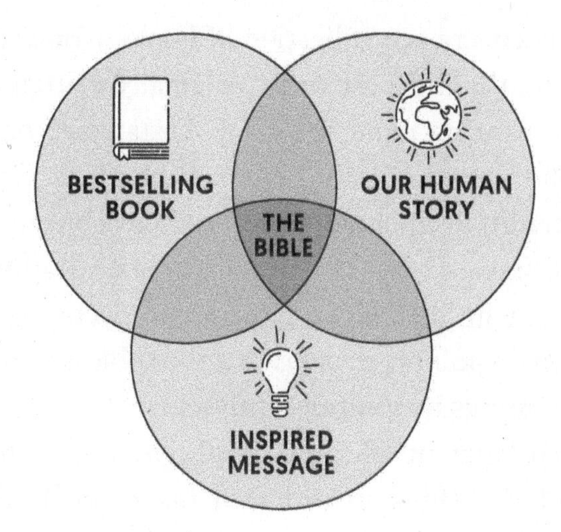


## Bestselling book

Most obviously, the Bible is a collection of writings. The word 'Bible' comes from an ordinary Greek word (*biblia*), which means 'books'. It's plural because the Bible is a multi-volume work. Equally, 'Scripture' comes from a Latin word (*scriptura*) meaning 'writings'. It's an everyday term for putting pen to paper. Today 'Bible' and 'Scripture' carry religious connotations. But strip back the jargon and the Bible is quite simply a bestselling book. In the British radio show *Desert Island Discs* a celebrity is invited to discuss the books, music and personal items they would take with them if marooned on a desert island. Interestingly, the Bible, along with the works of Shakespeare, is given as standard. The implication? Such an iconic piece of literature should be on everyone's reading list, whether a 'believer' or not.

### A small ancient library

The Bible was composed by at least forty different authors over a thousand years and only later collated into one volume.

Between the covers is a collection of books arranged into two main sections: the Old Testament, originally written in Hebrew (with some Aramaic) and the New Testament, originally in Greek (with snippets of Latin). Some Bibles from Catholic and Orthodox traditions include additional books but we will focus on the core sixty-six books that all Christian traditions agree on: thirty-nine in the Old Testament and twenty-seven in the New. The main point to grasp is that the Bible is a small library of ancient writings by multiple authors.

The word 'ancient' alerts us to the need to interpret the language of the Bible in order to make good sense of it. Words and idioms evolve over time and from culture to culture. When, for example, Queen Anne visited the newly completed St Paul's Cathedral in the late seventeenth century, she allegedly declared it: 'amusing, awful and artificial'. Yet the architect, Sir Christopher Wren, was delighted. Back then 'amusing' meant amazing, 'awful' meant awe-inspiring and 'artificial' complimented the artistic genius. Words and idioms change over time. Today, Bible translators have done much of the heavy lifting by translating the ancient texts into equivalent modern words and phrases. However, we still need to read the Bible with a sensitivity to its original meaning.

Equally, cultural practices in biblical times varied enormously from nowadays, but we can still learn from them. It's similar to the ways different cultures behave today. For example, last summer my children found it highly amusing when a French man greeted me with a kiss on both cheeks. In response to their sniggers, he gently pointed out: 'There are many things about British culture that I don't understand – cricket for example!' The French are arguably more biblical as they follow a clear command in the Bible: 'Greet one another with a holy kiss' (Romans 16:16). However, the fact that we Brits offer a handshake does not mean we are anti-Bible: we've distinguished the underlying principle (give a generous welcome) from the specific practice (holy kiss). There are plenty of other traditions in the Bible that may seem strange to us: foot-washing, animal sacrifices, head-covering. This book will provide coaching along the way so that we can learn how to interpret the Bible's ancient wisdom today.

Let me share one key principle for making sense of the Bible: *understand the text in its original context*. As the saying goes: if you take a *text* out of *context* you will be left with a *con*! It may shock you to hear that a few years ago I threw my wedding ring away in front of my wife. But before you close this book in disgust, let me put that text in context. We were at a friend's winter wedding. I was making snowballs during endless rounds of photos. My hands got cold. My fingers shrank. My wedding ring slipped off into one of those snowballs. So I literally threw my wedding ring away in front of my wife. Any text, if taken out of context, can be made to sound ridiculous, even offensive. The Bible is no exception. Throughout this book we will revisit the ancient contexts from which the Bible emerged. As we do so, we will discover that things that otherwise seem strange, actually make sense.

**Diverse styles of communication**

When we turn on our mobile devices we're used to seeing a whole range of icons representing weather apps, social media feeds, emails, online shopping, news reports. Rather embarrassingly my daughter's iTunes account syncs with my phone so I get regular updates from 'Fitness Girl' on my screen! When you open the Contents page in a Bible, imagine it like a home screen with an array of apps, each with different communication styles:

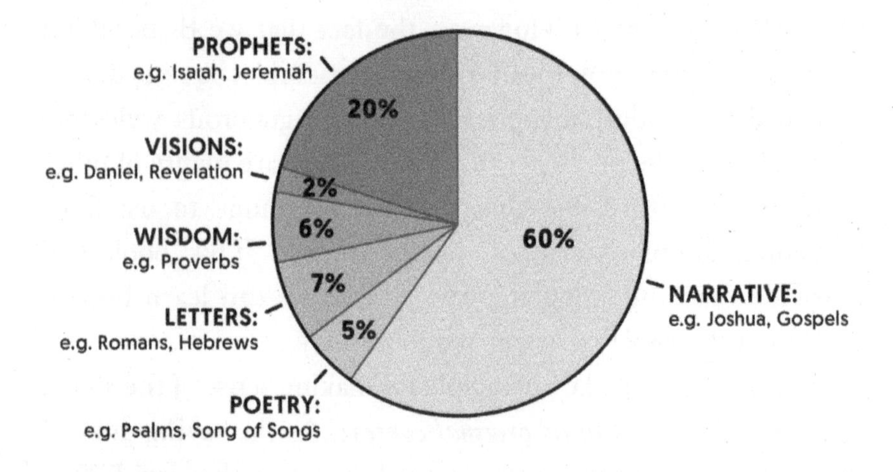


To make sense of the Bible we need to develop sensitivity to these different styles of writing. For example, poets use words figuratively to stir emotion: 'love is as strong as death' (Song of Songs 8:6), teachers use metaphors to inspire imagination: 'I am the good shepherd' (John 10:14), whereas historical description can be interpreted literally: 'Jesus wept' (John 11:35). With digital devices, we quickly learn to navigate the various apps when we use them regularly. With practice, identifying the different styles of writing in the Bible will become just as intuitive.

For all the advances of Western civilisation, nothing seems to replace the writings in the Bible. The wisdom contained in the proverbs of Solomon or the teachings of Jesus are timeless. When it comes to sacred occasions and rites of passage – births, marriages, funerals – the Bible is still our go-to. How many weddings, including royal ones, have drawn on 1 Corinthians 13: 'Love is patient, love is kind . . .'? I was officiating at a ceremony recently where this passage was read. Afterwards, someone came up to me and asked: 'Where did you get that poem from? It was bloody beautiful!' Perhaps we've overlooked how 'bloody beautiful' the Bible can be. Throughout this journey we will discover passages that still contain unrivalled depths of truth, wisdom and inspiration.

## Our human story

One of the least appreciated facts about the Bible is that this library of books forms one overarching *story*. The Bible is not a random collection of pious sayings or moral lessons. There is a coherent plotline from start to finish. At first glance this seems improbable. If you visit a local library or bookstore, you do not expect each title, written by so many different authors, to form one master narrative. There may be multi-volume series by the same author – Harry Potter novels or *Lord of the Rings* – but the entire contents of the library forming one compelling plotline? Impossible.

So where does the Bible get its coherence from?

My journey to answering that question began with a rather hostile exchange on a beach. As an enthusiastic seventeen-year-old, I somehow managed to strike up a conversation with a passerby about the Bible. 'It's full of contradictions,' the man declared. 'No it isn't,' I retorted, eager to defend the Bible. 'Oh yes it is!' he replied. 'Oh no it isn't!' By this point other people were listening in to this spontaneous Punch and Judy show. Finally my opponent landed a killer question: 'Have you actually read it?' Sensing my hesitation, he continued to probe: 'Have you read all of it?' I finally mumbled a 'No' of defeat to which my opponent replied: 'Well how do you know there aren't contradictions then?'

End of conversation.

Beginning of adventure.

Thanks to that provocation, over the next few months I read the Bible from cover to cover. I'll be honest: at times I really struggled. But other nights I couldn't put it down. Once I'd finished the whole thing, I arrived at two conclusions that remain to this day. First, the Bible is *complex*. There are indeed apparent contradictions, and ugly bits and mysterious sections. People who think it was all fabricated to make the church look good clearly haven't read it. No rose-tinted filter has been applied. Instead, it retains rough edges and loose ends that give it a rugged, authentic charm. If we really engage with the Bible it may feel more like a wrestling match than a cosy read. Second, the Bible has a *mysterious harmony*. The scenario I described earlier and deemed impossible – a library of writings by multiple authors spread across centuries that forms one compelling story – that is the Bible! After multiple readings I am more amazed than ever by its inexplicable harmony. How does a small ancient library become one coherent story and still make so much sense two thousand years later?

The rest of this book will journey through the storyline to discover how it hangs together. However, before we dive in it's helpful to pull up to a higher altitude and get a glimpse of the big picture. I'm a visual learner. I need to *see it* in order to *get it*. Over the years I've developed visual ways to imagine the whole Bible. Think of it like a sat-nav: when you first punch in the postcode of your destination, it shows the entire route on one screen before zooming in. So before we start at the beginning, let's get a vision of the whole Bible storyline.

Part 1 Origins: Our human desire for meaning

How a story opens and closes frames the whole narrative. The beginning of the Bible takes us back to the dawn of time. Notice the scale: it's not a story about a Christian country or religious cult; in Genesis we discover the origins of the whole universe, all of nature, the human race, evil and death. The Bible's origins story answers our deepest questions: *Where have we come from? Why are we here?*

Part 2 Exodus: Our human quest for freedom

The story zooms in on one Middle-Eastern man (Abraham) and his descendants (Israel). Through Joseph and his technicoloured coat, they end up enslaved in Egypt. Their experience captures our predicament. We may not be in physical chains but we can feel trapped by anxiety, guilt, anger, injustice. Through an event known as Exodus, God rescued Israel. Their subsequent journey to the Promised Land reveals how to *get out* of destructive patterns and *enter into* a fully liberated life.

Part 3 Exile: Our human cry for peace

Once in the Promised Land, Israel enjoy an era of peace and prosperity under kings like David and Solomon. However, it all goes to pot and they are eventually forced from their homeland and taken as exiles to Babylon (modern-day Iraq). Israel's longing for home echoes our cry for a world without suffering, injustice and pain. The story of exile reveals how we can experience peace through the storms of life.

Part 4 Messiah: Our human need for love

In the New Testament, the long-awaited hero arrives. Jesus is God's love in person. He healed the sick, raised the dead and put the marginalised centre stage. He gave a glimpse of how beautiful this world could be. But his popularity aroused opposition from religious leaders. They plotted his downfall in brutal fashion – Roman crucifixion. However, through the hatred, a more mysterious plot was unfolding. The story of Jesus reveals the invincible power of God's love.

Part 5 Spirit: Our human thirst for community

After Jesus returned to heaven, God's presence was released in a whole new way. From a small group of Jews, this good news went viral. New communities sprang up all over the known world. The Spirit united slaves and masters, females and males, Gentiles and Jews as one family. This is where we fit into the story: God's Spirit is still at work in the world today and we have a part to play.

## Part 6 Hope: Our human longing for home

We are hope-oriented creatures. Without a desirable future we lose the will to live. In the face of much uncertainty – environmental, economic, societal – the Bible speaks hope over our story. It concludes with visions of remade humans inhabiting a perfect world. Paradise lost will be regained. This story of hope gives us the resources we need to live bold and generous lives to the end.

I want to suggest that this story makes sense of who we are and how we experience life in the real world. Of course we don't live in Bible times. For Moses a tablet was made of stone; for us it's a digital device. Things have changed. But our deepest needs and desires remain constant: *meaning*, *freedom*, *peace*, *love*, *community*, *hope*. That's why the world's bestseller has an enduring shelflife and timeless relevance. As the clinical psychologist Jordan Peterson has noted, 'These great [Bible] stories are part of the substructure of our society . . . the further I delve into them, the deeper they get and that never ends.'[4]

The Bible is not a dusty book only relevant to vicars and nuns; it's our human story. When on an episode of *Desert Island Discs*, English comedian Lee Mack learned that the Bible came as standard, he replied: 'I would definitely take the Bible. After all if aliens landed on planet earth and asked what's life all about, I'd say, "Well there's this book that purports to have the answers."' He went on to admit: 'I've not actually read it. Isn't that crazy!'[5] I think Lee Mack has a better understanding of the Bible than most religious people. It's not just a collection of pious sayings and moral rules. In its own unique way, the Bible purports to explain nothing less than human life on planet earth. If that were the case, it would be crazy not to explore it.

##  An inspired message

This third point is a bit more controversial. The Bible is divinely inspired, with a transcendence and power that cannot be rationally explained. A verse within the Bible captures the essential idea: 'All Scripture is *inspired* by God' or literally 'God-breathed' (2 Timothy 3:16). Something mysterious happens when people engage with the Bible. I realise that may sound a bit weird or mystical but bear with me for a moment. People of all ages, IQ levels and cultures have discovered within the Bible a living message that defies its ancient origins.

Take Danny, for example. I first met him when he ran away from London and got off the train in Cornwall. Danny had been in a gang, started using cocaine and was now running away from the madness. To cut a long story short, he decided to try our church. He later told me that when he arrived outside, he was too frightened to come in: 'I thought I would burst into flames.' So Danny went home and started reading the Bible instead. Now bear in mind that by his own admission he had never read anything more than a comic. When we finally met up, I faced an avalanche of questions. The Bible had cut through the craziness and hit home. We started reading it together and discussing it each week. I think I learned more from him than he did from me. The Bible seemed to speak right into his soul. As Danny himself put it: 'I've taken a lot of medicine and been on lots of programmes. But the Bible has fixed me up on the inside.' We lost contact for a while after that, but I spoke to Danny on the phone recently. He told me he had just finished reading the New Testament again. Not bad for a kid who dropped out of education aged fourteen.

The Bible pulsates with a strange energy. Its words seem animated at times. They flex and morph to encounter us in surprising ways. I have been reading, studying and grappling with it for over two decades but I can never master it. As Napoleon put it: 'The Bible is no mere book, but a living creature, with a power to conquer all who oppose it.'[6] When I think I am reading the Bible, I discover that it's reading me. As I make sense of it, it makes sense of me.

My father died a couple of years ago. It's the hardest experience life has thrown at me to date. At times I thought I would fall over and not be able to get up again. But through it all, a verse in the Bible has been like a hand rail that I've grabbed hold of many times:

> The LORD upholds all who fall
> and lifts up all who are bowed down.
>
> *Psalm 145:14*

To you it may just sound like a *verse*. But for me it's been a *voice*, an inspired message speaking strength and hope. The Bible is like that. So be attentive. Read carefully. Tune in and the Bible may provide vital resources of wisdom, courage and hope for life's challenges. Of course, I can't put that in a test-tube and prove it. But why not experiment for yourself? Through this book, give the world's bestseller a try. At the end of each chapter there is a suggested short passage from the Bible. Don't wait until you believe it all. Try it on for size. See if it fits and makes sense of you.

PART 1

# ORIGINS

## Our human desire for meaning

# Introducing origins

*Who do you think you are?* is the question posed by a popular British TV series, in which celebrities trace their ancestry and discover secrets about their past. As the title suggests, there is an important relationship between our origins and our identity, *where* we've come from and *who* we are. Through DNA testing and powerful search engines, it's easier than ever to retrace our family tree back through the centuries and discover some surprising relations. My American mother-in-law is a past master at this. She claims to have hard evidence that my wife, Charlotte, is related to Pocahontas and Lady Godiva . . . that's right, not just a Disney character. Pocahontas was a real Indian princess, the daughter of Powhatan, who married an English settler called John Rolfe. And yes, that's right, Countess Godiva allegedly rode naked through Coventry on a horse. Anyway, let's not lose our train of thought. The question of origins is not a retired, antiquarian interest. We humans want to feel part of a larger story that secures a deeper sense of belonging in the world. That's why ancestry.co.uk has the slogan: 'Bring your backstory to life'. Tracing our origins is crucial to knowing who we are and where we fit.

Back in the Middle Ages, this would have been more straightforward as family stories were etched on to a small footprint of land, generation to generation. But in our modern era of mobile living and family breakdown, our sense of heritage and belonging has become fragmented. We know where we live but that's not the same as knowing where we belong. Personally, I find it hard in polite conversation to answer the simple question: 'Where do you come from?' I normally reply 'Lancashire' as this northern county in England is where the Ollerton family originates. It's where my granddad taught me to skim stones and my grandma shot a rabbit with her air rifle. But the truth is, I've never lived there. My parents relocated before I was born and now I live somewhere different again. But I say 'Lancashire' because it summons a sense of heritage that runs deeper than my own short existence.[1]

The opening scenes of the Bible provide a narrative portal through which to revisit our ultimate origins. The first book is entitled *Genesis*, which means 'origins' or 'beginnings'.[2] It takes us back to the dawn of time and tells the story of how the universe came into being, who we are as humans and how we can discover meaning in this complex world. By meditating on these opening sequences we can situate our small, fragile lives within a larger story that is coherent and enduring. Genesis therefore sets up the backstory to our entire human story and makes sense of many realities we still face today: work and rest, family and society, nature and culture, birth and death.

Have you ever wondered why life is such a rollercoaster of emotions? Moments of intense beauty and pleasure – birds tweeting, lovers loving, your team winning – leave us singing with Louis Armstrong, 'What a wonderful world'. But then life throws a curve ball and suddenly we face dark realities – the boss issuing redundancy, the doctor telling us it's malignant, our partner announcing it's over. Now we're singing with Travis, 'Why does it always rain on me?' The Bible doesn't shy away from these complexities or hide them in a corner. It faces up to reality and provides the best explanation for why our world is so *beautiful* and *broken* all at the same time. The book of Ecclesiastes in the Old Testament puts it succinctly:

> There is . . .
> a time to be born and a time to die . . .
> a time to weep and a time to laugh,
> a time to mourn and a time to dance . . .
> a time to search and a time to give up . . .
> a time for war and a time for peace.
>
> *Ecclesiastes 3:1–8*

In order to live with a secure sense of meaning amid the paradoxes of life, we need to rewind our story to the beginning. While science can investigate our physical origins and explain so much of the natural world, it cannot answer deeper questions that itch away in the human soul. As cultural critic Neil Postman argued:

> In the end science does not provide the answers most of us require. The story of our origins and our end is, to say the least, unsatisfactory. To the question 'how did it all begin?' science answers 'probably by accident' and to the question 'how will it all end?' science answers, 'probably by accident'. And to many people the accidental life is not worth living.[3]

When Charlotte and I tuck our kids into bed at night and whisper that we love them, we are affirming that they are not mere accidents or primates. They have purpose and significance beyond their material composition. Of course, genetically they may be advanced mammals whose short existence traces back to our DNA. But relationally and spiritually, there is another story to tell and deeper truths that need to be affirmed if they are to become emotionally healthy and socially responsible. I believe the ancient text of Genesis gives a compelling narrative of our ultimate origins, with profound truths that enable humans to flourish.

This section will explore the opening eleven chapters of Genesis, which form the backdrop to the rest of the Bible. Most of the Old Testament follows the story of one particular nation (Israel). But Genesis 1–11 starts further back and tells the story of the world through epic scenes of creation, temptation, a great flood and a Babylonian tower. In doing so, Genesis attempts to answer deep existential questions: *Where have we come from? What does it mean to be human? What is the key to flourishing in the world?* This last question is increasingly critical. As environmental commentators such as David Attenborough and Greta Thunberg testify, human mismanagement is jeopardising the future of our planet. Could it be that Genesis can help us recover a way of being human that models sustainable stewardship? Equally, as we experience the unpleasant symptoms of our social fabric unravelling – loneliness, family breakdown, stress and anxiety – perhaps revisiting our origins story can root our fragile lives in a more transcendent source of meaning and hope. According to Genesis, the universe is not a cold empty space, an unfortunate accident or a sick joke. If we trace our family history all the way back to its source, we discover things about ourselves and where we've come from that satisfy our human desire for meaning.

# 1

# Origins and Genesis

*Reading an ancient text today*

The other day I overheard our two sons having an argument in their bedroom. At school they'd been learning the difference between 'fiction' and 'non-fiction' and decided to rearrange their bookshelves accordingly. However, a dispute arose over where to house their illustrated edition of the Bible. My oldest son was convinced it belonged on the non-fiction shelf, insisting, 'It's true!' But my youngest son was not convinced, pointing to a cartoon picture of Noah's ark with a giraffe poking out of one window and a polar bear in the other. It was left for me to settle the matter. In a cowardly move, I suggested the Bible belonged on their bedside table in pride of place not on ordinary shelves anyway.

However, the underlying issue of whether the Bible can be taken seriously is not going away. In particular, the credibility of Genesis has been relentlessly challenged in our scientific age. The famous atheist Richard Dawkins mocked Genesis, claiming: 'It has no more special status than the belief of a particular West African tribe that the world was created from the excrement of ants.'[4] His underlying assumption is that science has disproved the Bible and we need to grow up and move on. Perhaps you respond like my eldest son: 'It's true . . . no matter what science says.' But that response risks making a false choice: the Bible *or* science? Instead, if we understand Genesis on its own terms, we realise that it operates at a deeper level than a scientific explanation of our origins. Before we dive into the detail, this section considers how to make sense of an ancient text like Genesis today.

I should confess that I've gleaned the following principles from other scholars over the years. In particular, I am grateful to my former tutor, Dr Ernest Lucas, a kind-hearted genius who holds two PhDs – one in scientific research and the other in Old Testament studies. When I was grappling with the credibility of Genesis, he taught me to appreciate the dual horizons of ancient Scripture and modern science without dismissing either.[5] He is one of many committed Christians over the centuries whose faith actually inspired scientific enterprise – think Galileo, Kepler, Boyle and Newton. More recently, a Christian called Francis Collins was head of the Human Genome Project and winner of the 2020 Templeton Prize. He concluded: 'The God of the Bible is also the God of the genome. He can be worshipped in the cathedral and in the laboratory.'[6] There is no necessary contradiction. Both science and the Bible can be true in their different ways.

**Genesis is more about *why* than *how***

Have you ever been in a shop and asked an attendant, 'How much is this?' only to be politely told by a bemused customer: 'Sorry, I don't work here!' There was nothing wrong with the question, except that it was misdirected. When it comes to questions about origins, science may be the best place to go for *how* questions: *How old is the universe? How do plants photosynthesise? How does DNA reproduce over time?* Precisely because there is a God who gives order and meaning to the universe, science and mathematics can reveal the inner logic and coherence of the natural world. As C. S. Lewis noted, humans 'became scientific because they expected Law in Nature, and they expected Law in Nature because they believed in a Law Giver'.[7]

However, if we ask a rather different set of questions, we can expect a blank look. Science cannot answer the deeper *why* questions that even children ask: *Why is there something rather than nothing? Why am I me? Why is there good and evil?* These first-order questions reflect our human desire for meaning. As Mark Twain allegedly quipped, the two most important days in your life are the day you were born and the day you find out why! To capture the difference between *how* and *why* questions, John Lennox, a retired mathematics professor at the University of Oxford, uses the illustration of a cake baked by Aunt Matilda. Nutritional scientists can analyse the ingredients; physicists the temperature and duration in the oven; mathematicians the behaviour of particles under those conditions. Science can tell us *how* the cake was made but only Aunt Matilda can tell us *why* she baked it. Perhaps it was to celebrate her grandson's birthday?[8] Science can read DNA coding and apply carbon dating but Genesis meets our deeper need for meaning.

**Genesis was written *for* us but not *to* us**

בְּרֵאשִׁ֖ית בָּרָ֣א אֱלֹהִ֑ים אֵ֥ת הַשָּׁמַ֖יִם וְאֵ֥ת הָאָֽרֶץ׃

I sometimes show the original Hebrew text of Genesis 1:1 to my English-speaking students to make a simple point: Genesis was not originally written *to* us. I believe it is highly relevant *for* us but it originated in a quite different language and culture from ours.[9] Genesis may have been written as early as the second millennium BC. Traditionally it is thought Moses was the author, though it went through subsequent stages of editing. We should not be surprised if some aspects of its world-view are quite different from ours. For example, Genesis seems to imagine the earth as a flat disc with the sky as a solid dome or 'firmament' and the stars fixed to it like studded diamonds. However, this is how things appear to someone standing on planet earth without the Hubble telescope to hand. Despite all we now know about cosmology, we still refer to 'sunrise' and 'sunset' because from our perspective that's what's happening. So Genesis is not 'wrong' but its message was accommodated to the audience it was written to.

Genesis was also not the only origins story in the ancient world. Each culture narrated myths about gods, humans, floods and fertility. The Babylonian myth, *Enuma Elish* traced the origins of the world to a fight between rival gods. Having slayed the evil goddess Omoroca, the male god Marduk fashioned earth and sky from her carcass. Either way, it was widely assumed that a pantheon of capricious gods controlled the fate of humans and used them as slaves. In this ancient context, Genesis was a counter-narrative, providing a radically different account of our human origins. According to Genesis, one all-powerful God brought order out of chaos simply by speaking. He did not use violence to create the world nor does he keep humans as slaves. Instead, he is a loving God who can turn our chaos into order and bring beauty out of brokenness. When we understand Genesis in its original context (not *to us*), it still makes sense of life (*for us*).

**Genesis is a *telescope* not a *microscope***

In one short chapter, a mere thirty-one verses, Genesis captures epic scenes of the entire cosmos coming into being. One throw-away phrase sums up galaxies and light years: '[God] also made the stars' (Genesis 1:16). The rather conservative word count is actually a clue: the author is not attempting an in-depth description of exactly how God made the world; instead, the focus falls on the way humans should relate to God, each other and the natural environment in order to flourish.

So don't get stuck dissecting the details. The creation accounts in Genesis are not a functional description taken from a manual. Think of it more like the Hubble telescope, providing footage of distant galaxies and worlds without end. Precisely because of the scale, it is able to capture the enchanting beauty of our universe. I was listening to a podcast recently with the British astronaut Tim Peake talking about his mission to the International Space Station. Apparently, when astronauts step outside, they are so overcome by the view that NASA now build 'awe-time' into their schedule. Before they can do any work they need a few moments just to take it all in. Then even mundane tasks take on a whole new significance. In a similar way, Genesis gives an expansive vision that stirs a sense of awe and wonder. As you read it, build in awe-time to reflect on the beauty of our world and the significance of human life. Then even mundane tasks will take on a whole new meaning.

READ: Genesis 1:1–5.

REFLECT: Take a leaf out of NASA's book and schedule in five minutes of awe-time today. Remind yourself of things that amaze you and recover a sense of wonder within your routines.

2

# Origins and God

*The source and centre of everything*

In the beginning God created the heavens and the earth.

*Genesis 1:1*

Every author searches for a killer opening line. Genesis remains the most famous ever penned. Immediately, it tells us that we are not accidental blobs of carbon floating alone in an empty universe. We are not the product of nothingness or an impersonal matter-making machine. Our origins trace back to a divine being who brought order out of chaos and beauty from nothingness.

In 1543 Copernicus published a theory that sparked a revolution. The prevailing assumption had been that planet earth was the centre of the solar system and the sun revolved around us. This was not only inaccurate, it was also unhelpful. We humans don't flourish when we think we're the centre. Instead, this belief produces a cocktail of arrogance and control, anxiety and despair. It was time for a revolution that reimagined the world with the earth orbiting the sun and not the other way round. Today, our selfie culture could do with something similar – a spiritual revolution that puts God back at the centre. It's actually the way things really are. But when we lose touch with reality we become drunk on ideas that lead us astray. To help clear our heads, Genesis declares: 'In the beginning God . . .' Before you and I, before society and social media, before nations and iPhones . . . GOD.

Being honest, what would you say is the real centre of your life? Genesis invites us to experience a revolution. Think about the radical implications for how we see the world if God is the centre: Is the world a cold empty space or a beautifully designed home? Is the natural environment raw material for profit or a divine gift to steward responsibly? Am I merely evolving DNA or a sacred being with eternal significance? When you hold a newborn baby or stand at the graveside of a loved one, which makes most sense? In my experience, it's when we centre our lives on God that we are able to explain so many deeply held values that seem obvious to us. As the talk show host Justin Brierley concludes, after a decade of conversations with atheists, it's belief in God that 'makes sense' of human existence, human value and human purpose.[10]

So if there is a divine being at the centre of everything, what is this God like? After all, the word 'God' comes with a lot of baggage. I was talking to a parent while our sons played football recently. During the course of conversation she told me she didn't believe in God. Instead of letting it go, I asked what kind of God she didn't believe in. When she described a sort of hybrid deity, part strict Victorian and part fairy godmother, I confirmed: 'I don't believe in that God either.' The God of the Bible defies stereotypes and bullet-point descriptions. So Genesis doesn't begin with a one-dimensional bio; instead, like a film that cuts straight to the main character, the first thing we encounter is God in action, creating the cosmos that we experience today. From this we learn three things about the divine being who is at the centre of everything.

**God is supremely powerful**

As science enlarges our understanding of the scale of the universe, it is mind-boggling. There are somewhere between 100 and 400 billion stars in our galaxy alone. To get a sense of perspective, imagine we shrank the entire Milky Way down to the size of North America. According to that scale, our solar system (the sun, Mars, Venus, etc.) would be the size of a coffee cup and planet earth a mere bubble spinning round inside.

Awe-time.

Now people respond differently at this point. For some, it's proof that the universe is even emptier than we thought. As Professor Brian Cox put it: 'We humans represent an isolated island of meaning, in a meaningless universe.'[11] But notice the irony here: despite the empty space around us, we struggle to conclude that *our* existence is meaningless. We know deep in our bones that human life is more significant than that. So what if we are not an isolated island but a specially formed planet with a unique purpose? Now the vastness points to the greatness and power of God who 'also made the stars ' (Genesis 1:16). Now the significance of human life is a source of wonder. Imagine if the God of all galaxies knows and cares about us.

On a recent trip to New Zealand, I was determined to enjoy some stargazing under the southern night sky. So I found a field away from electric lights and lay down. Soon layer upon layer of depth and beauty revealed itself. Filled with wonder, I recited one of my favourite poems from the Bible:

When I consider your heavens,
the work of your fingers,
the moon and the stars,
which you have set in place,
what is mankind that you are mindful of them,
human beings that you care for them?

*Psalm 8:3–4*

The scale of the universe is mind-boggling. But what stunned the ancient poet is that a supremely powerful God, who controls galaxies with his fingers, cares about human beings. We may be very small but we are greatly loved. The universe is not such a cold empty space after all.

**God is a prolific artist**

As a piece of artwork reveals the artist, so the natural world reveals the character of God. Another poem in the Bible puts it this way:

The heavens declare the glory of God;
the skies proclaim the work of his hands.

*Psalm 19:1*

Every flower displays the beauty of its designer. There are over 25,000 varieties of orchids and the orchid is just one of 270,000 species of flowers. If the natural world is a clue to the nature of God then, despite all the rumours he is not a miserable killjoy, but an extravagantly generous creator. He delights in colour, symmetry, beauty and variety. He is a generous and joyful artist, the source of all beauty and goodness. So if we centre ourselves on this God, maybe life won't be so miserable after all? Perhaps we could live with joyful generosity like him?

**God is wisdom personified**

If this world has been designed by a divine genius then we will flourish when we follow his original purpose. Think of life like a plank of wood: there is an integral pattern or grain running through it. As any carpenter knows, to avoid splinters you've got to go with the grain. Genesis reveals deeply ingrained patterns relating to work and rest, sexuality and gender, ecology and technology. There is a way to live in the world that avoids a lot of pain and regret. It's called wisdom. But when we stray from our original purpose, we pull the ceiling down on ourselves. Modern attempts to transcend natural limits and to exploit the environment only result in social and ecological disaster. We need to follow the way of wisdom in order to flourish in the world.

No matter our past, Genesis invites us into a new future – a life centred on God. We are not alone in the universe. Even if we have turned our back on our maker and wandered into trouble, God reaches out to us. He is closer than we think. Another poem from the Bible puts it like this:

> You have searched me, LORD,
> and you know me.
> You know when I sit and when I rise . . .
> Where can I go from your Spirit?
> Where can I flee from your presence?
>
> *Psalm 139:1–2, 7*

A few years ago, my wife and I were waiting in the departure lounge at an airport with our two-year-old daughter. Keeping a toddler entertained is hard work at the best of times. On this occasion, she kept wandering off as if she had somewhere important to go. In the end, out of sheer frustration and some curiosity, I decided to let her go and see how far she would get.

I tracked her for some distance, hiding behind plants and suitcases, never more than a couple of metres away. At one point, she glanced over her shoulder with a look of panic, realising that she was alone in a sea of unfamiliar faces. Undeterred, she carried on but now anxiously bumping into things. I wondered how long to let the experiment continue. As she boarded Flight 281 to Istanbul (only joking) I decided enough was enough and burst out of my hiding place. She gave me the biggest hug imaginable. The sheer relief of knowing you are not alone is a powerful thing. The opening line of Genesis reassures us that even though we cannot see God, he is watching over us. If we centre our lives on God, we can experience an embrace of love and a purpose for life that satisfies our deepest need. Let the revolution begin.

READ: Psalm 8.

REFLECT: Take a moment to centre yourself on God. Find a quiet place and reach out to God, asking for help and wisdom.

## 3

# Origins and beauty

*Why is the world so well designed?*

We all experience moments when a vista opens up and stops us in our tracks. I was driving home from work recently when a pheasant ran into the road and was hit by the car in front. There is a little-known law in Britain, that the car behind the vehicle that knocks down the bird can claim the road-kill . . . so I did. With the dead pheasant now in the boot of my car, I sent a text to my wife: 'Don't worry about dinner. I'll pick something up on the way home!' As the joke wore off, I began to search online for instructions about how to pluck a pheasant. When a long turquoise feather came off in my hand, I had one of those moments. I found myself mesmerised. Even in this world of evil, suffering and road-kill, there is enough beauty in a single feather to sense that our world is enchanted with a glory beyond itself.

Have you ever stopped to think: Where did all the beauty come from? Order, shape, symmetry and colour don't just happen. If you see a magnificent garden, there's probably a gardener. If you enjoy a delicious meal, there will be a talented chef working behind the scenes, not a random explosion in the kitchen. In fact, the Second Law of Thermodynamics, also known as entropy, states that without intervention things deteriorate into chaos. Gardens become overrun by weeds; kitchens become cluttered and messy. Understandably, we often ask why there is so much suffering in the world. But it's even more remarkable that there is so much beauty, love and justice. If it's not natural, where did it originate?

> Now the earth was formless and empty, darkness was over the surface of the deep . . . And God said, 'Let there be light,' and there was light.
>
> *Genesis 1:2–3*

This verse takes us back to a primeval moment at the dawn of time. The material world had been brought into existence but remained a scene of dark watery chaos. Then God simply speaks and commands order and beauty into being. It's a remarkable formula, more effortless than Mary Poppins tidying up the nursery. God simply spoke and creation poured forth. Think of God's strength more like authority than horsepower. Imagine a well-trained dog that immediately responds to the whistle of its owner. In Genesis, God speaks and matter responds, recognising the voice of its master. By contrast, the gods of the ancient world were often depicted grappling with forces of nature that threatened to run away with them. In particular, sea monsters such as Leviathan were thought to embody chaos itself. In ancient mythologies, the gods struggled to get them under control, like a pet owner chasing after their runaway dog. But Genesis simply states: 'God created the great creatures of the sea' (1:21).

As the rest of the Bible unfolds, it becomes clear that nothing in the material universe is out of God's control. When he whistles, a great fish obediently swallows up a runaway prophet

(Jonah). When he speaks, tumultuous waves and storm-force winds instantly die down (Jesus). The creation narrative frames our human story with a good God in complete control of all he has made. If instead we imagine the universe to be ruled by random forces of chance and chaos, we will become anxious, oscillating between obsessive tendencies to control and fearful superstitions. But if we believe in a good and powerful God then we can sleep peacefully and live confidently. There's something to be said for humbly accepting our place in the universe as creatures rather than battling with the stress of trying to control everything.

| God brings form | God brings fullness |
| --- | --- |
| **Day 1** Separation of light and darkness | **Day 4** The creation of the lights to fill the day and night |
| **Day 2** Separation of the waters to form the sky and the sea | **Day 5** The creation of the birds and the fish to fill the sky and sea |
| **Day 3** Separation of the sea from the dry land and creation of plants | **Day 6** The creation of the animals and humans to fill the land |
| **Day 7** The heavens and the earth were finished and God rested | |

The rest of Genesis 1 provides a beautiful account of six days of creation. It uses a poetic structure to convey the order and harmony that God established in the world. The first three days bring shape and definition to that which was 'formless'. Then in the second half of the week, God set about populating the 'empty' sky, land and sea with living creatures. This narrative symmetry captures the way God turned a scene of messy chaos into a world of beauty and order. Genesis is not providing a DIY guide for how to build a universe. If the sun and moon don't appear until day four, that doesn't imply that God was working in the dark for three days. The larger point is that God carefully choreographed the beauty of this world and created everything in it. Just as most products these days seem to have 'Made in China' written on them, the entire natural world has God's ownership stamped all over it. Consequently, nothing in the universe is inherently evil, as surely as God made it good. Equally, nothing in the universe is divine. Instead, all things are to be enjoyed as *good* but not to be worshipped as *god*. Again, Genesis is taking on rival claims here. In the ancient world it was common to worship the sun and moon as deities and to believe they controlled your fate. So Genesis doesn't even use their proper names. It simply refers to them as 'the greater' and 'the lesser light' (1:16) as if to say: 'Don't worship the sun and moon. Worship the God who created them!' Our destiny is not in the hands of blind fate but a loving God. Though we may not know what the future holds we can rest secure in the One who holds the future.

The account of creation in Genesis 1 raises a knotty question: Were these six days literal twenty-four hour periods? If so, this would indicate that planet earth is much younger than modern science suggests. However, it's worth noting that the Hebrew word for 'day' (*yom*) has a variety of meanings. Genesis 2:4 speaks of *the* 'day [*yom*]' of creation, suggesting it could also refer to an instantaneous act. Understandably therefore, Christian leaders over the centuries have interpreted Genesis 1 in a variety of ways. St Augustine favoured the idea that God made all things instantaneously. Others, like Professor John Lennox, suggest there were six literal days of intense creation, with extended periods of time in between. Pope Francis believes God worked through long periods of evolution.

The important thing is not to miss the point. Remember, Genesis is more about the *why* than the *how* questions. The clear intention is to frame the entire world as a masterpiece, the work of a creative genius who delights in all that he has made. After each day of creation, God is overheard to declare: 'It is good.' Once humanity is in place it goes up a level: 'It's very good!' These declarations are not just functional, as though creation has passed factory testing. This is an overflow of divine delight and pleasure in the goodness of the world. We experience moments like this too – a coffee lover sipping a flat white, a football player celebrating the winning goal, lovers reclining after intimate pleasure. God delights in the world he has made and he wants humans to enjoy it with him.

As we recover this vision, life takes on new meaning. The material world is not merely functional but sacred space. Every piece of fruit is a gift. Every flower is a work of art. The natural world, from a pheasant's feather to a turquoise ocean, forms a tremendous symphony of praise. If we look up from our phones and pay attention, we can hear their chorus. As Elizabeth Barrett Browning declares:

> Earth's crammed with heaven,
> and every common bush afire with God;
> but only he who sees, takes off his shoes;
> the rest sit round it, and pluck blackberries.[12]

My wife and I recently enjoyed a meal at a top restaurant. The food was so good that we said to the waiter: 'Please pass our compliments to the cook.' The next thing we knew, the Michelin-star chef appeared in person. He joined us for a conversation and ordered our glasses to be topped up on the house. It reminded me of two things that sum up the message of Genesis 1. Just as a delicious meal has a chef, this world has a creator. That's why it's so beautiful. Moreover, this good and generous maker promises to draw close and fill our cups to overflowing. As the most famous poem in the Bible concludes:

> The LORD is my shepherd, I lack nothing . . .
> You prepare a table before me . . .
> my cup overflows.
>
> *Psalm 23:1, 5*

READ: Genesis 1:6–25.

REFLECT: Take hold of an object that displays natural beauty (a leaf, a feather, a piece of fruit). Examine it carefully and allow wonder and gratitude to stir.

# 4

# Origins and human identity

*What does it mean to be human?*

The birth of our first child is indelibly etched on my memory. After some research, we opted for a water birth in a nearby maternity unit. I imagined myself catching up on some reading while Charlotte enjoyed a free hot tub. But it didn't work out like that. Instead, due to complications, we were sent to the main hospital where it became apparent that the umbilical cord was wrapped around the baby. Every time contractions came, the baby's heart rate plummeted and our stress levels rose. Before I knew what was happening, the nurse pulled a red cord, doctors came running in and five minutes later Charlotte was having an emergency C-section. Needless to say, I got a lot less reading in than planned.

After the stress came the moment every parent anticipates: a vulnerable little bundle was gently placed into my arms. As I looked down, two beautiful eyes stared back. I cried. Charlotte required further treatment, so I got to hold our daughter for the first hour of her life. She never stopped staring at me. Even the midwife remarked how freakishly alert she was. The gaze of a newborn makes you reflect on some deeper questions: What is this we have brought into the world? Why do I feel such love for someone I've only just met? We can study many theories, but when you hold a newborn, you feel something deeper. We humans are more than mere DNA. We carry a significance that transcends our short lifespan.

In this section, we step back to ask: What does it mean to be human? In our cultural moment this question fizzes with new significance. The traditional script has been torn up as previously unimaginable possibilities emerge for how humans can live in the world. In his book *Human Universe*, Professor Brian Cox sums it up in a pithy way: 'Two million years ago we were ape-men. Now we are space men!'[13] Whether you agree with these evolutionary beliefs or not, human progress is extraordinary. We communicate via satellites that orbit space, we fly in compressed cabins at 40,000 feet (with WiFi), we live with resident robots that recognise our voice: 'Alexa, play "Dance Monkey".' We have a relentless capacity to develop the world through arts, culture, science, sports, industry, medicine and technology. Humans are not merely top of the food chain. We are in a league of our own. As Shakespeare put it in *Hamlet*:

> What a piece of work is a man! How noble in reason, how infinite in faculty! The beauty of the world. The paragon of animals. And yet, to me, what is this quintessence of dust?
>
> *Act 2, Scene 2*

Hamlet's speech highlights a paradox. Despite our capacity for intellectual genius and moral goodness, according to chemical composition we are dust. The average human body contains sufficient carbon to make 900 pencils, enough fat to make seventy-five candles and enough sulphur to kill all the fleas on an average dog. When reduced to mere atoms: 'dust you are and to dust you will return' (Genesis 3:19).

So when the gaze of a newborn melts your heart, what is it that you are sensing? If they are just highly evolved matter why does their life hold such significance? When a loved one dies, we intuitively feel that they were much more than dust. After the famous Beatles singer, John Lennon, was shot dead in 1980, his wife, Yoko Ono, penned some poignant words of lament:

> Why do I miss you so if you're just a spec of dust
> Floating endlessly amongst the billion stars?[14]

According to Genesis, every human person must be evaluated according to divine origins, which transcend material composition.

> So God created mankind in his own image,
> in the image of God he created them;
> male and female he created them.
>
> *Genesis 1:27*

There are hidden depths to our humanity. Our value cannot be reduced to image and physique or personal achievements and CV. At the point of conception, a divine status is conferred and a sacred being is formed. A vulnerable newborn bundle is a gift and a miracle.

This claim was controversial in the ancient world. Other rival stories considered only male kings to be a reflection of the divine image. It set them apart from the riff-raff and justified their totalitarian rule. But Genesis democratises the idea so that all humanity is created equal: 'male and female'. There is no *essential* hierarchy. Right at the outset of our human story, a theological foundation is being laid upon which a flourishing society can be built. Even when the ugly curses of slavery, racism and bigotry have blighted our story, Genesis has provided an arsenal of truth to defeat oppression. The first person publicly to oppose the ancient system of slavery was a Christian leader called Gregory of Nyssa. Around AD 370 he preached a sermon that posed subversive questions: 'How much gold for the image of God? How much silver for selling the God-formed human being? Who can buy a man or sell a man made in the image of God?'[15] Centuries later, Martin Luther King gave his famous speech entitled 'The American Dream':

> There are no gradations in the image of God. Every human from a treble white to a bass black is significant on God's keyboard. This is why we must fight segregation with all of our non-violent might![16]

Hard-fought ideals of human dignity, equality, freedom of speech, civil and constitutional rights are deeply rooted in the Bible's definition of a human being. As Tom Holland has argued in his book *Dominion*, so many values that Western culture treasures are explained by 'the formidable – indeed the inescapable – influence of Christianity'.[17] To ditch the Bible in the name of progress is therefore to saw off the very branch we are sitting on. In order to safeguard the very values we cherish, we should root our understanding of a human being in theology not just biology. Genesis affirms the innate worth of every person and provides a more solid basis for insisting that *Black Lives Matter* and the poor and vulnerable deserve to be defended. A few months ago, I witnessed a well-dressed businessman in a London park urgently communicating with a 999 operative regarding a seemingly lifeless body slumped on a bench. The concern of the man for his fellow human being may seem obvious. But if we are only highly evolved dust, there is little rationale for the strong to help the weak. That businessman was embodying the values of Genesis: whether rich or poor, black or white, drunk or sober, every human is sacred.

When we grasp this vision, we treat other people differently, regardless of their social standing or current behaviour. As C. S. Lewis concluded: 'There are no ordinary people. You have never talked to a mere mortal.'[18] We must resist dehumanising practices that treat people like dirt or commercial property or sex objects. According to Genesis, the marginalised and broken have been made in the image of the King. That's why in Roman culture, when it was perfectly acceptable to leave unwanted babies at the rubbish dump, Christians adopted them as their own. That's why Mother Teresa served hopeless beggars in Calcutta, persuaded that 'a beautiful death is for people who lived like animals to die like angels – loved and wanted'.[19] That's why Dame Cicely Saunders, founder of the modern hospice movement, believed we should wash the feet of those who will not walk again. Humans carry eternal significance.

According to Genesis, our original standing before God is not that of ant to human but image to original, friend to maker. The closest you could get to God in creation would be to come face to face with another human being. That's why Israel was not to make any replica of God as a statue or idol. The only thing on earth legitimately god-like was a human. We can become so over-familiar with this and forget the sacred nature of human life. To help remind us, here's a piece of poetry that captures the wonder of being human:

For you created my inmost being;
you knit me together in my mother's womb.
I praise you because I am fearfully and wonderfully made.

*Psalm 139:13–14*

READ: Genesis 1:26–2:4; Psalm 139:1–17.

REFLECT: Try saying Psalm 139:13–14 to yourself in the mirror. How does it change the way you see yourself? How can you see other people through this lens too?

# 5

# Origins and human purpose

*What was our original vocation?*

If we are made in the 'image and likeness' of God, how should we humans live on planet earth? What does success look like according to Genesis? American rifle shooter Matt Emmons was one shot away from winning his second gold medal at the 2004 Olympic Games. He was so far ahead, his bullet just needed to hit the target. Anywhere. With nerves of steel he took a deep breath and pulled the trigger. Bull's-eye! But when Emmons looked at the scoreboard, no lights appeared. Nothing registered. The judges came over and questions were asked. Did the gun misfire? Was the scoreboard broken? None of the above. It turns out Emmons hit the wrong target. Standing in lane two, he had fired at the target for lane three. He couldn't have been more accurate but in the wrong direction. Nil points.[20]

How would you define lasting success in life? It's possible to achieve wealth and fame but still feel like we've missed the mark. Genesis helps us understand what true success looks like by revisiting our original purpose. After Genesis 1 provided a wide-angle introduction to the universe as a whole, Genesis 2 cuts to the lead characters – Adam and Eve. The Bible considers this original couple to be the root and ancestry of the entire human race. Reconciling this with modern evolutionary theories is complex. Some interpret the account in Genesis 2 literally, others more figuratively. Whichever conclusion you reach, remember Genesis is more about the *why* questions. Its concern is that we hit the right target.

**Purpose 1: Enjoy knowing God**

To be made in the image and likeness of God implies a level of similarity between humans and God that is quite shocking. Just as we might say 'like father like son', so humanity was created to be the spitting image of God. Of course, God is eternal Spirit so this does not refer to physical qualities. It's more about character, desire and a shared outlook on life. Our middle child always wanted to be with his dad. He practically became my shadow: if I knelt down to do press-ups, he would do the same. If I climbed up on the garage roof, he shook off fear and followed me up. One time I was giving a talk on a stage and suddenly he appeared by my side. Like father like son.

According to Genesis, success for a human is to know God as our Father and become like him in character. To enable this close relationship, God imparted his own Spirit to the first humans so that they could share life together.

> The LORD God formed a man from the dust of the ground and breathed into his nostrils the breath of life.
>
> *Genesis 2:7*

Humans are indeed dust. The very name 'Adam' means 'ground' or 'dirt'. He could just as easily have been called Dusty. However, God breathed his personal Spirit into him. This sets humans apart from the animals. We have the unique capacity to host God's presence and to know him personally, closer than our own shadow. Later in Genesis, God walks with Adam and Eve in the garden. Just imagine that. We are hardwired to know God, not as a distant fact but as a kindred spirit.

According to Genesis, this is what success looks like. Any other life will become dehumanising and disappointing, even if we're very good at it. Our human desire for meaning cannot be satisfied by money, pleasure or fame. As St Augustine famously concluded: 'You made us for yourself, O God, and our hearts will always be restless until they find rest in you.'[21]

**Purpose 2: Flourish in relationships**

Buried within the account of our origins is a mystery that has puzzled theologians over the centuries: 'Let *us* make man in *our* image.' Who is speaking and, more importantly, who are they speaking to? Some argue that God is addressing a heavenly court of angels. But others sense something deeper here. Within God himself there is a community of persons in conversation. Later this idea will be referred to as the *Trinity*. But for now, simply note that our human origins do not trace back to a lonely bearded figure in the skies but to a divine conversation that suggests real relationship. This explains a lot about why we are such talkative, sociable creatures who flourish in families and communities.

For a brief period in Genesis there is a solitary figure, Adam, surrounded by a hosts of animals. Brace yourself if you're a doting pet owner. God declares: 'It is not good for the man to be alone' (Genesis 2:18). Unfortunately, our highly sophisticated culture has valued productivity and consumption ahead of family and friendship. Now we face a scourge of our own making: loneliness. Despite the stereotype of an older person stuck in a flat, isolation is now plaguing younger generations too. With earpods in and screens on, we are nurturing an increasingly lonely society. Ironically, we are tempted to solve the problem through more technology. In Japan, early trials are using Artificial Intelligence and robotics to simulate human presence and offset feelings of isolation. Instead, we need to revisit our origins and re-evaluate the priority of family and community. As Desmond Tutu put it: 'The solitary human being is a contradiction in terms . . . We are created for a delicate network of relationships, of interdependence with our fellow human beings.'[22]

When we experience true friendship we realise it is more than meets the eye. It's an echo of the divine community that we originate from. I met up with an old friend in Oxford recently. It's one of those friendships where you pick up right where you left off, even if a year later. We've journeyed through so much together, from being bachelors to getting married. From the pain of not being able to have children, to our families going on holiday together. I sometimes think I haven't got time for friendship. But after experiencing its renewing qualities, I realise that my tendency towards isolation is shooting at the wrong target. We met in a pub called The Eagle and Child, where J. R. R. Tolkien and C. S. Lewis used to meet with a group of their friends who became known as the Inklings. Imagine them catching up over a pint and sharing updates on their stories. Over the bar there's a plaque attributed to Lewis: 'My happiest hours are spent with three or four friends in old clothes, tramping together and putting up in small pubs.' Now that's the image of God talking.

**Purpose 3: Steward the earth's resources**

As well as being hard-wired for *relationships*, the image of God also carries *responsibility*. In the ancient world, kings set up statues in their image in order to convey their presence and authority throughout the realm. Humans are living statues, called to administer God's stewardship over the earth. Genesis does not depict a world where God gets everything sorted and humans lie around on sun loungers with angels serving piña coladas. The 'image of God' conveys a sense of *vocation* (Latin for 'calling'). Before anything went wrong with the world, humans had work to do.

In Genesis 2, God planted a beautiful garden called Eden as a base for Adam and Eve to call home. Eden means 'delight'. It was a paradigm for how humans could live in harmony with the natural world. But having set them up with a starter-home, God also commissioned them with a more adventurous task:

> Be fruitful and increase in number; fill the earth and subdue it.
>
> *Genesis 1:28*

Think of Eden less as a typical back garden and more like the beautiful home and walled garden at the centre of a large estate or National Trust property. Further out the landscape becomes increasingly rugged with wilderness encroaching at the perimeter. God commissioned humanity to take the beauty of Eden and extend it to the rest of the world, subduing chaos and bringing order. So the world Adam and Eve inherited was not a vacant show-home. It was an ambitious project that humans were to undertake in partnership with God. Our desire for purpose goes all the way back. God is not 'super-spiritual', only interested in religious services and transcendental meditation. According to Genesis, *all of life* is spiritual and *every task* is in some sense sacred. Part of our human vocation was to build sustainable societies whether through agriculture, music, textiles, architecture or other industry.

As we'll see, our human story soon took a turn for the worse. But pause for a moment and reflect on the strategic role humans were originally given. We were made to enjoy a relationship with God and to reflect his beauty to the world. The entire cosmos was to be a sacred home, a shared living space for God and humans. Our original purpose was to bridge heaven and earth, nature and culture, God and the cosmos, so the whole world would flourish. That's what success looks like. Bull's-eye!

READ: Genesis 2:5–25.

REFLECT: Which of the three purposes are strongest and weakest in your life? Celebrate the strongest and write down a practical way to invest in the weakest.

# 6

# Origins and evil

*What's wrong with the world?*

The interesting thing about this question is that everyone's got an answer. From taxes to terrorism, from war and hatred to reality TV shows like *Love Island*, no one believes dysfunction is just natural. Religious types and secularists share a conviction that there is a way the world is supposed to work and this is not it. But where does this instinct come from? According to Genesis, it's a deep collective memory of a long-lost reality. Just as I say that I come from Lancashire even though I've never actually lived there, we humans know that we belong in a different world. Eden is in our blood and we miss it even though we've never lived there.[23] Things are not the way they're supposed to be. So what went wrong?

Recently, I visited Exeter Cathedral in south-west England. It boasts a majestic ceiling that was designed to draw people's attention upwards to God. However, in doing so it can also result in a pain in the neck! To prevent this, the Cathedral staff kindly supply trolleys with a mirrored surface. As I pushed my reflective cart round, taking in the beauty of the ceiling above, it dawned on me that this was our original purpose: made in the image of God, we are strategic mirrors, called to reflect the beauty of God above to the world around us. However, if the mirrors turn to the dark side and become tarnished, the world will descend into gloomy chaos. This is the story of Genesis 3. It explains the origins of evil in a way that makes sense. It's not dusty mythology. The snake in the grass, the voice of temptation, the choice between good and evil – aren't these realities we all still face? There is a way to live wisely and reflect divine beauty. But, as Yeats notes, when we turn away from it:

> Things fall apart,
> the centre cannot hold;
> mere anarchy is loosed upon the earth.[24]

In Genesis 3, Adam and Eve hear an unfamiliar voice that brings them to a fork in the road. The Bible doesn't dwell on where this shadowy influence came from. Later references suggest a fallen angel, also known as Satan, who set up a rival kingdom (Ezekiel 28:12–15). Either way, temptation in Eden comes in the form of a serpent or snake, which frankly is brilliant typecasting. Our son has a pet snake and even we don't trust it. There's something about the way they move that makes people instinctively recoil. At this point you may be wondering if there was literally a talking snake in Eden. My guess is that this archetypal story draws on the serpent as a widely recognised symbol of evil. So the talking snake may be a metaphor but the dark voice of temptation is a reality we still encounter today.

Either way, Genesis 3 boils down to the issue of trust as the serpent raises concerns about God's motive: 'Did God really say, "You must not eat from any tree in the garden?"'(v.1). Eve corrects the serpent, pointing out that only the 'tree of the knowledge of good and evil' was prohibited, with a warning of death. Otherwise, the whole verdant orchard was a gift to enjoy. And remember, fruit is a common metaphor for something else a naked couple might enjoy.

God is good. Life in the garden was very good. But the serpent was crafty.

Through a few devious questions, he managed to reframe their scenario as one of restriction, stirring in Adam and Eve a concern that modern psychologists have dubbed the Fear Of Missing Out (FOMO):

> God knows that the moment you eat from that tree, you'll see what's really going on. You'll be just like God, knowing everything.
>
> *Genesis 3:4–5 (The Message)*

Satan sows seeds of doubt to poison their minds. What if God is like an over-controlling parent, holding you back from self-actualisation? What if doing life God's way means you will miss out on all the fun? This line has been pretty persuasive ever since. Peer-pressure, commercial advertising and the world of entertainment all depict freedom and fulfilment as the complete opposite to God. The ancient voice of temptation therefore sounds incredibly contemporary: God is a killjoy; you're missing out.

> When the Woman saw that the tree looked like good eating and realized what she would get out of it – she'd know everything! – she took and ate the fruit.
>
> *Genesis 3:6 (The Message)*

However, when Adam and Eve bit into the forbidden fruit, their teeth were set on edge. It looked attractive on the outside – the wrong choice usually does – but it was rotten on the inside.

Theologians refer to this moment as 'the fall' because our human condition plummeted to an all-time low; the exact opposite of what the serpent promised. When humans fall for the voice of temptation and betray their maker, it always ends in a bad place.

What happened next captures the way evil penetrates and poisons all areas of life. First, they experienced estrangement from God.

> They hid from the LORD God among the trees of the garden. But the LORD God called to the man, 'Where are you?'
>
> *Genesis 3:8–9*

For the first time, God approaching engenders fear. A new instinct to run and hide kicks in. God is now a threat to be avoided: the headmaster in the corridor, flashing lights in the rear-view mirror, the hunter in the wild. Humanity is estranged from the original source of life, joy and beauty. That's not a good situation to be in. In fact, it's tantamount to spiritual death.

God's question – 'Where are you?' – is therefore a probing one. If you ever sense the Almighty asking a question, it's unlikely that he lacks information. Instead, he is inviting a moment of honest reflection. It's time to stop running and to face up to reality. Hope begins here.

Second, human relationships are fractured.

> Then the eyes of both of them were opened, and they realised that they were naked; so they sewed fig leaves together and made coverings.
>
> *Genesis 3:7*

Hopefully, the only place we might hang around naked is at *home*. That's the point of Genesis 3: Adam and Eve felt completely at home together, with nothing to hide and nothing to fear. Can you imagine that? But when they turn from God it fractures their intimacy. Suddenly they feel exposed in each other's presence and begin to cover up. Ever since, we humans have fought a running battle with feelings of shame and inadequacy. Instead of living with openness, we fear rejection and use subtle tactics to cover up weakness and impress others. We work hard to manage appearances and keep people at arm's length. This stuff goes all the way back. But in our image-obsessed age it seems to be getting worse. Sadly, it results in untold psychological damage, self-loathing and toxic relationships. Perhaps you know what this feels like?

Third, our rule over the world has become destructive:

> Cursed is the ground because of you; through painful toil you will eat food from it . . . dust you are and to dust you will return.
>
> *Genesis 3:17, 19*

Our work was meant to be enjoyable and fulfilling. Instead, it has become stressful and frustrating. We now live in a world of thorns and thistles, diseases and computer viruses, tax returns and risk assessment forms. We were supposed to extend the beauty and ecology of Eden to the rest of the planet. Instead, we have exploited and commodified nature with disastrous consequences. Deep-sea divers recently set a new record by descending 11 kilometres into the Mariana Trench.[25] Guess what they found at the bottom? A plastic bag and some sweet wrappers. Evil is like plastic pollution: completely pervasive and seemingly impossible to get rid of.

Genesis 3 is ultimately a story of human beings seeking independence from God. But this is not natural. We are not freelance operatives or autonomous dudes. We are creatures. As former Archbishop of Canterbury Rowan Williams argues: 'Negotiating what it means to be dependent is part of being human.'[26] In Eden, this was symbolised by the 'tree of life', a divine gift that provided a source of vitality based on trust. But now, access is denied:

> GOD expelled them from the Garden of Eden . . . and stationed angel-cherubim and a revolving sword of fire east of it, guarding the path to the Tree-of-Life.
>
> *Genesis 3:24 (The Message)*

Shut out from Eden, humans faced the prospect of death. Unless we live with God at the centre, we wither back to dust. This makes sense of painful moments of loss and grief when we feel more acutely than ever: *It wasn't supposed to be this way!* Genesis gives voice to what we know deep down. Something's gone wrong with the world and we are personally implicated. When angled mirrors turn away from the source of beauty and life, it spells disaster for the whole cosmos. Now the entire world feels different. Humanity is living East of Eden and can only look back with fond memories. However, though the world is marred by brokenness, there is still so much beauty. Alongside the loss, there are glimpses of hope. The story continues . . .

READ: Genesis 3:1–24.

REFLECT: In what ways are we tempted to doubt God's goodness and turn away from him? God called: 'Adam, where are you?' Put your name in there. How will we respond to God's call?

# 7

## Origins and hope

*The promise of a snake-crusher*

According to Genesis, our origins story has a simple headline: God made the world good but humans rebelled and things turned bad. This makes sense of life on a daily basis: good and evil, pleasure and pain, newborns and bereavements. However, these bi-polar realities will not simply cancel each other out. Life is not a zero-sum game. That's not the story we inhabit. We are hope-based creatures. We lean forward, anticipating something better on the horizon. Life is not a random tragedy or a pointless comedy. Life is a divine story full of meaning. That's why the best storytellers face the complexities of life with confidence that good will triumph in the end. As the children's author, Michael Morpurgo put it:

> Wherever my story takes me, however dark and difficult the theme, there is always some hope and redemption, not because readers like happy endings but because . . . the sun will rise in the morning and there is light at the end of every tunnel.[27]

After the fall of humanity, subsequent chapters (Genesis 4–11) are like a river that splits into two divergent paths. We will trace each in turn. On the one hand, evil spreads, the world is vandalised and God acts in judgement. On the other hand, the world is washed clean and a rainbow appears as a promise that good will triumph over evil in the end.

After falling for the voice of temptation, Adam and Eve are expelled from the beautiful garden and face life on the outside. Wilderness. Originally, 'God blessed them' (Genesis 1:28). But now life is severely disrupted. Childbearing is complex and painful. The ground is hard to cultivate and prone to weeds. Family life is fraught with tension. Key areas of our human vocation have been frustrated. Experiences of failure are now the 'new normal'. Adam and Eve were meant to extend the beauty of Eden. Instead, they emerge bringing curses and transmitting the deadly disease of sin to future generations.

The situation quickly snowballs, as one dark tale follows another:

- Genesis 4: Rivalry and violence
  Adam and Eve have two sons. Cain lures Abel into the field and murders him in cold blood. Imagine the sadness that descended on the human family that day. A descendant of Cain called Lamech then shamelessly boasts that he killed a man in cold-blooded revenge (Genesis 4:23–4).

- Genesis 11: Pride and division
  Early humans then attempt to reverse the fall by building up to heaven: the Tower of Babel. If God no longer comes close to them, they will ascend to God and take back control. The whole project is birthed out of a self-confessed desire to 'make a name for ourselves' (Genesis 11:4). The latest technology (bricks) gives a feeling of invincibility as they ascend

> to new heights. However, in a moment of irony, God has to 'come down' just to glimpse their life's work. God then confuses their languages (*babel* means 'confusion') and the human race fragments and disperses in tribalism – the origins of wars, racism and Spanish lessons!

When I've been away overnight with work, Charlotte sometimes brings the kids to pick me up from the train station and give me a lift home. One time we pulled up on the driveway and I was first in the front door. I saw our belongings strewn across the floor and the house ransacked: 'We've been burgled!' I gasped as I stared at the chaos. 'Don't be ridiculous,' Charlotte replied, brushing past me. 'The kids had a sleep-over and we haven't tidied up yet!' When God looked at the state of the world he must have felt something similar. He created it to be a beautiful home, a shared living space for God and humanity. But those he entrusted it to had vandalised and corrupted every corner. In Genesis 6 we get a rare glimpse into God's emotional response:

> The LORD regretted that he had made human beings on the earth, and his heart was deeply troubled.
>
> *Genesis 6:6*

When I return home to chaos, my reaction is often: 'Well I'm not the one who should have to clear this mess up.' But that's not how God responds. As the Bible plays out, the Great Author will write himself into the story and pay the ultimate price to end the chaos. Our generous maker will become a bloodied saviour. But before all that, Genesis records a dramatic promise and a beautiful sign that declare hope over our broken world.

In Genesis 3, God addressed the serpent who introduced temptation and chaos in the first place. Listen to the dramatic nature of this promise:

> And I will put enmity
> between you and the woman,
> and between your offspring and hers;
> he will crush your head
> and you will strike his heel.
>
> *Genesis 3:15*

An offspring of a woman is coming as a heroic serpent-crusher. A new Adam will resurrect our hope of Eden and break the power of evil. However, in the process he himself will absorb the deadly poison: 'you will strike his heel'. This enigmatic hope is without much detail at this stage. But suffice it to say the rest of the Old Testament is pregnant with the promise of his arrival.

Then, in Genesis 6, God sends judgement in an unprecedented deluge. Several ancient accounts outside the Bible also record a catastrophic flood in the region of Mesopotamia that wiped out human settlements. However, the key debate is why this devastation was necessary. According to other myths, the gods were angry with humans for making too much noise or failing to provide them with enough food. Remember, in the ancient world humans were considered to be slaves for the gods. Genesis hits back with a counter-narrative. The flood was indeed an act of divine judgement. But as with any loving parent who disciplines their child, a greater purpose of restoration was in mind.

God called Noah to build an ark in which to save not only his own family but also pairs of animals. The hope that is invested in this human family is not just that 'souls will be saved' but animals and wildlife too. At the height of the flood, we are told that 'the waters covered the surface of the earth'. Remember, that's exactly how the earth looked before God spoke order and beauty into creation (Genesis 1:2). So the flood brings the world back to a new beginning. It's like God hit the refresh button. When the ark settled on dry land, Noah emerged as a new Adam stepping into a new creation:

> Then God blessed Noah and his sons, saying to them, 'Be fruitful and increase in number and fill the earth.'
>
> *Genesis 9:1*

God then makes a promise to this human family through a colourful visual aid. A rainbow appeared as a symbol of peace, the shape resembling a war bow hung up in the sky. Mercy is pledged instead of judgement. Despite the spread of evil like cancer, God promises to find a way to cleanse our world without destroying humanity in the process. Spoiler alert. Turn to the final page of the Bible and you will see that our human story loops all the way round to a new beginning: 'On each side of the river stood *the tree of life*' (Revelation 22:2). This iconic symbol from Eden reappears at the end. Paradise lost will be regained. In fact, you could take the first two chapters of the Bible (in Genesis) and the last two chapters (in Revelation) and stitch them together. They form brackets around our entire human story and act as a promise: we have come from a good place and we will one day get back there, despite the struggle in between. As we journey through the rest of the Bible story (*Exodus*, *Exile*, *Messiah*, *Spirit*), we already know that good will triumph in the end. Because the snake-crusher took our poison on a Roman cross, we will one day regain access to the tree of life. As a line in the film, *The Best Exotic Marigold Hotel* puts it: 'Everything will be all right in the end . . . If it's not all right, then it is not the end!'

READ: Genesis 8:15–9:7.

REFLECT: Put a picture of a rainbow on the kitchen fridge or the office wall as a reminder that whatever challenge or chaos we face, with God there is always hope.

PART 2

# EXODUS

## Our human quest for freedom

# Introducing freedom

'Freedom!' It's a cry that makes the hair on the back of my neck stand up every time I watch *Braveheart*. Mel Gibson stars in this film about a Scottish freedom fighter (William Wallace) who is finally captured by the oppressive English army and is about to be brutally executed. But as the darkness closes in he lets rip with a majestic and somewhat paradoxical cry that resonates deep in the human soul: 'Freedom!'

Despite living in a 'free society' we experience subtle forms of entrapment – an oppressive boss, a miserable relationship, an incurable disease, a recurring debt. Equally, we can become enslaved by inner demons of anger and lust, suffocating levels of anxiety or toxic habits that we can't break. We can spend much of life pondering escape routes and exit strategies that will lead to increased happiness. We humans are on a quest for freedom. That's the big idea of the story of Exodus. The word means 'exit' or 'way out'. When Israel was enslaved under Pharaoh in Egypt, God stepped in and brought them *out*. Then, after years of wilderness wanderings, they finally settled *in* the Promised Land. It's perhaps the most iconic story in the Old Testament.

However, Exodus is more than a historical event. It is also a metaphor that captures a much larger reality: the God of the

Bible is a freedom fighter. Still today, he sides with the underdog and roars against the oppressor: 'Let my people go!' The story of Exodus has therefore inspired numerous liberation movements – William Wilberforce and the Abolitionists, Martin Luther King and the Civil Rights movement, modern-day anti-trafficking campaigns, like Christine Caine's A21 movement. 'Exodus' can also become part of our story. We may not be physically oppressed by a literal Pharaoh but we all have our 'Egypt' – tough situations and negative cycles that leave us feeling trapped. I wonder what that might mean for you? Exodus is about inner freedom as well as outward liberation. What God did for Israel in the Old Testament, Jesus has come to do for all humanity. He is the freedom-fighter who brings true Exodus. As Jesus promised:

> If the Son sets you free, you will be free indeed.
>
> *John 8:36*

Like a first date, freedom is something we instinctively want but without being sure how to make a success of it. So it's worth taking care to define what we mean before exploring the Exodus story. In Western culture over the past 200 years, freedom has increasingly been defined by the individual's right to self-determination or autonomy. The Enlightenment project vigorously pursued emancipation from political, social and religious coercion and resulted in many positive changes. *Vive la revolution!* These political changes combined with increased social mobility have caused a rapid expansion of choice for the individual: global travel, career options, sexual expression. Equally, the digital revolution has brought the world to our doorstep through online shopping and on-demand streaming. Increased choice is surely a good thing. Who wants to return to the medieval era before Amazon Prime and Netflix? However, it has also been accompanied by a new freedom narrative. Here's my version of it:

> Discovering my inner self is the key to happiness. I need to throw off constraint and follow my heart. When I am free to be myself, life will have meaning and fulfilment.

This freedom narrative is what sociologists refer to as 'expressive individualism'.[1] It makes self the centre of the story and seeks emancipation from limitations and constraints. It has become the dominant story in Western culture. As I write this, I am staying in an old cottage in a remote mountain location. Even here, the plaque in the hallway says: 'In a world where you could be anything, be yourself.' Self-actualisation and self-expression are the goal of life and a queue of product advertisers, life coaches and YouTube influencers are poised to sell the dream. However, there are a couple of flaws with this freedom narrative: first, it's not true and second, it doesn't work. Rabbi Jonathan Sacks sums up the problem brilliantly: 'The twenty-first century has left us with a maximum of choice and a minimum of meaning.'[2]

If freedom is found through increased levels of choice and opportunity, we should be living the dream by now. But the pursuit of expressive individualism has given us nightmares. Western society is experiencing a mental-health crisis on an unprecedented scale. Symptoms of stress and anxiety dominate medical prescriptions. In addition, many self-medicate through drinking, shopping, over-working and entertainment bingeing. We are a culture addicted to forms of escape and distraction. The failed pursuit of freedom through self-expression has left us emotionally fragile. Increased choice without a grander sense of purpose actually results in unmanageable pressure. As Australian cultural theorist Mark Sayers concludes, we become 'frozen with choice anxiety and the pressure to perform . . . we are drowning in freedoms but thirsting for meaning'.[3] Instead of playing a part in a larger story, the individual has become the story. But this inward turn to self-discovery actually results in increased fragmentation and individualism as we each pursue happiness in different directions.

Humans don't flourish when we are the centre of the story. This only leads to subtle forms of entrapment. As professor of psychiatry, Glynn Harrison concludes: 'Questions of value and self-worth need to be sorted out in the context of a larger story about our identity and purpose.'[4] If the origins story in Genesis is true, then freedom will be found when I am free to be who I was *made to be*. Think William Wallace. He's on the rack without any freedom of choice. But having situated himself within a larger story (Scottish independence), he has a freedom that even suffering and death cannot thwart. That may all sound a bit Hollywood but it's actually very Bible. Made in the image of God, we are hard-wired with a divine purpose and responsibility. No amount of self-expression can replace this.

Exodus therefore tells a different story, a better one. Freedom means more than just escaping the oppressive control of Pharaoh; it also means entering a covenant relationship that is truly liberating. It's *freedom from* Egypt and *freedom for* the Promised Land. It's the way *out* and the way *in*. True liberation is not mere escapism; it is much more powerful than that. It includes snapping chains of tyrannical oppression but also the shedding of blood, the giving of law, the journey of faith, the exercise of courage and restraint. As we dive into the detail, don't lose sight of the bigger picture. We belong in the beauty of Eden, but we've ended up enslaved in Egypt. Exodus is the God of the Bible acting decisively to bring us out of the chaos and darkness in order that we may fulfil our original purpose as image-bearers and angled mirrors, reflecting God's beauty to the world. That's who we were made to be. That's freedom.

8

# Exodus is a freedom story

*From Abraham to Israel to us*

We used to have a sheepdog called Ben. He was born in a barn and didn't see the light of day until we drove him off the farm nine months later. For the next year this rural collie was a nervous wreck, struggling to adjust to urban life. Then one afternoon on holiday I took Ben home, back to the farm he originally came from and the shepherd let him into a field of sheep for the first time. What happened next would have been a YouTube sensation if only I'd had the presence of mind to record it. Ben shot off like a black and white missile, circled round the sheep, assumed crouch-mode and moved towards the rather startled flock. They in turn obediently made their way to the shepherd. Somehow knowing that this was job done, Ben trotted over to me and sat down. From that day on, he displayed a new inner calm and confidence. Even back in the urban jungle he was a different dog. Lesson learned. When a sheepdog fulfils its original purpose, it discovers what freedom feels like.

The story of the Bible is ultimately about humans fulfilling their original purpose as image-bearers and reflective mirrors. When we do, like Ben we discover the exhilaration of being who we were made to be. However, since being banished from Eden, freedom has become problematic. We face the harsh realities of a broken and cursed world in which life feels more like an urban jungle than a safe garden. In short, by rejecting our maker, we lost our freedom and joy. The Exodus event reveals God's plan to restore all that we've lost. It's an epic story told from the vantage point of a marginal people (Israel), overshadowed by empires whom they outlast. The Exodus narrative is inherently political. Indeed, the whole Bible has a distinct bias toward the disadvantaged and celebrates moments when the poor are exalted and the mighty humbled.[5] The story of God and humanity is revealed not through superpowers but from the perspective of an oppressed people who experienced true freedom.

Before we get there, we need to join the dots from the story of our origins in Genesis to the particular story of Israel and Exodus. Despite the promise of a heroic snake-crusher, the last scene we witnessed in Genesis 1–11 was one of humans trying to take back control by building a tower to heaven. God's judgement came in the form of linguistic confusion. At the Tower of *Babel*, humanity lost its unity of speech and purpose. As a result, the human race fragmented into hostile tribes. So what next? How will humans recover their original freedom and purpose? Genesis 12 reveals a surprising answer that turns the drama of Scripture in a whole new direction. Until now, the story had been told on a global scale – creation, temptation, the flood, the Tower of Babel. But in Genesis 12 we reach the Bronze Age (*c*. 1800 BC) and the story zooms in on one individual living near modern-day Basra (Iraq). The global scenes in Genesis 1–11 now form the backstory for a particular family that begins with Abraham (previously Abram). However, as the horizons of the plot shrink down to this Middle-Eastern tent-dweller, somehow the whole world is still in view:

> The LORD had said to Abram, 'Go from your country, your people and your father's household to the land I will show you.
>
> I will make you into a great nation,
> and I will bless you . . .
> and *all peoples on earth*
> *will be blessed through you.*'
>
> *Genesis 12:1–3*

According to this promise, Abraham's family carries hope for 'all peoples on earth'. After evil entered the world in Genesis 3, the word 'curse' was spoken five times. But now, as God calls Abraham, he speaks blessing five times.[6] This word is the opposite of curse. It results in what modern ideas of 'success' and 'wellbeing' hint at. In other words, somehow Abraham's family is the launch of a divine plan to destroy evil and recover our original freedom. Abraham will become the patriarch, literally 'founding father', of the nation of Israel. From Israel will come the Messiah and through the Messiah God will launch a new humanity and a new creation. All that's gone wrong with the world will eventually be resolved through this chosen family. It's no exaggeration to say that the rest of the Bible is an outworking of these promises to Abraham in Genesis 12.

Think of it like the opening sequences of a Bond film. The early scenes are often epic in scale as an evil maniac stroking a cat is plotting world domination. Then suddenly the camera cuts to one individual, 007, some distance from the action. The viewer knows what this means: somehow James Bond will be the key to resolving the global crisis. But it won't be until the end of the film that we find out how. As the camera cuts to Abraham in Genesis 12, it's clear that God has a plan to rescue the entire world through his family. But it won't be until the New Testament that we find out how.

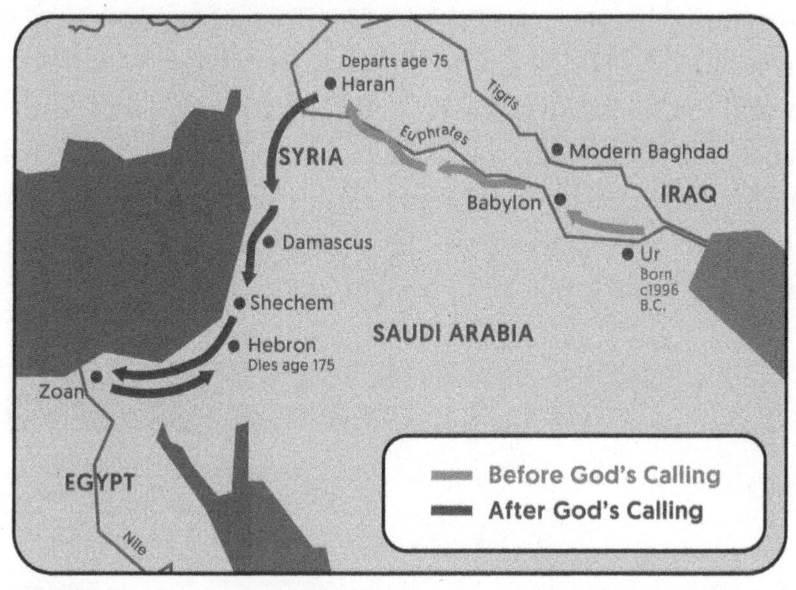


*Abraham's journey from Ur (Iraq) to the Promised Land (Hebron)*

With this larger backdrop in mind, Abraham and his wife Sarah relocate to a distant land and begin a new life. In the ancient world, to cut ties with your roots and leave the soil of your ancestors was a radical thing. In Abraham's case, at seventy-five years of age, he travelled 900 miles with his immediate family to the land of Canaan. This will later be known as the 'Promised Land' or 'Holy Land', roughly the combined territory of Israel and Palestine today. It's HQ for the rest of the Old Testament. Abraham's journey out of an old life and into something new provides an early glimpse of what liberation will involve. It anticipates the Exodus journey that his offspring, the nation of Israel, will make, out of Egypt, through the wilderness and into the Promised Land.

Abraham's radical relocation also captures the metaphorical journey that we must all make. If we want freedom, we cannot stay living the way we always have. God's call has a disruptive element to it. We must leave one story to be joined to another, no matter what the cost. I think of my friend David who grew up in a wealthy Hindu family. However, at university, he began to read the Bible and discovered the liberating power of Jesus. When David announced that he had become a Christian, his family disowned him and removed his name from the will. Despite the pain of rejection, David once said to me: 'You can't put a price on the freedom I have in Jesus.'

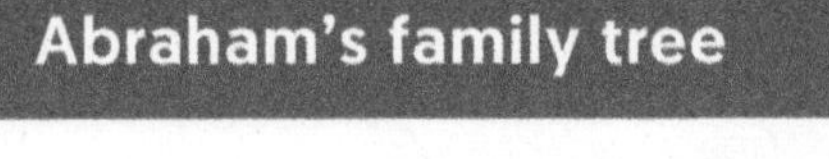


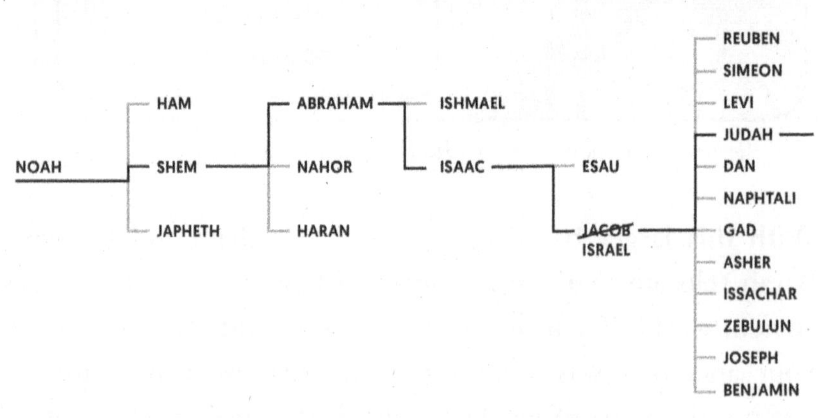


Back to the Bible. How do we get from Abraham relocating to the Promised Land to Israel enslaved down in Egypt? The rest of Genesis (chapters 12–50) tells the story in detail. But this book is about seeing the big picture. So here it is in a paragraph. Abraham and Sarah faced the pain and trauma of infertility until they were pensioners. But then God gave them a miracle child called Isaac who in turn had twins called Jacob and Esau. Jacob had twelve sons who form the basis for the twelve tribes of Israel. However, despite being the chosen family, they were pretty dysfunctional. Through a wicked tale of envy, violence and betrayal, Jacob's favourite son Joseph was sold as a slave by his own brothers and taken down to Egypt. Several decades later, they were reconciled and Jacob's entire family relocate to Egypt to be with Joseph – a happy ending to the book of Genesis. However, it wouldn't be long before the Egyptian powers-that-be turned against them. That's how to join the dots from Abraham in Canaan to Israel down in Egypt and in need of Exodus deliverance.

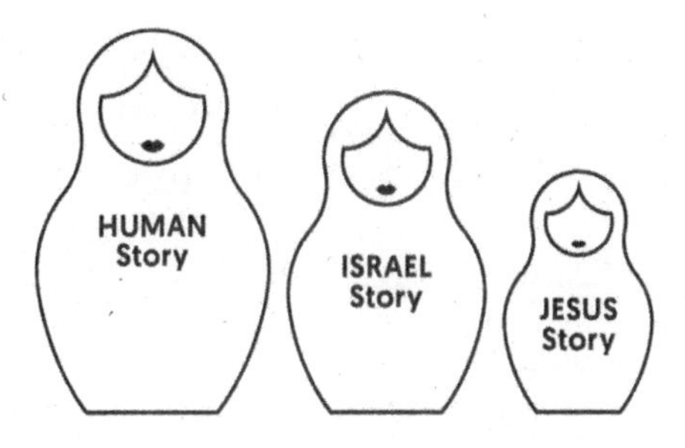


The call of Abraham and the story of Israel form part of a multi-layered story, much like a set of Russian dolls. The largest narrative is a universal story, which bookends the Bible at the start (Genesis) and at the end (Revelation). But in between a smaller plotline emerges from Genesis 12 onwards (Abraham and Israel). This in turn narrows down to one individual (the Messiah). However, as Jesus breaks the curses of evil, the story can expand out again to 'all people on earth'. His victory has opened up the way of freedom for all humanity. Just as a sheepdog comes alive working sheep, Exodus is about humans rediscovering the freedom and exhilaration of our original purpose. Irenaeus, a Christian leader in the second century, summed it up perfectly: 'The glory of God is a human being fully alive.'[7] Can you imagine what that would mean for you? That's why

God called Abraham, rescued Israel and sent Jesus. God wants us to experience true freedom through his liberating love.

READ: Genesis 12:1–7.

REFLECT: We are invited into this Exodus story. Write your name in the smallest Russian doll below and reflect on what true freedom could mean for you.

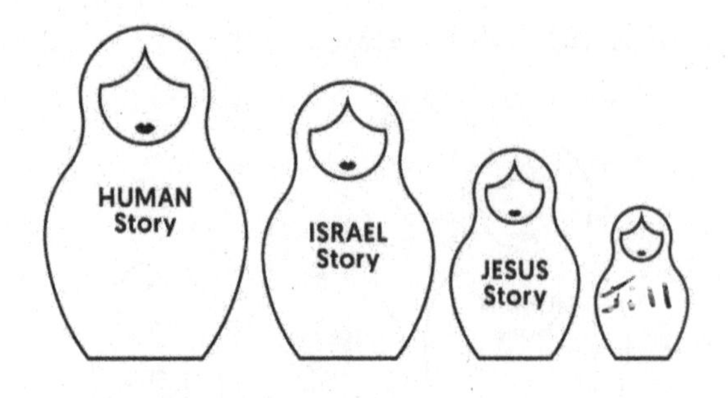

# 9

## Exodus begins with encounter

*Moses and the great I AM*

As we turn to Exodus, the second book of the Bible, the Israelites are trapped south of the River Nile. Four hundred years since Joseph came down to Egypt, the descendants of Abraham have grown so rapidly that Pharaoh considered them a threat to national security. So he enslaved them in labour camps, forcing them to meet impossible targets with diminishing resources. Now they are crying in the dark and desperate for a change. However, the narrator wants us to know that their plight has not been overlooked:

> God heard their groaning and he remembered his covenant with Abraham . . . So God looked on the Israelites and was concerned about them.
>
> *Exodus 2:24–5*

Notice the verbs: God 'heard', 'looked', 'remembered'. Though God doesn't have ears or eyes the narrator is communicating divine attentiveness. God cares. That's worth remembering when we feel forgotten in the dark. For myself, I can still remember the shock of redundancy and the feeling of being left on the shelf. Maybe this resonates with your experiences? However, precisely when Israel thought nothing was happening, God was preparing a dramatic rescue. Think of it like a play at the theatre. On stage sits a lone actor for whom the plot seems to have run out. But backstage there's a flurry of activity as crew and cast scramble into position ready for the next scene that will kick the story in a new direction. Israel's Exodus begins backstage with a compassionate God who cares for the oppressed.

We are now ready to meet the central character in the Exodus drama: Moses. His significance is captured by an easily overlooked detail. In order to save her baby from the threat of genocide, Moses' mother placed him in a basket. The idea stuck and parents still use 'Moses baskets' today. Interestingly, the word for 'basket' in Exodus is the same as 'ark' in Genesis. It's Russian dolls again. As Noah's ark rescued our human story from extinction, so Israel will be saved through this baby hidden in a basket on the River Nile. Sure enough, Pharaoh's daughter found him, took pity on Moses and brought him up in the palace. So Pharaoh unwittingly provided shelter for a Hebrew descendant of Abraham who will later become his successor's nemesis. He even funded Moses' mother to provide childcare for her own son. In Exodus, female characters consistently gain the upper hand over tyrannical males.

Fast-forward forty years and Moses has hit rock bottom. We find him hiding in the wilderness region of Horeb. It would have been as miserable as the name suggests. While living in Pharaoh's palace, Moses had witnessed an Egyptian beating a Hebrew slave. He saw red and murdered the Egyptian in a bungled attempt at justice and revenge. As word got round, Moses fled for fear of getting caught and ended up looking after sheep in the back of beyond. What happened next is key to the whole story of Exodus:

> There the angel of the LORD appeared to him in flames of fire from within a bush. Moses saw that though the bush was on fire it did not burn up . . . God called to him from within the bush, 'Moses! Moses!'
>
> *Exodus 3:2, 4*

Through this burning bush experience, Moses came face to face with two life-altering facts: *God knows my name* and *God has a name* (Exodus 3:14). The voice from the bush spoke on first-name terms: 'Moses! Moses!' That's both reassuring and disturbing. I recently met someone who had moved over to the UK from Kuala Lumpur. In order to exchange contact details, he told me his number and I dialled it. Suddenly, my number appeared on his screen with: 'Andrew Ollerton?' next to it. I was disturbed. How does a phone from Kuala Lumpur recognise my name and number? In an era BG (Before Google) Moses encountered the God who already had his name and number. This is the beginning of freedom for Moses: he realised in a personal way that God knew him and had a purpose for his life. If 'All the world's a stage' (Shakespeare), Moses just met the director (God). And despite all Moses' failings, God had written him into the script. That's deeply reassuring.

The problem with turning inwards to discover freedom is that we must come up with the script. The responsibility for life working out happily ever after is on our shoulders. That's a crushing weight. It can leave us paralysed with choice anxiety, jeopardising opportunities and relationships because we are unable to commit fully. We hedge our bets, paralysed at the thought of missing out on a happy ending. Moses had made his fair share of bad choices and no doubt concluded that the rest of his life was consigned to the 'unfortunate' category. But when God called his name, he was summoning him out of a sense of doom and failure. It was an invitation to anchor his fragile self to a much larger purpose that could not be thwarted. This is freedom. It begins when we encounter the director and surrender our scripts to him.

As the bush kept burning, God kept talking. In the course of conversation he revealed his own name: 'I AM WHO I AM. This is what you are to say to the Israelites: I AM has sent me to you' (Exodus 3:14). This rather odd name, I AM, comes from a Hebrew verb for 'existence' and is the root of the name *Yahweh* or *Jehovah*. This name was used to distinguish Israel's God from other so-called deities. After all, 'god' is just a title like 'Mrs' or 'Dr'. But, at the burning bush, God revealed his personal name. In most versions of the Bible today the capitalised word 'LORD' is used as a substitute. Why has someone left the Caps Lock on? It is to signify that the divine name is so sacred it should not be pronounced. The name 'I AM' therefore captures the holy and eternal nature of God. Like a fire that burns without fuel, God is utterly sufficient and complete in himself. Moses can count on this God to be all he needs, without fail.

So, there's fragile Moses, wracked with fear and failure but a solid God who is utterly sufficient. On this basis, Moses can take on Pharaoh. God's promise to him is simple: 'I will be with you!' His life can make a difference because God will always live up to his name. Feelings of inadequacy can hold us back and keep us indoors, scared that our weaknesses will be exposed. But when we encounter the great I AM, we discover a new source of confidence. This has been my experience. I lived in the shadow of fear for many years, too concerned about what my peers thought of me. Ironically, I never won their respect as I traded honour and integrity for showmanship. But when I encountered the great I AM it was a game-changer. His presence broke the stranglehold of fear and I discovered a new freedom to be who I was made to be.

Although Moses continued to struggle with feelings of inadequacy, along with a speech impediment and a criminal record, God was determined to partner with him to fulfil his Exodus mission. As a parent might invite their child to help them with a task they could easily accomplish on their own, so God calls inadequate people like us to work with him. It's God's primary way of getting things done. As St Augustine put it: 'Without God we cannot; without us he will not.'[8] Back in the nineteenth century, the missionary Lord Radstock was staying in a hotel in Norway when he heard a little girl playing the piano out of tune downstairs and it began to drive him mad: plonk . . . plink . . . plink . . . plonk. But then another man sat down and began playing alongside her, filling in the gaps. Soon the hotel was filled with the sound of beautiful music. Lord Radstock later discovered that the man was her father, Alexander Borodin, composer of the opera *Prince Igor*.[9]

When the great I AM comes alongside flawed people, he more than fills in the gaps. He is able to turn our plinking and plonking into something beautiful. Freedom begins when we encounter the God who *calls us by name* and *lives up to his name*. With the great I AM by our side, we can overcome our fears and bring about some beautiful change in the world.

READ: Exodus 2:23–3:15.

REFLECT: Can you summarise ways that you can make a difference in the world? Has God tasked you with anything? Don't let fear stop you, no matter how inadequate you feel.

10

# Exodus confronts idols

*Pharaoh and the plagues*

God's exit-strategy for Israel began in earnest when Moses returned to Egypt. He came fresh from the burning bush with a message for Pharaoh: 'Let my people go!' What followed is one of the greatest showdowns in world history. Each time Pharaoh refused, another plague struck Egypt. Finally, after ten rounds, Pharaoh threw in the towel. Behind the obvious physical plagues – frogs, gnats, boils, etc. – a spiritual confrontation was unfolding that is key to our freedom. The Egyptians believed in a pantheon of gods that they associated with the natural world. Imagine a children's story like *Thomas the Tank Engine* where inanimate objects such as trains have names, faces and personalities. For the Egyptians, the sun was a god called Ra who gave light to the world. So when the ninth plague brought darkness for three days it was not just a tanning issue; it was an affront to the Egyptian understanding of how the world works and who's in charge. As God said to Moses: 'I will bring judgment on all the gods of Egypt. I am the LORD.' (Exodus 12:12).

Equally, Pharaoh considered himself to be the son of Ra. As such Pharaoh was responsible for establishing what the

Egyptians called *ma'at*, order and peace. At the centre of this ideal was the River Nile. Its delta of fertility was the lifeblood of Egypt. So the first two plagues turned the Nile to blood and caused an infestation of frogs. These plagues ruthlessly exposed Pharaoh's inability to manage the world and secure *ma'at*. No wonder he stubbornly refused to accept defeat. His whole identity and status were at stake.

The showdown with Pharaoh therefore illustrates a much deeper aspect of freedom. Powerful forces are at work in our world with a vested interest in keeping us under their control. Imagine Pharaoh less as a particular person and more as a metaphor for what the Bible calls *idols*. That word may conjure up images of stone statues in the British Museum, but the Bible has something far more contemporary in mind. Think of Pharaoh as any rival to God, an alternative source of authority and trust in our lives. In the Bible an idol is anything or anyone that promises to meet our deepest needs for security and fulfilment in exchange for our service. Popular author Timothy Keller therefore refers to idols as 'counterfeit gods', which includes 'anything so central and essential to your life that, should you lose it, your life would feel hardly worth living'.[10] That's rugby and rogan josh curries for me. How about you? Joking aside, if we want to know whether we're serving idols, we need to follow the trail of our deepest passions, our time and money as well as potential threats that cause anxiety. At the other end of that trail are the idols or counterfeit gods that have captured our hearts.

What's particularly subtle is our ability to turn good things into ultimate things: family and children, sex and relationships, work and career, money and possessions, sports and exercise. All good, but none can bear the weight of 'everything'. When we make them our whole reason for living it damages us and them. For example, if we make financial security and material possessions our goal, we will never have enough and the fickle nature of money will run us ragged. If career becomes our source of self-esteem and measure of success, we will become stressed-out workaholics with a continual point to prove. It's not the work that's the problem; it's our need to be seen, to secure a successful reputation and future security that drives us into the ground. Like Pharaoh, idols are demanding: they want more bricks with less straw. No wonder anxiety is such a plague on our modern culture. We build our lives on fragile things like money, popularity, career and appearance. When we feel them giving way, we are shaken to the core. Frightening.

Eventually, the idols will fail us. When the plagues come (recession, sickness, bereavement) their shortcomings will be exposed and we will realise the things we worked so hard for were empty. The relationship we always wanted leaves us feeling trapped, the new house with hot tub becomes an empty nest, the business we ploughed everything into fails to take off. Idols always break the hearts of their worshippers.[11] The story of our origins revealed that humans only flourish with God at the centre. When other passions push him aside, we lose our centre of gravity and become as fragile as the things we have idolised. A poem in the Bible captures the danger:

> Those who make [idols] will be like them,
> and so will all who trust in them.
>
> *Psalm 135:18*

Pharaoh is a counterfeit, a rival in the way of true freedom. That's why Exodus requires a head-on confrontation. If we are to escape servile ways of living we must be freed from the power of idols to serve the living God: 'Let my people go *so that* they may worship me' (Exodus 8:1). When tough times come and things we have set our hopes on fail, it can be devastating. No one would choose the loss of a job, betrayal by a partner or a fight with cancer. But there's a strange kindness in the plagues God sends on the Egyptians. They expose the lies of Pharaoh and reveal a better place for our trust. As Timothy Keller concludes: 'The only way to free ourselves from the destructive influence of counterfeit gods is to turn back to the true one, the living God . . . He's the only one who if you find him, can truly fulfil you, and if you fail him, can truly forgive you.'[12]

As Moses came to Egypt to set the captives free, so Jesus came into our world to bring us true Exodus. So don't let Pharaoh intimidate you into staying put. The Messiah breaks the stranglehold of dark forces and ends the negative cycles that run us ragged. The football manager, Jürgen Klopp, has spoken about the liberating power of Jesus in his life. In an article, Klopp declared that his faith was far more important than football and for that reason he was free to enjoy the beautiful game: 'There is nothing so important to me that I cannot bear to lose it, and that is why I find I have no reason to fear.'[13]

Surprisingly, when Israel finally left Egypt, quite a few other people joined them, including some Egyptians (Exodus 12:38). The experience of the plagues had woken them up to reality. The emperor's got no clothes. Pharaoh cannot keep his promises. They had served the counterfeit long enough. It was time to get out. In the same way, we must choose to let go of our idols and embrace the way of freedom. In Robert Pirsig's novel, *Zen and the Art of Motorcycle Maintenance*, he describes the South Indian Monkey trap, an ingenious method for catching troublesome creatures. Chained to a tree is a hollowed-out coconut with a small hole and some rice inside. The monkey's paw can fit through the hole but his clenched fist full of rice cannot come back out. The monkey is trapped by its own desires. The instinct to grab as much rice as possible becomes enslaving. It's a brilliant picture of contemporary addictions and idols. The very things we hold on to so tightly threaten to destroy us. The very things we want more of leave us trapped. The story of Exodus is about letting go of false hopes and reaching out to the living God. Freedom ultimately comes down to what or who we chose to serve.

READ: Exodus 7:8–24.

REFLECT: What are you holding on to that is stopping you from being truly free? Clench your fist and imagine that thing. Now open your hand and release it to God.

## 11

# Exodus means crossing over

*The way out of bondage*

At some point around the fourteenth century BC there was a mass exodus from Egypt as Israel finally got the green light. Pharaoh gave in and let them go. After 400 years of slavery, they headed east towards the land God had promised Abraham centuries earlier. They were going home. However, no sooner had they set out but they found themselves trapped again, this time between an expanse of water called the Red Sea, and the Egyptian army closing in behind. That's right, Pharaoh changed his mind. Bullies often do. When they realise they've lost out they become angry and devious in a bid to reassert control. They can't live without it. That's why you mustn't buckle and go back. The worst thing you can do with a bully is back down. They'll apologise and say reassuring things you want to hear. Then it will start all over again.

Anyway, back to Israel. No way forwards and no way back. So the scene is set for a mighty act of deliverance that has been used as a metaphor for salvation ever since. Moses said to the Israelites:

> 'Stand firm and you will see the deliverance the LORD will bring you today. The Egyptians you see today you will never see again. The LORD will fight for you; you need only to be still' . . . Then Moses stretched out his hand over the sea, and all that night the LORD drove the sea back with a strong east wind and turned it into dry land. The waters were divided, and the Israelites went through the sea on dry ground, with a wall of water on their right and on their left.
>
> *Exodus 14:13–14, 21–2*

Interpreting the Bible is about exercising powers of imagination. Don't just read it. Feel it. Imagine these poor, tormented slaves, born under oppression, never expecting to taste freedom. Imagine them walking down that corridor of water and out into the light at the other end. This is the crux of Exodus. The Red Sea parting is the iconic event that captures our need for divine intervention.

I recently read an online article, which argued that the story of Exodus shows that human beings have the capacity to transform their circumstances. In fact, the overarching message of Exodus is the polar opposite. We could paraphrase Moses' speech as follows: 'Do nothing. You can't even begin to sort this out. Let God be God!' Of course, we have a part to play – we'll come to that. But first the Bible insists that we must stop striving and start trusting. Quit trying to sort it ourselves and make space for God. Some of us find this hard. Perhaps, like me, you are a fixer? Despite juggling unmanageable pressures, we still try and assert control and keep up appearances. But for as long as we rely on ourselves, we can't experience true Exodus. Self-help will never bring us to the other side. For that matter, neither will religion. Too often it's assumed that the message of the Bible is spiritual hoop jumping: if we perform certain rituals and duties and live a moral life, we can earn a position of acceptance with God:

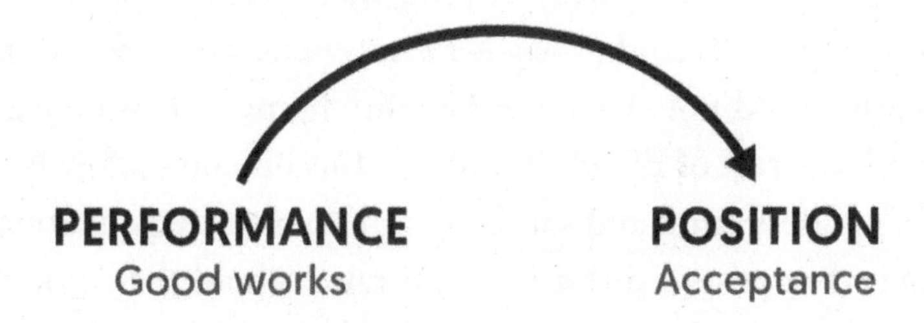


But Israel's Exodus worked in completely the opposite way. They had not even received the Ten Commandments at this point, let alone obeyed them. Without any performance or achievement on their part, God stepped in. Salvation is an undeserved gift, not a reward for good works. God didn't meet them halfway once they'd sorted themselves out. He made the first move and got them out. This is how the whole Bible works: God loves us and saves us upfront. Then, having found acceptance, we respond by living to please God:

This point becomes clear when we back up and remember what it took to break Pharaoh's hold in the first place. With Moses still locked in a stand-off with Pharaoh, God declared a tenth and final plague. The death of the first-born male. Nothing else could prize open Pharaoh's grip. Crucially, Israel was not immune from the threat. Despite being oppressed and abused they were also culpable. We should remember this. A victim mentality doesn't help anyone. The Israelites were still responsible for their failures and shortcomings. So they would have faced the tenth plague of judgement like everyone else.

However, an event known as *Passover* ensured that the angel of death would not strike the Israelite homes when he passed through the rest of Egypt. To secure this outcome, they had to take a spotless lamb and sacrifice it. The blood was daubed on to their doorposts using a hyssop branch (hold that thought). The angel of death would see the blood and *pass over* the house. Hence the name. While all this was going on outside, the family tucked into delicious roast lamb. The feast provided a foretaste of an imminent escape. They were to eat the meal with their shoes on, ready for the off (Exodus 12:11).

The Passover festival is still celebrated annually by Jewish families. It includes a meal that recalls the Exodus event through smell, taste and touch. Bitter herbs and salt water give a taste of oppression and tears; flat bread called *matzoh* symbolises their rushed departure without time for the dough to rise; cups of wine share in the celebration of freedom on the other side. And of course central to the whole thing is the lamb. Centuries later, Jesus shared a Passover meal with his friends. But in a shocking moment he reinterpreted the entire Exodus event around himself. He broke the matzoh bread and gave it to his disciples:

> 'Take and eat; *this is my body.*' Then he took a cup . . . 'Drink from it, all of you. *This is my blood* . . . for the forgiveness of sins.'
>
> *Matthew 26:26–8*

Ever since, bread and wine have become vivid Christian symbols. As Jesus died on the cross, he was the ultimate Passover lamb. As if to make the point, a cup of wine-vinegar was lifted to him on a hyssop branch (John 19:29). Remember that? The broken body and shed blood of Jesus provide a new Exodus, the way of freedom for all humanity.

Through the Passover lamb and the parting of the Red Sea, Israel crossed over to the other side. It was a decisive moment of transfer. Beforehand, they were slaves in Egypt; afterwards, they were free people, able to see themselves in a new light. In the ancient world, before modern bridges and tunnels, an expanse of water was an important boundary marker. Just crossing a river would feel like a significant change of location and jurisdiction. Even today there's something about crossing water on holiday that makes you feel like you've properly got away. For Israel, the Red Sea was like a birth canal. Coming out the other side, they entered a brand new existence.

The story of Exodus resonates deeply with our human quest for freedom. We want to leave behind old ways of living – regrets, addictions, anxiety – and cross to the other side. According to the New Testament, Israel's physical deliverance was a pattern of the freedom we can experience through Jesus. When he sets us free, it's like crossing over: we may live in the same physical location but spiritually we become new people. A friend of ours experienced repeated bullying at a young age. To escape anxiety and feel in control, she dabbled with Ouija boards and occult powers. But this only made things worse. At rock bottom she cried out to God for help. One Sunday she turned up at church, received prayer and invited Jesus into her life. She later described what happened next: 'I walked back along a familiar route but everything seemed new. I remember hearing the birds singing for the first time. When I got home and looked in the mirror, I saw a new me smiling back. By God's grace, it's become the new normal.' Through Jesus, we can experience the gift of Exodus. No longer slaves to Pharaoh or fear, we can live on the other side. As the New Testament puts it:

> If anyone is in Christ, the new creation has come: the old has gone, the new is here!
>
> *2 Corinthians 5:17*

READ: Exodus 14:10–22.

REFLECT: Why not go online and listen to the song 'No Longer Slaves' (Bethel Music) and allow the truth of it to sink in.

12

# Exodus brings us to God

*The covenant at Mount Sinai*

Having passed through the Red Sea, Israel made it to the other side. From this vantage point they sang freedom songs loud enough for any surviving Egyptians to hear. Israel's God had won an emphatic victory over all rivals and counterfeits. As birds sing after the storm, Moses and his sister Miriam burst into song:

> I will sing to the LORD,
> for he is highly exalted.
> Both horse and driver
> he has hurled into the sea.
> The LORD is my strength and my defence;
> he has become my salvation.

*Exodus 15:1–2*

This is the first song in the Bible and the first of many. Singing is a powerful way to express our freedom. The Exodus story has inspired whole genres of music as enslaved African-Americans wrote songs of hope and resistance in the face of oppression. Perhaps the most famous spiritual was called 'Go down, Moses!' and included the Exodus refrain: 'Let my people go!' When we face fears and challenges, songs that celebrate God's power and victory can change the atmosphere. After all, you can't worship and worry at the same time. One will always give way to the other.

So Israel sang and celebrated. But as the party fever wore off . . . what next? Escaping Pharaoh's control in Egypt was only the first half of Exodus. Freedom *from* oppression and loosing the chains of injustice are vital. However, we must also experience freedom *for* a new purpose. Western culture tends to appreciate the first but reduces the second to empty sound bites like 'Be yourself'. Once we are driving away from Pharaoh with the wind in our hair we are classified as free. But the Bible tells a more inspiring story. It's *freedom from* Pharaoh's regime and *freedom for* God's purpose: 'Let my people go, *so that* they may worship me' (Exodus 8:1). Human beings are hard-wired to worship or serve. In the Bible, the same word is used for both. The question is who or what

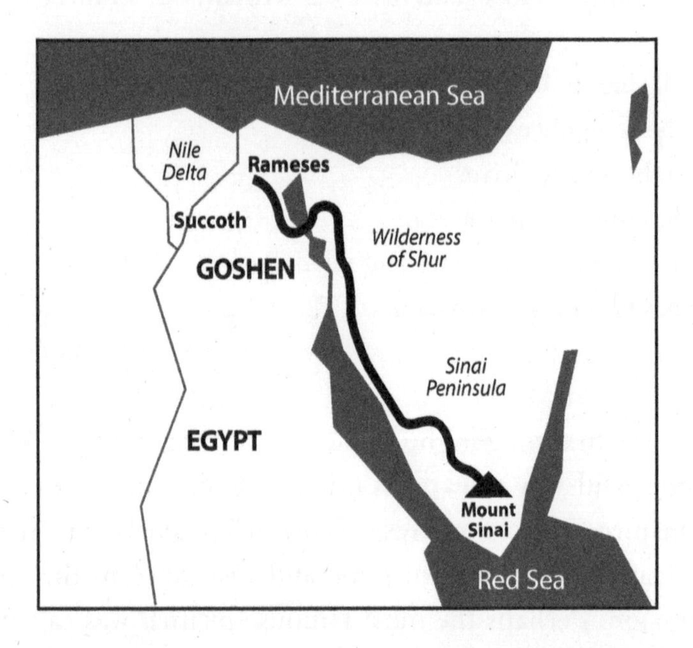


*The likely route Israel took from Egypt to Mount Sinai*

will we worship? Bob Dylan sang it this way: 'You gotta serve somebody. It may be the devil or it may be the Lord but you gotta serve somebody.'[14] In the Exodus story, freedom is being released from serving the tyrant (Pharaoh) to serve the liberator instead (God).

Before the Exodus event really got going, God had already said to Moses: 'I have promised to bring you up *out* of your misery in Egypt *into*. . . a land flowing with milk and honey' (Exodus 3:17). In the ancient world, milk and honey were symbols of richness and rest. Even if you are lactose intolerant that's pretty good news for ex-slaves. Given how straightforward it all sounds, the Israelites probably assumed that after a successful jailbreak they would be in the Promised Land by nightfall. But real change doesn't work like that. Exodus is a more honest guide to freedom. Nelson Mandela's biography was entitled *Long Walk to Freedom*. That's about right. Not just for Mandela and Israel but also for us.

**Three months later . . .**

After wandering through the harsh wilderness and facing numerous challenges for weeks, Israel finally arrived at the foot of a mountain. This was not any old peak but Mount Sinai or Mount Horeb. Can you hear the echo back to Exodus 3 and the burning bush? Moses has returned to the place where God first called him, only now he is accompanied by a whole nation of ex-slaves. This time, God came down on the mountain and revealed himself to all Israel in an experience they would never forget.

How do you imagine God? Take your time on this one. It's perhaps the most revealing thing about us. Religious depictions often assume a miserable Victorian deity, austere and repressive. Cultural stereotypes swing the other way and assume God would be a liberal-minded sugar daddy. Exodus 19 shatters both illusions. God declares himself so loving Israel can trust him *and* so holy Israel should fear him. In a series of pyrotechnic eruptions, God revealed his fearsome holiness (Exodus 19:16–19). We'll return to that shortly. But first, through surprisingly intimate metaphors, God reassured Israel that they could trust him:

> 'You yourselves have seen what I did to Egypt, and how I carried you on eagles' wings and brought you to myself. Now if you obey me fully and keep my covenant, then out of all nations you will be my treasured possession. Although the whole earth is mine, you will be for me a kingdom of priests.'
>
> *Exodus 19:4–6*

Imagine a fluttering eaglet being hounded by predators. Suddenly a mother eagle swoops in, scares off the bullies and carries the eaglet to safety on her wings. Think *Lord of the Rings.* In a closing scene, Frodo and Sam lie exhausted and in danger. Suddenly, mighty eagles arrive and carry them home to the safety of Gondor. When we feel harassed and vulnerable, God says, 'I am like a mother eagle, defending, protecting, carrying.' The second metaphor is even more personal: 'you will be my treasured possession'. Imagine a monarch with great wealth at their disposal. Yet they have a sentimental item that means more than all the rest, a necklace from their grandmother perhaps or a ring from their father. This is their 'treasured possession'. The Hebrew word is *segulla*, which is a popular child's name in Israel. As a monarch wears a personal item round their neck, as a parent scans a crowded playground for their special treasure, so God declares his covenant love for this rabble of ex-slaves. He is the eagle who will defend and carry them; they are his *segulla*.

Israel needed to hear this. They were fresh out of a pretty abusive situation and no doubt they emerged with trust issues. Read Exodus 16: just three days after leaving, at the first sign of hardship, they considered returning to Egypt. There's no resilience. Emotionally they're all over the place. Have you ever felt like that? Well out in the wilderness, with Israel feeling exposed and vulnerable, God declares his loving intentions towards them. Unlike Pharaoh, God does not use threats or compulsion; he does not even apply a payback model (*you owe me for the Red Sea parting*). Instead, he commits to loving them out of their servile and fearful disposition and into a relationship of dignity and honour.

You may have experienced bullying, abuse or other forms of trauma. We shouldn't underestimate the healing required. Trust issues can run deep. They cause us to recoil from the world and adopt a negative stance that assumes the worst. The world is unpredictable, people can't be trusted and predators are lurking. As a result, we live on a high state of alert, with continuous background anxiety that leaves us exhausted. Alcohol, drugs, and casual sex may help escape for an evening. But then comes the hangover. Exodus 19 reveals a better way. God promises to love us back to strength:

> Now if you obey me fully and keep my *covenant*, . . . you will be my treasured possession [*segulla*].
>
> *Exodus 19:5*

A covenant in the ancient world was a binding agreement between two parties. It was sealed with an oath and an outward symbol. The closest we come today is marriage, a legal ceremony with binding vows and a ring on the finger. A wedding ring is not just a circle of metal. It's a pledge of love and commitment that goes right back to those vows. At Mount Sinai, God Almighty is down on one knee. He is inviting Israel to put their trust exclusively in him and to experience healing through a loving covenant relationship. The Bible's vision of freedom is nothing less than this.

God also had a larger purpose in mind: 'you will be . . . a kingdom of priests'. A priest was an intermediary who reflected God's presence to the world. Remember, that was our original calling as angled mirrors. Through choosing Israel and setting them free, God intended to release his healing power to all peoples. In a broken world, Israel would recover what it meant to be human. They would enjoy such freedom that they would set others free in the process. This was God's invitation to Israel. Through Jesus, it is an open invitation to us: 'This cup is the *new covenant* in my blood.' Jesus bled and died to get us out of Pharaoh's grip and to restore our original dignity and purpose. By pledging ourselves to him, we experience true Exodus. It's freedom *from* and freedom *for*. It's coming *out* and entering *in*. Lyrics by the British band Mumford & Sons capture the beauty of this liberating love that is the heart of the Exodus story.

> Love that will not betray you, dismay or enslave you,
> it will set you free.
> Be more like the man you were made to be.
> There is a design,
> an alignment, a cry of my heart to see
> the beauty of love as it was made to be.[15]

READ: Exodus 19:1–8.

REFLECT: How do you imagine God? How might this need to change in the light of what you've just read?

13

# Exodus sets boundaries

*The Ten Commandments*

In our front garden there's a proverbial line that our kids must not cross on their own. If they do, we enforce severe sanctions, like a whole day without screen time. The other side of the line is a busy road. We put this rule in place because we want to protect our children. In the context of loving relationships, clear boundaries ensure safety and freedom. Equally, the technology giant, Apple, recently introduced a screen limit function to help people set boundaries on their devices. It seems the constant buzzing of notifications has been damaging our mental health. If commercial companies are prepared to set limits on their products to safeguard the user, how much more would we expect an all-wise creator God to establish boundaries for the sake of our wellbeing?

So after making a covenant with Israel on Mount Sinai (Exodus 19), God reveals Ten Commandments as a foundation for human flourishing (Exodus 20). These were never intended as a DIY rescue plan or a self-help guide; they were a gift to a chosen nation that had been delivered from slavery. Now that they'd been *set free*, the law was given to help them *live free*. The Bible celebrates God's law or *Torah* (Hebrew for 'instruction') as 'more precious than rubies' (Proverbs 8:11) and 'sweeter than honey' (Psalm 119:103). However, in our cultural context, external rules and moral authority are considered a threat to our freedom, like controlling parents or the nanny state. Of course, some regimes can be oppressive but God has our best interests at heart. His laws were designed to help ex-slaves flourish again as human beings. As we consider the Ten Commandments, expect to discover great wisdom that resonates deeply but also a voice of doubt: *Isn't freedom about following your heart, not a set of rules?* For Adam and Eve, Moses and Israel, you and me, it comes down to who we trust.

Here's a condensed summary of the Ten Commandments:

> You shall have no other gods before me.
> Do not make any graven image.
> Do not take the name of the LORD in vain.
> Remember the Sabbath day.
> Honour your father and your mother.
> Do not murder.
> Do not commit adultery.
> Do not steal.
> Do not bear false witness.
> Do not covet.

The first three commandments ensure that Israel's God (Yahweh) has pride of place. Nothing else should rival him and no attempt should be made to replicate him. These specific commands came with a powerful demonstration of God's majesty. In Exodus 19, God came down on Mount Sinai with fiery eruptions that split rocks and caused the mountain to tremble. The Israelites were given front-row seats to witness this terrifying display. Yahweh is not a village god who can be kept under control. This is the creator who spoke forth reality and split open the sea.

So, to revisit an earlier question, how do you imagine God? The Bible carefully blends two truths that must be held in tension: God is *so loving* we can trust him and *so holy* we should fear him. C. S. Lewis captured it beautifully in *The Lion, the Witch and the Wardrobe*. Mr Beaver tells Susan that Aslan (the ruler of Narnia) is a great lion. Susan is surprised and asks Mr Beaver, 'Is he safe?' Mr Beaver laughs, 'Safe? Who said anything about safe? Of course he isn't safe. But he's good. He's the King.' The Ten Commandments remind us that God is not a cute domesticated deity. He is frightfully holy.

According to the Bible, if we want to live in freedom, this is an essential starting point: 'The fear of the LORD is the beginning of wisdom' (Proverbs 9:10). This 'fear' is not a negative phobia like a night terror but a reverence that positively shapes the way we live. When we experience something awesome it is energising. No one stands under Niagara Falls and thinks: 'I'm so great!' Instead, we visit these places to experience something sublime and so much greater than ourselves. I love climbing high mountains precisely because the grandeur puts me in my place and makes me feel more alive. In the same way, when humans experience the majesty of God it's liberating. A healthy, holy fear of God can deliver us from a multitude of other anxieties. Imagine you had to travel through a dangerous jungle. There may be many possible threats to worry about. But if you rode on the back of a mighty lion, there would be only one thing to fear: the lion! That's what the ancient poet had in mind when he declared:

> The Lord is with me; I will not be afraid.
> What can mere mortals do to me?
>
> *Psalm 118:6*

Having insisted on the total supremacy of God, the remaining commandments emphasise the dignity of human beings. The fourth commandment, 'Remember the Sabbath day', echoes back to Genesis when God made the world in six days and blessed the seventh. The Hebrew word *Shabbat* means 'rest' or 'cease'. From this we get 'Sabbath'. It's the principle that each week we need a switch-off day. Time to down tools, turn off emails and remember that we are humans not machines. When I was in Israel recently, I was surprised how strictly this custom is still observed. From sunset on Friday evening, we found ourselves alone on empty highways as the nation locked down. Our hosts explained that Sabbath is a fiercely guarded time for family, worship and rest. It was clearly the highlight of their week.

Interestingly, in the creation account the seventh day was left open-ended as if this beautiful quality of life was meant to continue indefinitely (Genesis 2:2–3). Sabbath is how the world was meant to function, with work and rest in perfect equilibrium. For Israel, Sabbath therefore became a symbol of hope. One day the world will be right again. Meanwhile, a day of complete rest was part of their retraining programme. These ex-slaves were no longer Pharaoh's machines but God's precious children. Their value was no longer measured by sheer productivity. In our hurried and distracted world, Sabbath remains a vital practice. It reinforces profound truths that are otherwise eroded by the constant pressures of modern living:

> I am not a machine. I am loved regardless of my output.
> I am not God. I can rest because it doesn't all depend on me.

Writing in the eighteenth century, the political activist William Wilberforce noted at the end of an intense week: 'Blessed be God for this day of rest . . . wherein earthly things assume their true size and ambition is stunted.' He went on to say regarding other colleagues in Parliament: 'With peaceful Sundays, the strings would never have snapped as they did from over-tension.'[16] When we choose to observe a day of rest we establish vital rhythms that bring freedom. Is this something you may need to reconsider?

The remaining commandments seek to cultivate honourable relationships. Unlike other ancient treatises that focused on property rights, the Ten Commandments value people. To steal, kill, lie or cheat is not merely a moral failure; it is a violation of the image of God. The porn industry, human trafficking and clickbait advertising turn humans into objects that can be commodified. God's law rebukes every attempt to *use people* as things instead of *using things* to serve people.

The final commandment is of a different order. Instead of external actions ('Do not kill') it addresses our desires and motives: 'Do not covet'. It reminds us that God's vision for our freedom cannot be reduced to a tick-list. Human liberty is about well-ordered desires, free from the tyranny of continual comparison. As numerous studies have shown, over-exposure to advertising and social media causes depression, self-loathing and anxiety. Airbrushed images of 'what everyone else is doing' fuel insatiable desires that are detrimental to our wellbeing. 'Do not covet' has never been more apt. We need intentionally to cultivate gratitude to counter the drag of comparison and greed. I have seen this in myself. So I try to think of three things to give thanks for every day. It helps me focus on what I *have* rather than what I *want*. Well-ordered desires are at the heart of true freedom.

The Ten Commandments were given out of love. The lines were drawn to ensure safety and flourishing. They speak wisdom into all areas of life: who we worship, how we work, who we sleep with, what we most desire. Exodus is not just coming out of Egypt; it's embracing a new way of living. Freedom is not just escaping Pharaoh's tyranny but belonging to a new master who has a beautiful vision for our lives. I went into a shop the other week and noticed a sign on the door: 'Under new ownership'. Chatting to the assistant at the counter, I asked how it was going: 'Fantastic!' she replied. 'The old boss was a right ***. But the new one really cares, and not just about profits!' Freed from Pharaoh and bound to God, I think Israel would have said something similar. Since putting my trust in Jesus Christ, that's been my experience too.

READ: Exodus 20:1–21.

REFLECT: Revisit the Ten Commandments. Which of them seem particularly relevant to you right now? How could they help you experience greater freedom?

14

# Exodus is a journey

*Faith enters the Promised Land*

After receiving the Ten Commandments on Mount Sinai (modern-day Egypt), Israel set off for the Promised Land. What happened next has inspired songs and sermons ever since. A few months ago, I took my two boys to watch a rugby match between Wales and Australia. As we entered the stadium we were offered a sheet with lyrics so we could join forces with 70,000 home supporters singing their team to victory. The hymn most associated with Welsh rugby sums up the entire Exodus experience. Here are some highlights:

Guide me, O Thou great Redeemer,
pilgrim through this barren land.
I am weak but thou art mighty,
hold me with thy powerful hand.
Bread of heaven, bread of heaven,
feed me till I want no more!

When I tread the verge of Jordan,
bid my anxious fears subside.
Death of death and hell's destruction

Land me safe on Canaan's side.
Songs of praises, songs of praises
I will ever give to thee!

The song recalls the journey Israel made from slavery in Egypt to freedom in the Promised Land of Canaan. It also reminds us that the story of Exodus is like a set of Russian dolls. Inside Israel's story is a greater story of freedom that we can experience today through Jesus Christ. He delivers us from being slaves to being children of God. As the New Testament puts it:

> God rescued us from dead-end alleys and dark dungeons. He's set us up in the kingdom of the Son he loves so much, the Son who got us out of the pit we were in, got rid of the sins we were doomed to keep repeating.
>
> *Colossians 1:13–14 (The Message)*

However, as the 'Bread of Heaven' hymn also suggests, we must now make our way through the wilderness towards home. One day, we will finally cross the Jordan River (an analogy for death) and land safely on Canaan's side (the hope of a perfect world). In the meantime, there is some complex terrain to navigate. Between Egypt and the Promised Land we must 'pilgrim through this barren land'. Exodus is a journey of faith.

For Israel, the route home was more complicated than it should have been. From Mount Sinai to the Promised Land should have been an eleven-day trek. It ended up taking just over forty years. How on earth did that happen? Well, Israel arrived on the brink of the Promised Land in good time and sent in a reconnaissance team of twelve spies. They brought back grapes so large it took two men to carry each cluster. They were symbols of the goodness of a land that was intended to be

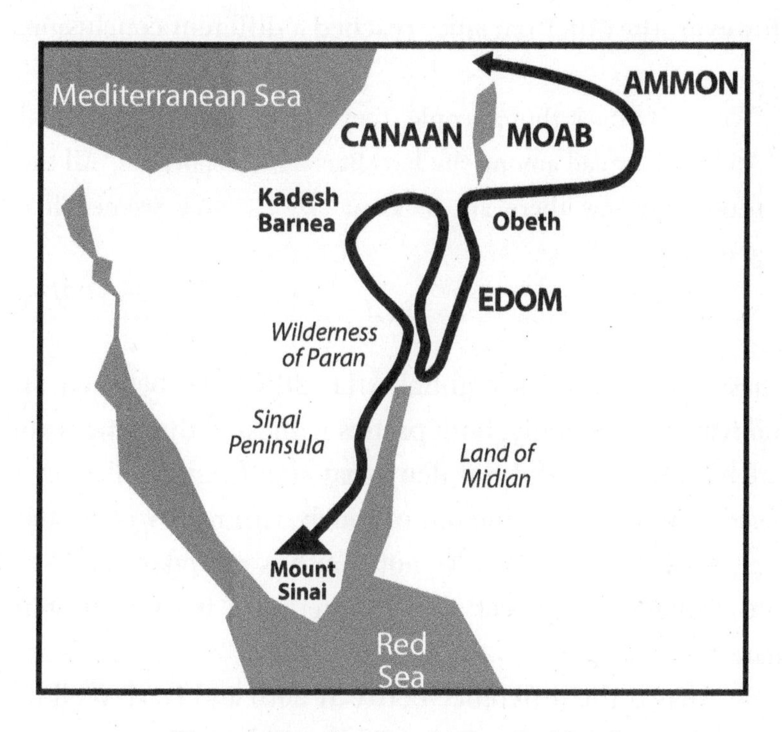


*The route Israel took to the Promised Land*

like a new Eden (I hope they were seedless grapes). However, the spies also reported giant-sized challenges. The Canaanite inhabitants looked menacing and their cities were heavily fortified. Doesn't that sound like life? It's full of opportunities (big grapes) and threats (big giants). As with Israel, the determining factor is how we respond.

Two of the spies, Caleb and Joshua, were full of faith and made one of the great speeches in the Bible:

> If the LORD is pleased with us, he will lead us into that land, a land flowing with milk and honey, and will give it to us. Only do not rebel against the LORD. And do not be afraid of the people of the land . . . the LORD is with us.
>
> *Numbers 14:8–9*

However, the other ten spies reached a different conclusion:

> 'We can't attack those people; they are stronger than we are.' And they spread among the Israelites a bad report . . . 'All the people we saw there are of great size . . . We seemed like grasshoppers.'
>
> *Numbers 13:31–3*

These two responses highlight the difference between faith and fear. Interestingly, both parties witnessed the same reality. Caleb and Joshua did not deny that significant challenges lay ahead. Faith is not being out of touch with reality or pretending you're fine when you're not. Faith is not faking it. We all face challenges and feel afraid sometimes. It's OK to admit that.

So what is the difference between faith and fear? Well it all comes down to how we make decisions. The ten spies lost sight of God and concluded that his call was impossible. For them it was simple:

**ME < LIFE'S CHALLENGES**

Having left God out of the equation, the Israelites got so worked up with fear that they even contemplated returning to Egypt. How irrational! When we forget God, we lose all perspective and start worrying about scenarios that don't exist. Psychologists call this catastrophising. Your spouse is late home from work . . . it's a fatal car crash. Your boss wants to see you . . . it's redundancy. You feel a lump . . . it must be terminal. How much energy have we wasted worrying and shadowboxing? As one old man put it: 'I've had a lot of troubles in my life, most of which never happened!'

By contrast, faith puts God at the centre of the equation and reaches a different conclusion. As Caleb said: 'The LORD is with us. We can certainly do this!'

## ME + GOD > LIFE'S CHALLENGES

Faith doesn't deny our fears but it introduces a higher thought. As a verse in the New Testament puts it:

> If God is for us, who can be against us?
>
> *Romans 8:31*

When I feel anxious, I often draw on verses like this to silence the voice of fear. This puts God back at the centre and stops me losing perspective. I wonder what giants you're facing? It's OK to feel some fear; I'm sure Joshua and Caleb did. But we mustn't leave God out of the equation and give in to the intimidation. As Joyce Meyer explains: 'Courage is fear that has said its prayers and decided to go forward anyway.'[17] So don't be bullied by fear. The great I AM promises to be with us all the way.

Sadly, in Israel's case the voices of fear prevailed. They retreated from the edge of the Promised Land and turned back into the wilderness. There they wandered aimlessly for decades while a whole generation died off. Joshua and Caleb were the only exceptions. Finally, forty years later than planned, a new generation of Israelites crossed the Jordan River and entered the land of Canaan. They were led by Moses' successor, Joshua. In Hebrew, Joshua happens to be the same name as Jesus (*Yeshua*). Jesus is our Joshua. He is the way out of Egypt *and* the way into the Promised Land. The Welsh rugby anthem was spot on. Israel's journey was a prototype of our freedom story. When we were enslaved, God intervened. Jesus is the great Moses who took down our Pharaohs of evil and death. Jesus is the Passover lamb, who shed his blood for our deliverance. Jesus is the bread of heaven who sustains us on the journey home. Exodus is a Russian doll: inside Israel's story is our story.

There is an exit strategy for everyone enslaved in addiction, anxiety, guilt and shame. The way of true freedom is open to all humanity. And it's not mere freedom of choice or following our hearts. That's just wandering in the wilderness. Jesus brings us into a covenant relationship with Almighty God. That's how we discover our original purpose. As a sheepdog is wired to work sheep, we humans were made to love and serve God. This is the fulfilment of our human quest for freedom.

READ: Numbers 13:1–2; 13:26–14:9.

REFLECT: Try committing to memory Romans 8:31: *If God is for us, who can be against us?* Next time fear rises up, speak this truth to silence it.

PART 3

# EXILE

## Our human cry for peace

# Introducing peace

'Can I please get some peace and quiet round here!' As a parent of three, I shout this all too often. Our daughter's practising the keyboard, our boys are booting a football against the garage door. And they've left Alexa blasting Ed Sheeran in the kitchen. In a chaotic family, the cry for peace means a reduction of noise and mayhem. In the face of more brutal realities – war, crime, office bullying, anxiety-disorders – the cry for peace means escape from conflict and fear. In the Bible, the word 'peace' includes all of this and so much more. The Hebrew word for peace is *shalom.*[1] It's still a warm greeting between close friends in Israel today. The word conjures up the idea of health, wholeness and wellbeing – the world working as it's supposed to. It can also be used as an adjective to describe inanimate objects like a piece of pottery that has no cracks, or defensive walls with no weak points. To experience *shalom* is to live with inner and outer peace. More than the absence of *wrongness* (conflict and chaos), it's the presence of *rightness* (justice and beauty). *Shalom* integrates the natural environment, human relationships and our inner self into an ecosystem of peace. Human life on planet earth was meant to be like this.

But it's not.

Deep down we know that all is not well with the world. Life is not *shalom*. Instead, a cry stirs deep within us, not just for 'world peace' but for inner peace. The cry surfaces in Google searches, doctor's prescriptions, Amazon Prime orders and holiday brochures. Despite Western affluence, it seems to be getting louder. Being well-off and experiencing true *wellbeing* are really not the same thing. Growing levels of anxiety and loneliness plague even the most advanced countries on an unprecedented scale.[2] Experts have dubbed ours the 'age of anxiety'.[3] No wonder there is such demand for classes, techniques, diets and lifestyles that promise inner calm: from philosophies such as Zen Buddism to yoga, meditation and mindfulness techniques, as well as various approaches to minimalist lifestyles (e.g. Lagom and KonMari methods). In different ways, they all attempt to strip back the clutter and chaos, dim the noise and craziness and return to an original state of peace.

However, the reason for our loss of *shalom* is not as simple as messy kids, too much technology or environmental mismanagement. The Bible draws on the theme of exile to give a more satisfying explanation. In Part 1 (Origins), we saw that we were made to live in a beautiful garden called Eden. As well as existing as a real place, in the Bible Eden functions as an archetype for *shalom* – the way the world was supposed to be. Think of it like your dream home. Eden was intended to be a beautiful shared living space in which God and humans were together in perfect harmony. In the story, however, as humans turned away from God and pursued fulfilment through independence, they were escorted off the premises and forced to live East of Eden in the harsh wilderness. In other words, humanity was banished or *exiled*.

Now remember: the Bible is shaped like Russian dolls. Inside the larger human story of exile, Israel also faced the painful experience of being expelled from their homeland. In Israel's case it came centuries after the high point of Exodus. As we've already seen, Moses led Israel *out* of the clutches of Pharaoh and then Joshua led them *into* the Promised Land of Canaan. It was meant to be a foretaste of humanity's homecoming, the restoration of a new Eden. But after several centuries of Israel disobeying God and being led astray by unfaithful kings (Adam and Eve on repeat), their homeland was destroyed by the Babylonians and they were forced to live in exile. In the Bible, exile therefore refers to Israel's traumatic experience *as well as* the more general condition of human life outside Eden. So the story of Israel helps us reflect on tough realities we still experience today:

> We were made for this world but it's quite hostile.
> We were made for community but life can feel lonely.
> We were made for God but he can seem remote.

Do these words resonate with you? Why is this so? The Bible's answer is that we are exiles, living away from our true home. We belong in a place that we can't seem to get back to. We brush up against it in moments of real intimacy and sense it in true friendship. C. S. Lewis referred to it as 'the desire for a far-off country'. It's the longing of someone made to live in one reality (Eden) but who finds themselves in another (exile). Lewis goes on to warn against trying to resolve the situation superficially:

> These things – the beauty, the memory of our own past – are good images of what we really desire; but if they are mistaken for the thing itself they turn into dumb idols, breaking the

> hearts of their worshippers. For they are not the thing itself; they are only the scent of a flower we have not found, the echo of a tune we have not heard, news from a country we have never yet visited.[4]

We human beings have a deep collective sense of how the world should be. *Shalom*. But East of Eden we try and satisfy this longing through substitutes and distractions. We search for intimacy only to discover that neither casual sex nor long-term commitment fulfils the underlying desire. We work for promotion and accolades but they fail to offset the crushing need to belong. Even if we're the fortunate one who marries the prince, lives in the castle and raises beautiful kids, it still falls short. When we pin our hopes on this material world, the 'dumb idols' only break our hearts. As exiles, our deepest longing will only be satisfied when we return home.

Cue the Prince of Peace . . .

While we were languishing in exile, in a far-off country, God heard our cry and intervened in person to restore our broken world and bring us peace. The final chapter of this book will consider how the Bible story ends with an ultimate homecoming in eternity. But in the meantime, the Scriptures introduce Jesus as the one who can restore peace to our hearts here and now. He is the 'Prince of Peace' or literally the 'Prince of *Shalom*' (Isaiah 9:6). The Bible is replete with the promise that even in exile, when life is tough and hostile, we can experience true peace that runs deeper than our circumstances and keeps us buoyant in the storms. As the New Testament puts it:

> The peace of God, which transcends all understanding, will guard your hearts and your minds in Christ Jesus.
>
> *Philippians 4:7*

So how can we live with a greater experience of peace? As we've noted before, hidden away in Israel's story of exile are some key principles that still make sense today. In 586 BC the Babylonian Empire sacked Jerusalem and led the majority of its inhabitants as forced refugees to Babylon (near modern-day Baghdad). There they endured seventy years of captivity. In this section we will draw on Israel's exile in order to interpret our own experiences of loss and yearning for peace. We will cover centuries of history from Israel entering the Promised Land after the Exodus (*c*. 1300 BC) to being thrown out of it during the Exile (*c*. 600 BC). This section of the Old Testament is a complex saga and we will only cover some of the main characters and events. It's also a period marked by much failure and frustration. However, God heard Israel's cry for peace. Now we live as exiles in a hostile world. Will the Prince of *Shalom* not also hear our cry?

15

# Peace breaks the negative cycles

*The era of Joshua and the Judges*

*Exodus* and *exile*. These two words nicely sum up the complex story of God's people in the Old Testament. But how do these themes touch down in our lives today? As we've seen, Exodus is all about freedom and victory – God getting Israel out of Egypt and into the Promised Land. However, exile is more about suffering and defeat – the Israelites held captive in a foreign land. This theme remains profoundly relevant and helps make sense of those moments when life throws us a curve ball and we experience trauma and loss. To understand the metaphor of exile therefore requires taking the long view. So let's rewind to the time of the Judges and then make our way through the era of the Kings (David and Solomon) before arriving at the exile itself.

Around 1300 BC, a newly liberated people-group was formed into a nation and emerged out of the wilderness. Under the leadership of Moses' successor, Joshua, the Israelites crossed the River Jordan and entered the land of Canaan. Through unusual military tactics, Israel conquered Jericho and other strategic cities before dividing up the land between the twelve tribes and settling in. The clear sense in the book of Joshua is that after centuries of sojourning in Egypt, Israel had finally come home. For this strip of Middle-Eastern land – known also as Canaan – was the plot God had promised to Abraham and his offspring, hence 'Promised Land'. Now Israel was called to be a model nation, displaying obedience to God's commandments and radiating God's light to the world. In this sense, the Promised Land was to be like a patch of new creation on the old earth, a recovery of Eden and *shalom* in the midst of chaos and sin.

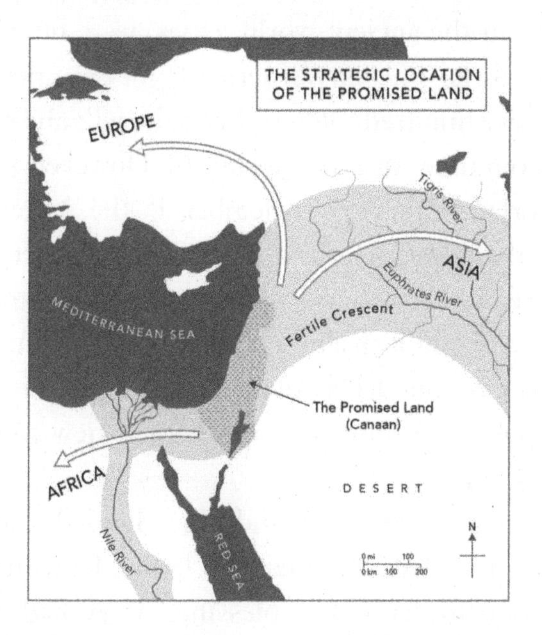


This bigger vision helps makes sense of why Israel was given such a strategic plot of land, right on the crossroads of three continents – Europe, Africa and Asia. The Promised Land was not a secluded paradise island where Israel could get away from it all. It was one of the most prominent locations in the ancient world. It amounted to 20,000 square kilometres, equivalent to the nation of Wales. Though the mountainous regions were less accessible, lower down on the coastal plains there was an international highway with heavy traffic. If Israel was to fulfil her vocation to be a light to the nations, this was a strategic piece of real estate.

But with that came a problem. The land was already occupied and its inhabitants (the Canaanites) were not looking to vacate. So the book of Joshua records a series of battles as Israel fought their way in. Personally, I find this is one of the most troubling sections in the Bible. How can a God of peace allow his people to declare war?[5] While this is a complex issue deserving of a longer answer, it's worth noting that the cities conquered by Israel were not urban centres with large populations as we have today. In the ancient world 'cities' were often defensive garrisons or forts. The 'city of Jericho', for example, primarily housed about a hundred soldiers; hence Israel's ability to march round it seven times in a day (Joshua 6). However, perhaps the most important thing to remember is the larger purpose. Removing the Canaanites and their sinful practices of shrine prostitution and child sacrifice was vital in order to purge the land of evil and establish a new culture of *shalom*. As the Allied troops used force on D-Day to liberate Europe from the Nazis, so Israel took the Promised Land with a view to setting up *Shalom* HQ.

So, having conquered the land, they divided it up between the tribes and settled into their new home. Israel had become a great nation under God's blessing. They had the law or Torah as a source of wisdom and now the Promised Land as a base. What could go wrong? To answer that, we need to listen carefully to Joshua's famous last words to Israel before he died:

> Now fear the LORD and serve him with all faithfulness. Throw away the gods your ancestors worshipped . . . and yield your hearts to the LORD, the God of Israel.
>
> *Joshua 24:14, 23*

As we've noted, true peace is more than the absence of conflict. It has to do with the integration of life around *one* unifying source, 'the God of Israel'. Joshua's speech warned Israel that if *one* should become *two* it would spell disaster. If instead of being 'whole-hearted', Israel became half-hearted, following Yahweh *and* pursuing other idols, they would vandalise *shalom*.[6]

Sadly, this is precisely what happened. During the era of the Judges (*c*. 1350–1050 BC), Israel went off the rails and ended up in a dark place. Called to be the solution, they quickly became part of the problem. Set on a hill to reflect God's light, they were engulfed by the darkness. God's people compromised with the surrounding nations and ended up living like everyone else. The book of Judges is a disturbing read, a downward spiral culminating in gang rape, murder and civil war. It all got a bit *Game of Thrones*. Through its twisted narrative, the book of Judges therefore conveys one simple warning: *When we turn away from God, we vandalise* shalom *and end up in chaos.* This track is played on repeat throughout the book as generation after generation gets stuck in negative cycles:

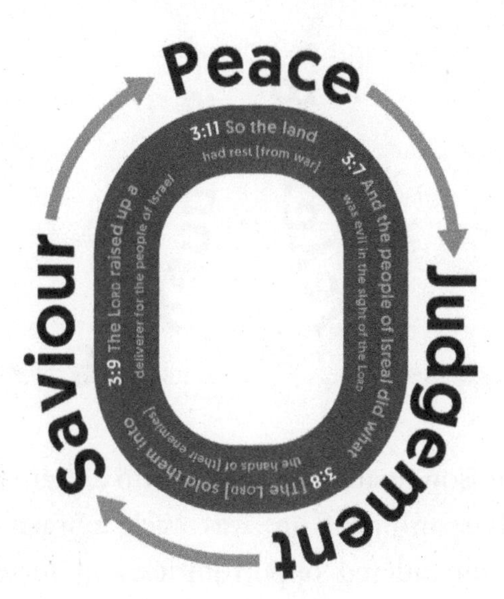

Whenever Israel compromised with the Canaanite culture they ended up oppressed, so God raised up a judge to intervene. By the way, when picturing the judges, think military leaders wielding swords not law-court judges banging gavels. Othniel, Deborah, Gideon and Samson were fascinating characters, desperately trying to restore peace in the midst of chaos. But after each judge died, the next generation turned away from God and round we go again. It's a sad story of repeat offending that leaves Israel stuck in a downward spiral, further and further away from *shalom*.

Towards the end of the book, it gets so bad that even the presiding judge, who is meant to be the hero, becomes complicit with the chaos and compromise. Samson was one of those annoying types – unbelievably muscular and gifted from birth. But instead of using his strength to cultivate *shalom*, he got caught in negative cycles:

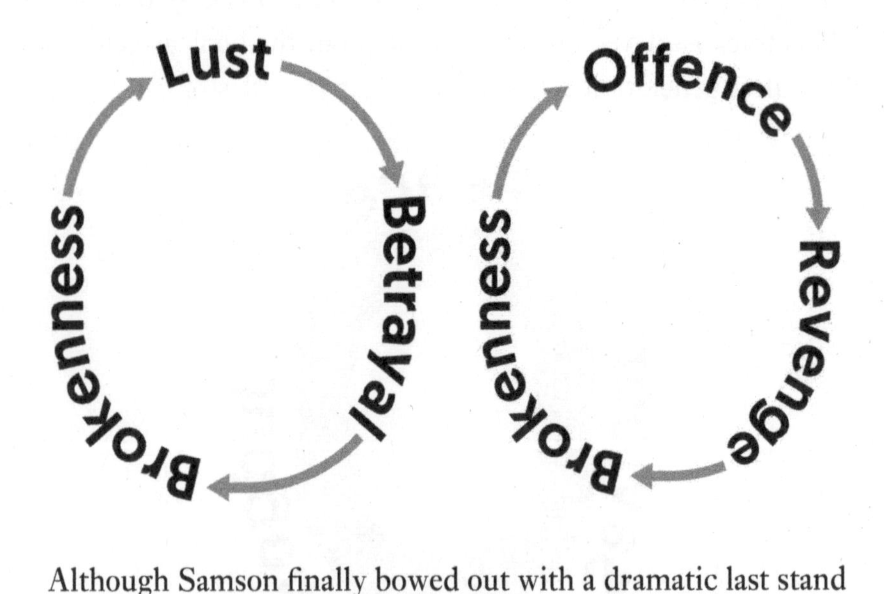


Although Samson finally bowed out with a dramatic last stand for God, his soap-opera life was such a waste (see Judges 13–16). He squandered opportunities and forfeited *shalom*, pursuing passions that were never satisfied. That's what happens when we live for *two* not *one* – half following God but also rival dreams and fantasies. Instead of living an integrated life of honour, we get caught between things. Imagine someone trying to walk in two different directions at the same time and ending up in the splits. That's Samson.

Before we go pointing the finger, the book of Judges hands us a mirror in which to examine our own lives. Are we living wholeheartedly for God or caught chasing rival dreams? Are we cultivating *shalom* or stuck in negative cycles that are destructive? It's all too easy to waste our precious lives in downward spirals of lust, greed, envy and bitterness. We mess up, cry out to God for forgiveness and make all kinds of promises if he will deliver us. But soon we become complacent and loop back on to the negative cycle. It's such a demoralising way to live. We neither enjoy the sin nor experience *shalom*.

So what to do? Let's revisit the words of Joshua: 'Throw away the foreign gods . . . and yield your hearts to the LORD.' Key to breaking negative cycles and dwelling in peace is to renounce destructive patterns that leave us estranged. When we fully yield ourselves to God, we experience inner integration and harmony. When all of life is under the *One* we no longer feel torn in *two*. Here are some commitments that I have found helpful to break negative cycles and live an integrated life:

> I will not allow my desires for comfort, pleasure or gratification to rule me. I choose to exercise self-control and live with honour.
> I will not embrace feelings of envy or rivalry that stop me enjoying what I have. I choose to be grateful and generous.
> I will not harbour bitterness or seek revenge against those who hurt me. I choose the way of forgiveness and peace.

This *shalom* lifestyle is really challenging and there will be plenty of setbacks along the way. But Israel's story reveals a God who doesn't give up on his people, despite all the negative cycles. Moreover, in Jesus Christ we have the ultimate Judge who not only forgives our sins but also gives us power to change. Our lives do not have to sound like a broken record. The Prince of Peace can break negative cycles and restore *shalom* to our hearts. As the New Testament puts it: 'There is now no condemnation for those who are in Christ Jesus' (Romans 8:1).

READ: Judges 13:1–7; 16:1–22.

REFLECT: Take a moment to write your own personal pledges. Ask God to help you avoid negative cycles so that you live his way and experience greater *shalom*.

16

# Peace silences the giants

*The life of King David*

Growing up, one of my childhood fears was that an evil person would break into our family home and steal my train set. Of course the fear wasn't just about the potential loss of my Intercity 125 (for all you train spotters). It was a more basic angst that we all experience when the place we call home doesn't feel secure. We may live in a hostile world, but if home is a haven of safety and acceptance we function from a place of peace. As any child psychologist knows, though, when we experience bullying, abuse, neglect or the crushing weight of parental expectation, it leaves us feeling like exiles in our own home. If you've experienced this, your cry for *shalom* may come from a very deep place. If you are currently living in a home marked by brokenness, remember there is a Prince of Peace who hears you.

As we have seen, during the time of the Judges Israel got stuck in cycles of compromise. This left the spiritual door unlocked and their enemies kept breaking in. The main threat came from the Philistines, a super-sized tribe of warriors who came down from Europe and invaded territories near the Promised Land (like the Vikings invading Britain). Living in the shadow of these bullies, Israel was a nation in fear. Their homes were not safe so they hid in caves and holes in the ground (Judges 6). Israel was on its knees; it was time for a change. So the last of the Judges, Samuel, anointed the first king over Israel in a bid to unite the tribes and restore security. To cut a long and painful story short, Saul, the first king, failed. So Samuel got out his ram's horn again, filled it with olive oil and set off to find a replacement. His search ended in an unlikely village (Bethlehem) where, to Samuel's surprise, God told him to anoint the youngest son of a man called Jesse. David was a shepherd boy without a lot going for him. But the message was clear:

> The LORD does not look at the things people look at. People look at the outward appearance, but the LORD looks at the heart.
>
> *1 Samuel 16:7*

Now there's a challenge for our celebrity-obsessed, image-saturated gym culture: David got noticed not because of his external appearance but because he was 'a man after [God's] own heart' (Acts 13:22). I wonder what we try and get noticed for?

David went on to become something of a legend in Israel's history, a foretaste of the long-awaited Messiah. In fact, the term 'messiah' derives from the Hebrew word *mashiach*, which means 'anointed one'. In those days, coronation did not involve a crown but oil poured over the head as a symbol of the divine Spirit empowering the king to rule. It's worth noting that the Greek equivalent of Messiah is *Christos* – they both refer to God's anointed king. So when we hear about Jesus *Christ*, that's not his surname; it's his title and job description. He is God's ultimate king who has come to do for the entire world what David did for Israel – defeat our enemies and bring us peace. It's Russian dolls again.

David's first major challenge came in the form of a man-mountain called Goliath. This Philistine warrior caused terror in the ranks of Israel's army, who were trapped in the valley of Elah. Imagine the scene: the Philistine army dug in on one side and Israel on the other. Twice a day, morning and evening, Goliath came down into the valley and taunted them, demanding a duel with their best fighter. Needless to say, there were no volunteers: 'On hearing the Philistine's words, Saul and all the Israelites were dismayed and terrified' (1 Samuel 17:11). I wonder what Goliaths you are facing right now? When we come up against giant-sized problems – debt, redundancy, sickness, betrayal – it can leave us feeling powerless and scared. The voice of fear is often particularly loud in the morning, making us feel like we can't face the day, or at night-time when we can't get to sleep. A Holocaust survivor called Corrie Ten Boom, who knew a thing or two about giants, described anxiety as 'a cycle of inefficient thoughts whirling around a centre of fear'.[7] I'm sure we've all been there, trapped by circumstances we can't handle, bullied by fear.

Cue David . . .

On to the scene comes the young shepherd boy whose initial task was simply to deliver groceries to the real soldiers. But on hearing the giant roar and witnessing the terrified retreat of Israel, David felt a rising defiance that quickly led to decisive action.

Brook. Pebbles. Sling shot. Forehead. Beheaded. Victory! (See 1 Samuel 17 for the gory details.)

It wouldn't have felt quite so straightforward but the net effect was the same. David felled the mighty Goliath with a single stone and led Israel in a decisive victory that restored peace. This incident has since become legendary. Still today we say 'it hit me between the eyes' and sports commentators refer to mismatches as 'David versus Goliath'. But what's the relevance of this underdog story for us?

Given what we said earlier, David and Goliath is a window through which to glimpse the ultimate Messiah. Like David, Jesus was born in Bethlehem. Like David, he stepped on to our battlefield to take on the insurmountable challenges we face – evil, fear and death itself. On a Roman cross, Jesus became locked in mortal combat with the great enemies of our human story. Through his resurrection, he defeated them and won a decisive victory. David's individual triumph was then shared by the rest of God's people, who surged forwards and defeated the remaining Philistines. In the same way, we can share in Jesus' victory and live with confidence, even when we pass through giant country.

I once got into a fight at secondary school, but before we could finish it the teacher broke us up. So we arranged to meet outside the school gates to settle the matter. Now I want you to know that I could have had him! But when I turned up to fight, he approached with a smug grin of defiance. Standing behind him was his older brother who played rugby for the school team. Needless to say, I walked away. Not because of my assailant but because of who was with him. The key to peace is to align ourselves with the Prince of Peace. If Jesus is with us, then fear need not dominate us. As David declared in one of many psalms he wrote:

> The LORD is my light and my salvation –
> whom shall I fear?
> The LORD is the stronghold of my life –
> of whom shall I be afraid?

*Psalm 27:1*

Next time fear bullies you in the morning or keeps you awake at night, try reciting this verse and calling on the Prince of Peace. I gave this advice to a friend recently. He's not a Christian but the bottom had just fallen out of his world and, despite heavy drinking, he wasn't sleeping. As a last resort, one evening he tried reading Psalm 27 and saying the Lord's Prayer. 'Bloody hell!' he said, as he told me what happened, 'I felt this tranquil feeling pass down through me and back up again. The next thing I knew, it was morning.'

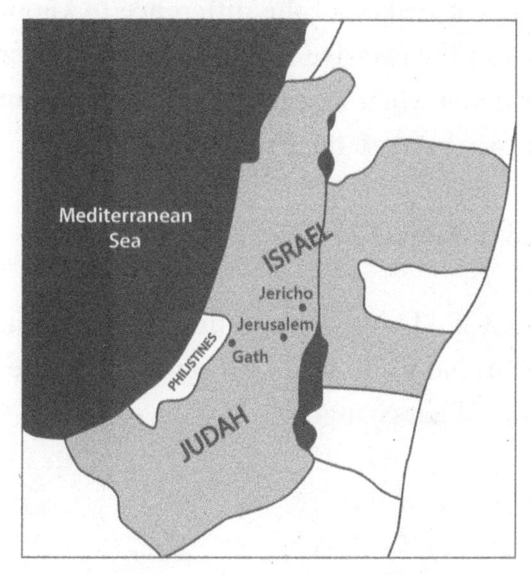


*The territory of Israel during the reign of King David*

From around 1000 BC, David became king over all Israel and united the twelve tribes into one nation. He went on to win further battles that stopped the encroachment of raiding parties and secured the borders. With David on the throne, Israel could sleep at night and flourish in the daytime. He also captured a hill fort called Mount Zion and set it up as the new capital city. In the process, they came up with a name that encapsulated Israel's calling: *Jerusalem* which means 'city of peace' – *salem* is derived from *shalom*. Jerusalem was to be an epicentre of world peace, radiating light and hope to all nations. For a brief window mid-way through the Old Testament, God's people were feeling at home in the world.

Note that *shalom* is more than the absence of conflict; it's the world working as it's supposed to. True peace enables us to feel secure in an uncertain world. For Israel, King David the 'anointed one' made all the difference – from hiding in caves to living with confidence. In a hostile world with plenty of threats and challenges, it makes all the difference to know that Jesus has already won the decisive victory. So we don't need to hide away in fear. Even when we pass through giant country we can journey in peace because the Prince is with us.

READ: 1 Samuel 17:17–50; Psalm 27:1–3.

REFLECT: Think of a specific challenge you are facing at the moment. Now visualise God standing beside you, ready to defend you. What changes?

## 17

# Peace is found in God's presence

*King Solomon, wisdom and the temple*

After seeing David take down Goliath and establish Jerusalem, the 'city of *shalom*', the Jews at the time might have wondered: Is he the Messiah, the long-awaited prince who will crush the evil serpent? (Genesis 3:15). The second half of David's life gives a pretty emphatic answer. David committed adultery with Bathsheba, then had her husband murdered in an elaborate cover-up. Needless to say, when a prophet finally exposed the scandal it was sensational news that rocked Israel to the core. Instead of closing out his life in *shalom*, David was soon betrayed by his own son and faced a period of exile in the wilderness. The royal family became a broken home. However, despite David's failure, God restated his promise that the snake-crusher would come through his family line and establish a kingdom of peace (2 Samuel 7). As a token of this amazing grace, one of the children born out of David's adulterous relationship became the next king of Israel. David's son, Solomon, was living proof that the God of the Bible is into recycling: he can make something new even out of our failures. Do you carry shame and regret from the past? Why not draw on David's psalm of repentance:

> Have mercy on me, O God,
> according to your unfailing love . . .
> Create in me a pure heart, O God,
> and renew a steadfast spirit within me.
>
> *Psalm 51:1, 10*

**The wisdom of Solomon**

The reign of King Solomon became known for a couple of outstanding features. The first was his wisdom. Solomon had a dream in which God came to him like Aladdin's genie in a lamp: 'Make a wish!' Now pause there for a moment. If you could have anything, what would you ask for? To his credit, Solomon didn't wish to be a millionaire but to be wise (1 Kings 3). So God gave him the gift of exceptional wisdom. Ironically, he also became a multi-millionaire. During his reign, there was so much gold that silver was not considered of any value – it was just metal. However, the crucial principle revealed through the life of Solomon is that money cannot buy you true success. For that you need wisdom. As the book of Proverbs puts it:

> Wisdom is more precious than rubies,
> and nothing you desire can compare with her.
>
> *Proverbs 8:11*

The book of Proverbs in the Bible is well worth exploring. It's a compendium of wisdom that draws on the teaching of Solomon and other sages. Full of short, memorable sayings, Proverbs speaks into all areas of life – money, sex, work, anger management, parenting, socialising, alcohol consumption.[8] It considers all of life to be interwoven with a spiritual dimension. The root idea of wisdom traces right back to our origins; the world was designed like a beautifully woven garment. Life is an incredibly complex network of interrelated threads: when we live with wisdom it results in personal, social and environmental integration and harmony:

**WISE CHOICES = *SHALOM***

But when we make poor decisions that turn away from God, the very fabric of our lives begins to unravel:

**POOR CHOICES = ANTI-*SHALOM***

Wisdom in the Bible is not mere intellectual knowledge. As Miles Kington put it, 'Knowledge is knowing a tomato is a fruit. Wisdom is not putting it in the fruit salad.'[9] You can have a very high IQ but still make poor life choices. Like steering a car, wisdom helps us navigate through life so we avoid common pitfalls and arrive safely at our destination. Wisdom literature in the Bible is therefore a great resource to consult regarding decisions in our personal life, relationships, work or for society as a whole.

### Solomon's Temple

The other noteworthy feature of Solomon's reign was the construction of a vast temple on the mountain overlooking Jerusalem. In the ancient world, high places were often sites of worship. So Solomon's temple provided Israel with a focal point for holy pilgrimage. Think of it less like a local parish church and more as a campus facility, containing law courts, teaching spaces, priestly quarters and the national bank.

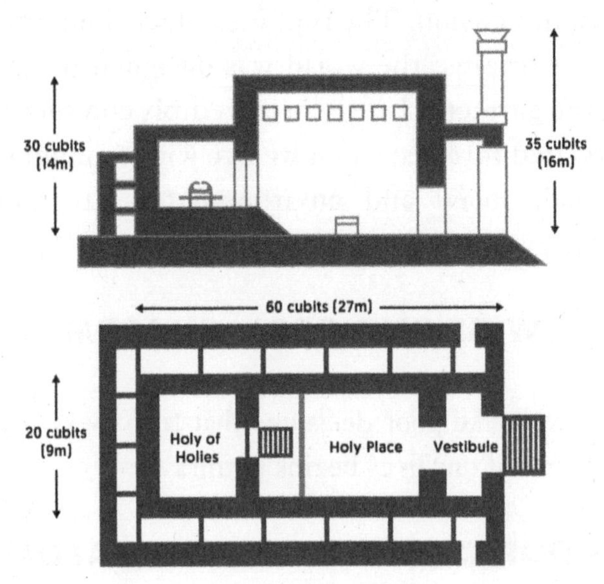


*The proportions and layout of Solomon's Temple*

The epicentre of it all was the Holy of Holies or Most Holy place. This was thought to be God's private throne room, where only the high priest was permitted to enter once a year. A wall of curtain blocked the way in for everyone else. After Solomon completed the building work, he offered sacrifices to God. Suddenly, a mysterious glory cloud appeared and flooded the inner spaces of the temple so that even the priests had to leave the building (1 Kings 8:11). God had taken up residence. The temple was not really about the building but the presence. It was the house of God, where heaven touched earth. It gave the Almighty a postcode in Israel's neighbourhood.

Now remember, the way it was in the temple was how the whole world was supposed to be. We were made to live as priests enjoying the immediate presence of God, but after being banished from Eden, we humans have been on the outside. Our cry for *shalom* is ultimately a desire to experience the glory and presence again. Solomon's temple was therefore a symbol of hope in a world of exile. There on Mount Zion was a residual patch of *shalom*. This explains why the interior design included echoes of Eden – pomegranate trees, oxen, flowers and cherubim to name a few. Israel's cry for peace could be directed to the temple, which (of course) was built facing east, pointing back to Eden.

Let's briefly fast-forward to the New Testament. As the Messiah died for the sin that causes exile: 'The curtain of the temple was torn in two from top to bottom' (Matthew 27:51). This curtain symbolically separated human beings from God. But the death of Jesus opened up access again into his presence. We are no longer shut out but invited to experience the love of a heavenly Father who welcomes us home. In my experience, only this embrace can end our inner exile and restore true peace. On the other side of the curtain is the answer to our deepest longings. Not a million pounds, but *Shalom* himself waiting to embrace us.

With all this in mind, let's revisit Aladdin's cave and the genie's question: 'If you could have anything, what would you want?' Where is true *shalom* to be found? Despite getting the answer right first time, in later life Solomon lost his way and forsook the path of wisdom. Sadly, he became convinced that more wealth, status and pleasure would lead to flourishing. Instead, he ended up lonely and empty. The book of Ecclesiastes draws on Solomon's experience as a case study to expose the myth that being *well-off* equates to having *wellbeing*. Ecclesiastes invites us to imagine the person who has everything – they excel in education, become a multi-millionaire, get the pick of the beautiful and are idolised by the rest. But without God, the conclusion at the end of their life is bleak: 'This to is meaningless, a chasing after the wind'

(Ecclesiastes 2:26). In our contemporary culture that idolises the celebrity lifestyle, we need to hear this. As the famous actor Jim Carrey concluded: 'I wish everybody could get rich and famous and do everything they ever dreamed of so they could see for themselves that it's not the answer.'[10] If we want true wellbeing we must break the cultural spell that blinds us. True peace cannot be found through acquisition or accomplishment. The source of peace is the presence of God. Only on the other side of the curtain will our deepest longings be met.

A few years ago my wife and I became friends with a housekeeper who worked nearby. Initially she seemed a bit cautious but after a while we got invited to tea. The house turned out to be an Aladdin's cave. There were original oil paintings by the Italian Renaissance artist Titian, a huge model ship that was a personal gift from Queen Victoria and a polar bear rug. 'But,' said our friend gesturing to two small vases on the mantelpiece, 'these are worth more than the rest. They are an extremely rare pair of Goya on glass, valued at £10 million. And I have to clean them every week!' Over tea she mentioned two other things that I've not forgotten. First, the family who owned it had never stopped arguing about inheritance issues. Aladdin's cave was not a happy place. And the other thing . . . a few months previously some burglars had broken in. Somewhat ignorant as to the value of all that lay before them, they crept past the paintings and vases, and made off with the TV! That thought has brought a smile to my face ever since. The irony of it. All that could have been theirs if only they had known what was truly valuable. So go on, answer the genie: *What do you really want? Where is true peace found?*

READ: 1 Kings 3:1–15; Ecclesiastes 1:1–11.

REFLECT: Imagine God gave you one request. What would you ask for? What do you *really* need? Pray for the gift of wisdom to discern what's truly valuable in life.

## 18

# Peace in the storm

*The trauma of exile*

After the glory days of David and Solomon, Israel descended into the dark ages. From 900 BC onwards, their story is one of division, civil war and defeat. Despite noteworthy exceptions (e.g. Hezekiah, Josiah), Israel's kings compromised with the surrounding nations and ignored the warnings of prophets like Elijah or Isaiah. It all came to a head in 587 BC when the Babylonians sacked Jerusalem, smashed down the city that David had established and burned down the temple Solomon had built. Jerusalem was left in ruins and God's people were forced out of their homeland and deported to Babylon.

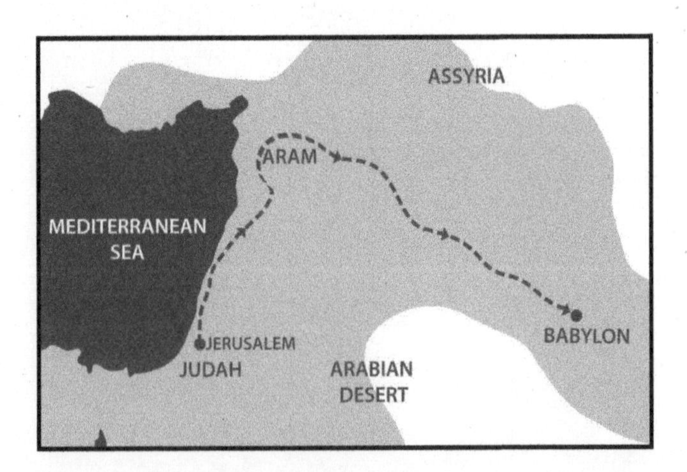


*The route into exile from Jerusalem to Babylon*

When God first called Abraham in Genesis 12, he was living in Babylon (modern-day Iraq). He then made his way up through Syria and down to Canaan. Now Abraham's descendants are marched back round to Babylon. A story with such promise seemed to come to an abrupt end, back where it started.

Imagine the Jewish exiles arriving in a foreign land, disorientated and utterly broken. A psalm in the Bible, made famous by Boney M, captures the mood:

> By the rivers of Babylon we sat and wept
> when we remembered Zion [Jerusalem] . . .
> for there our captors asked us for songs . . .
> they said, 'Sing us one of the songs of Zion!'
> How can we sing the songs of the LORD
> while in a foreign land?
>
> *Psalm 137:1–4*

The agony of exile for Israel provides a moment for honest reflection on our most perplexing and painful experiences. Remember the Russian dolls. Our human story is also in a state of exile. Life is punctuated by inexplicable moments of loss and pain when our cry for peace becomes almost deafening. Before leaving for Babylon, the Jews were rounded up into a temporary refugee camp in a place called Ramah, just north of Jerusalem. The prophet Jeremiah captured the dreadful sounds from inside the camp:

> A voice is heard in Ramah,
> mourning and great weeping,
> Rachel weeping for her children
> and refusing to be comforted,
> because they are no more.
>
> *Jeremiah 31:15*

A few years ago, while a church leader, I received one of those phone calls in the early hours of the morning: 'My brother has drowned,' said the voice on the other end. He'd been drinking with friends and decided to have a late-night swim in the sea. He never made it back. A week or so later, while taking the funeral, I said the committal, 'ashes to ashes, dust to dust', and pressed the button. As the curtain closed around the coffin, his mother wailed, doubled over with grief. It was a deep guttural sound that only a mother could make as her boy disappeared from view for the last time: 'A voice is heard in Ramah, mourning and great weeping.'

When tragedy and suffering hit, we are left with roughly the same questions Israel would have had: Why has this happened? Where is God? How are we going to cope? From a historical perspective, the answer to the first question is fairly straightforward. Babylon was the new super-power on the block, intent on world domination. Israel happened to be in their way – wrong place, wrong time. Similarly, so much human suffering appears to be random: cancer, redundancy, crime and violence. The atheist Richard Dawkins captured this view of life in his aptly named book *River Out of Eden*: 'In a universe of blind physical forces and genetic replication, some people are going to get hurt, other people are going to get lucky, and you won't find rhyme or reason in it.'[11] However, we humans are not satisfied by everything being placed in the 'random' or 'unfortunate' category. Are we really just DNA machines, subject to chance?

In Israel's case, God had raised up a series of prophets to provide a more satisfying if challenging explanation. Read the oracles of prophets like Isaiah or Jeremiah and you will hear the repeated warning that Israel's disobedience is pulling the ceiling down on their own heads. Israel's prophets were like the nation's conscience, calling out home truths that those in power tried to ignore. The Israelites were culpable in their own downfall. The Bible therefore attributes exile *both* to the brutal Babylonians *and* the judgement of God because of their unfaithfulness. Harsh though this may seem, it's worth pausing to reflect on how much suffering today is related to human sinfulness and injustice. Why should the poorest suffer simply because of postcode lotteries? We still need the uncomfortable rebuke of modern-day prophets and social activists. Life is not just random-chance; negative choices cause ourselves and others to suffer, resulting in brokenness, injustice and environmental damage that characterise our world today.[12]

However, when Israel progressed from 'Why did this happen?' to 'Where is God?' the answer was surprising. Given a string of ignored warnings, they might have expected to hear: 'Well, I told you so!' as God stepped back and watched it unfold. When we suffer, we only increase the pain if we imagine events this way. We assume God has abandoned us to our fate. We interpret painful experiences as clear evidence that God no longer cares. But that simply isn't true. The very same prophets who warned of judgement also declared something mysterious. God would go with Israel into exile and walk them through it:

> When you pass through the waters,
> *I will be with you*;
> and when you pass through the rivers,
> they will not sweep over you.
> When you walk through the fire,
> you will not be burned . . .
> Do not be afraid, for I am with you.
>
> *Isaiah 43:2, 5*

This may sound strange, but exile proved to be a time when God drew close. On one occasion, three exiles were thrown into a furnace by the Babylonian king for refusing to bow down to his statue. In a literal fulfilment of this prophecy, the flames did not set them ablaze. Instead, a fourth figure stood with them in the furnace: one 'like a son of the gods' (Daniel 3:25). This incident beautifully captures what so many have experienced. Even in the furnace of suffering, God draws close, closer than we've known before. I think of a friend whose husband recently left her: 'God has been so near through this. I've never felt alone.' I think of a colleague whose teenage daughter recently tried to commit suicide: 'Even in the darkness, God is with us. Like a miner's lamp he keeps lighting up the next step on the path.'

C. S. Lewis summed it up: 'God whispers to us in our pleasures, speaks in our conscience, but shouts in our pain.'[13] There are some truths you can only *really* know when it's all that you've got left – God is faithful. There are profound things you can only *fully* experience in a storm – the peace of God. There are character traits and negative behaviours that only *truly* change in the furnace. In the ancient world fire was a purifying agent. It burned away impurities, known as dross, resulting in something much more valuable. The Bible depicts God as a skilful refiner, using the heat of tough times to purify our lives:

> [God] knows the way that I take;
> When he has tested me, I shall come forth as gold.
>
> *Job 23:10*

Final question: How should we respond when the bottom falls out of life? Perhaps the best advice I have been given is to bring it all to God – tear-soaked tissues, raw prayers and real doubts.

Have you read any of the psalms of lament in the Bible? Try Psalms 42, 43 and 44. They are unbelievably honest. God is not scared of our questions or embarrassed by our tears or afraid of our anger. The Bible never shies away from the gritty stuff. Its pages openly publish Israel's heartfelt laments as an ongoing resource to help us process grief and pain today.

When my father died it felt like exile. His presence made me feel at home and secure in the world. His absence was a cruel blow. Life felt like frozen ground. But through the tears and grief, I have experienced God's love in more intimate ways. Instead of an awkward God who doesn't know what to do when we cry, we have a heavenly Father who himself has tasted grief and pain. The Messiah, God's Son, died in agony on a Roman cross. He faced the ultimate exile, shut out in darkness. So God knows how we feel. He can sit with us in our pain. Precisely because so much of the Bible has been shaped by exile and suffering it becomes a source of strength in tough times. Through the comfort of the Scriptures we can live with peace even when the bottom falls out of life.

READ: Jeremiah 25:1–11; Psalm 137:1–9; Isaiah 43:1–7.

REFLECT: It's easy to suppress negative experiences and emotions, but the Bible encourages us to bring them to God. Write a prayer expressing your honest emotions and inviting God into the pain.

19

# Peace away from home

*Daniel and life in Babylon*

As we've established, during the sixth century BC God's people were forced to live as exiles in Babylon. To get a more personal perspective on this major upheaval, let's trace the story of a young man called Daniel. Born in Israel and raised among the elite in Jerusalem, Daniel would have been immersed in Jewish culture from a young age. But then the Babylonian king, Nebuchadnezzar, conquered Jerusalem and deported the gifted and talented to Babylon (*c.* 605 BC). So Daniel was snatched away from domestic safety and all that was familiar and forced to adjust to life in a foreign land. He must have felt like he'd been kidnapped from his homeland and left to fend for himself.

Several years ago, I was kidnapped. Late one night, eight men attacked me, stripped me down to my boxer shorts and threw me into the back of a minibus. Blindfolded, I was driven some distance before being forced to stand with my back against a tree. Then I heard the minibus drive off and I was alone. Managing to get the blindfold off, I found myself in a village that I didn't recognise. I tried desperately to get my bearings, but even the road signs seemed foreign. However, despite feeling disorientated, I had a strange sense of peace. Deep down, I knew it was all going to be OK. In my case, the sense of composure came from the fact that it was my stag-do in North Wales, which explains the problem reading the road signs! My so-called friends thought abandoning me in a random Welsh village in the early hours of the morning would somehow prepare me for marriage. Either way, it gave me peace to know that despite the apparent chaos, things were not completely out of control; my best man had made arrangements to ensure I survived the ordeal and arrived back in time for the wedding.

Disorientated in a foreign land, Daniel and the exiles also had reasons for confidence. Exile was not a random catastrophe; it was part of a divinely orchestrated plan that had been foretold long ago. The prophet Jeremiah even gave quite detailed instructions from God regarding how the exiles should conduct themselves when the time came:

> 'Seek the peace and prosperity of the city to which I have carried you into exile . . . For I know the plans I have for you,' declares the LORD, 'plans to prosper you and not to harm you, plans to give you hope and a future.'
>
> *Jeremiah 29:7, 11*

For the exiles, it must have been incredibly reassuring to hear that God still had 'plans to prosper' his people. In the meantime, they were not to panic or become despondent. Instead, they were to embrace the opportunity to trust in God's faithfulness while in a foreign land. In sporting terms, they were to prove that God's people can 'win away from home' and succeed even in hostile circumstances.

Daniel's challenge is now our challenge. We are exiles, called to succeed against the prevailing culture. In the Bible, 'Babylon' is not limited to an ancient city; instead, Babylon symbolises all that is in opposition to the way God intended people to live. It goes right back to the Tower of Babel, that symbol of human pride in Genesis 11. The name *Babel* is the stem from which we get the word 'Babylon'. They were located in the same place (near Baghdad in Iraq) and represent the same big idea: when humans rebel against God they use their skill and ingenuity to set up rival empires and 'worldly' cultures. By the first century AD, 'Babylon' had become Christian code for the Roman Empire. A first-century letter therefore considered God's people to be in a state of exile under Roman rule:

> Dear friends, I urge you, as foreigners and *exiles*, to abstain from sinful desires, which wage war against your soul.
>
> *1 Peter 2:11*

In one sense this has been the general state of play for God's people ever since. However, in our cultural moment the metaphor of exile is becoming increasingly relevant. Within my lifetime (born in 1978 in case you were wondering) a major cultural shift has occurred. Just as Daniel moved from living in Jerusalem to Babylon, so Western society has migrated from a culture primarily shaped by a Judeo-Christian worldview to a post-Christian or secular culture. During the 1980s and 1990s, shops were shut on Sundays, the Bible featured heavily in schools and sexual ethics were still largely defined by Christian values. Now don't misunderstand me. Nominal Christianity and a churchified culture was hardly Utopia. Nevertheless, those who metaphorically grew up in Jerusalem must now work out our faith in a context where Christianity has been pushed to the margins and secular humanism dominates.[14] Modern-day Babylon is an intoxicating experience, offering powers of knowledge, technology and entertainment unrivalled in world history. However, this culture is shallow and pulls us away from the truth of the Bible. So if you desire to live God's way, consider yourself a modern-day exile. Like it or not, we no longer live in Jerusalem. We are residents in what David Kinnaman from Barna Research refers to as 'digital Babylon'.[15]

Framed this way, the stories of Daniel and other exiles become highly relevant. They show us that it is still possible to win away from home no matter how much pressure we come under. They also help us adjust our expectations to a different set of challenges that we now face in digital Babylon. If we are to succeed in exile, we must adopt the *posture* and *practices* of exiles like Daniel.

The distinct *posture* that Daniel adopted was one of radical allegiance to God, while seeking to bless the Babylonian Empire. This may sound like a contradiction but it's the sort of tension that exiles have to get comfortable with. On arrival, Daniel and his Jewish compatriots were issued with Babylonian names and had to learn a new language and culture (Daniel 1:4). By embracing these challenges, they established trust and reassured their new boss that they were not adopting a hostile stance. In fact, they 'distinguished' themselves (Daniel 6:3) and became known as the best civil servants in Babylon. However, when the Babylonians tried to involve them in pagan worship (Daniel 3) or served up food that had probably been sacrificed to idols (Daniel 1:8) they refused point blank. Anything that compromised their absolute allegiance to God crossed a line. As three exiles said to Nebuchadnezzar shortly before being thrown into a furnace:

> The God we serve is able to deliver us . . . But even if he does not, we want you to know, Your Majesty, that we will not serve your gods.
>
> *Daniel 3:17–18*

Isn't that brilliant? Polite and respectful ('Your Majesty') and yet utterly defiant ('we will not . . .'). That's how exiles win away from home. A friend of mine was overseas on business. After a day of hard negotiating, the CEO from the other company pulled him aside. Once in private she said: 'I think we have a deal. But let's sleep on it first. Your room or mine?' As a Christian, he refused. She was slighted and threatened to call off the deal the next day. My friend replied: 'If I am prepared to cheat with you, I might cheat on you. And nobody wants that.' He has gone on to flourish, despite operating in a rather toxic business environment. To thrive in exile you've got to be upfront about who you ultimately work for and where you draw the line.

Successful exiles also adopt regular spiritual *practices* to sustain their faith in a hostile culture. In Daniel's case, despite a busy and demanding job, he prayed three times every day. Maybe in Jerusalem you wouldn't need to be quite so disciplined, but in Babylon it's essential to keep the right perspective. Ironically, it was this practice that soon got Daniel into trouble. The king passed an edict that anyone caught praying would be thrown into the lions' den. Daniel's response?

> He went home to his upstairs room where the windows opened towards Jerusalem. Three times a day he got down on his knees and prayed, giving thanks to his God, just as he had done before.
>
> *Daniel 6:10*

When exiled in a hostile culture, prayer is a lifeline. Every time Daniel opened his window to Jerusalem and called out to God he reasserted his true identity and remembered his ultimate calling. Through disciplined use of spiritual practices exiles can resist the pressure to assimilate. A friend who is an MP said to me recently that he has learned the necessity of switching off from news and social media for a twenty-four-hour period each week. It gives breathing space and a weekly reminder that though the people elected him, he answers to God. Prayer, Sabbath, worship – these are vital spiritual practices in exile. They enable us to be a blessing to our culture while living with God as our ultimate master. That's how exiles like Daniel can win away from home.

READ: Daniel 6:1–28.

REFLECT: How do we experience the pressure to conform? Do we give in too easily? As exiles, what specific practices might we need to adopt in order to 'win away from home'?

20

# Rebuilding peace

*Nehemiah and the hope of restoration*

After seventy years of suffering in a foreign land and succeeding against the odds, it was finally time to go home. In 538 BC the Persians defeated the Babylonians. Cyrus the Great ruled the new super-power with a very different foreign policy. Out of respect for local cultures, the Persians encouraged Jewish captives to head home with their blessing and even some financial support. So by 520 BC, several waves of Jewish exiles made the long journey back to their homeland. There they set about rebuilding and restoring until it felt like home again. Like so many *Grand Designs* projects, it was both a remarkable achievement and tinged with some disappointment. Here we focus on the successful renovation phase; in the following section we will see how their unfinished business highlighted the need for a coming messiah.

Imagine being in the sandals of a Jewish exile as they turned the corner and Jerusalem came into sight. They would have known the legends and prophecies that gave this city iconic status. However, as they drew closer, they discovered that the 'City of God' was a pile of charred rubble. Talk about mixed emotions: the joy of arriving home and yet the reality of a broken home. The story of Jewish exiles returning to find their homeland ruined reflects our larger human story. Planet earth was intended to be a home filled with *shalom* and yet we encounter so much brokenness. Like the walls of Jerusalem, key areas of our lives can feel broken and dysfunctional. We dream of a simple, ordered, tidy life but the reality is more like a pile of rubble. It's easy to slump into negative responses: anger, self-pity, resentment or despair. Perhaps you're feeling some of that right now?

This is precisely why we need the Bible. It's a story of hope and restoration from start to finish. When life feels like chaos and rubble, God's word lifts us out of despair. Through the story of Israel in the fifth century BC, we witness the miraculous restoration of Jerusalem from a pile of rubble to a new home. And we discover that their *story* holds *promise* for us – the same God who acted decisively on their behalf can rebuild our lives and restore *shalom*. Whatever areas of brokenness you may be living with, even if you've experienced stress and breakdown or life feels ruined right now, take heart. Whatever the mess, there's always hope. The rubble can become a home and peace can be restored.

To get a handle on how this works, let's zoom in on Nehemiah, an exile who returned to Jerusalem around 450 BC. He was an extraordinary leader who successfully mobilised a construction company from scratch that rebuilt Jerusalem in just fifty-two days. If you've ever experienced building works first hand you will appreciate what a miracle that is . . . when the builders finish ahead of schedule, under budget and without major snagging issues, it must be God!

The first thing Nehemiah reveals about how to transform rubble is *the importance of Spirit-inspired imagination*. Nehemiah had been living in Persia as chief cupbearer to the king. This was a well-paid job and rather cushy – getting paid for wine-tasting. But Nehemiah was a Jew who really belonged in Jerusalem. One day he got news that his homeland lay in ruins:

> When I heard these things, I sat down and wept. For some days I mourned and fasted and prayed before the God of heaven.
>
> *Nehemiah 1:4*

God's Spirit was clearly disturbing Nehemiah's comfort zone and inspiring his imagination for Jerusalem. Soon Nehemiah would be galloping back from Persia having handed in his resignation. He appeared to be risking everything for a ruin. But where others saw rubble, Nehemiah saw raw material and the hope of restoration. He was so captivated by the vision that it ruined his taste for fine wine and motivated him to take the risk. So don't feel sorry for him; he wasn't doing it out of a sense of duty or obligation. Instead, it was a vocation: 'what my God had put in my heart to do' (Nehemiah 2:12). It's the invigorating feeling you get when you're part of a really worthwhile cause. If anything, feel sorry for those who felt a similar call but never plucked up the courage to take action. After all, what's one of the most common deathbed regrets? 'I wish I'd taken more risks.'

Once back in Jerusalem, Nehemiah took time to inspect the ruined state of the walls. A Spirit-inspired imagination does not hide from reality. However, Nehemiah's assessment was framed by a deeper conviction. An extract of his speech to the inhabitants of Jerusalem captures his inspiring sense of vision:

> 'Come, let us rebuild the wall of Jerusalem, and we will no longer be in disgrace.' I also told them about the gracious hand of my God on me.
>
> *Nehemiah 2:17–18*

The people he was addressing returned from exile much earlier than Nehemiah. By now, they'd been living in the rubble for years. They'd got used to it and normalised it. No doubt they could reel off excuses as to why they lived in a ruin. 'We prefer it open-planned . . . so much easier to clean.' The major difference between the rubble-dwellers and Nehemiah was Spirit-inspired imagination that aspired to something better. The first key to converting rubble into *shalom* is to refuse to settle for it – the dysfunctional marriage, cycles of debt, a bitter stand-off with a friend or family member, the hidden addiction. If the gracious hand of God is upon us, let's quit making excuses and thinking it's normal. There's a better way to live.

The second key to restoration is *start with the rubble in front of you*. When faced with enormous challenges, the hardest thing can be knowing where to begin. Problems appear so overwhelming that we cannot imagine making any real difference. This can be demoralising. It stops us taking action and we procrastinate instead. So having inspired the people with a vision of *where we want to be* Nehemiah rolled out a strategy for *how to get there*. Detailed planning is not my strong point, but I've learned over the years that without it even Spirit-inspired visions remain mere daydreams. Unless there's a clear and practical plan, nothing changes. If we are in debt, we need a repayment plan. If we are out of shape, we need an exercise plan. If our marriage is broken, we need a relationship plan.

Nehemiah's plan involved each family taking responsibility for the rubble outside their own front door (Nehemiah 3). This ensured quality control – you won't sleep well if your section of the wall is weak. It also encouraged people to put their own house in order before sorting out the rest of Jerusalem. As clinical psychologist Dr Jordan Peterson puts it: 'My sense is that if you want to change the world, start by tidying your room and work out from there . . . If you can't even clean up your own room, who the hell are you to give advice to the rest of the world?'[16] For Malkijah and his family, this involved a particularly unpleasant task. They lived opposite the *Dung Gate* in Jerusalem, so these unsung heroes rebuilt it (Nehemiah 3:14). Round of applause please. If we want to see our rubble become *shalom* we will have to get our hands dirty. Precisely because the gracious hand of God is upon us, we must roll up our sleeves and take responsibility. So, let's stop procrastinating and beating ourselves up for all the things we can't do. Start with some small changes, stick with them, and soon you will see a big difference.

The final principle from Nehemiah is *don't quit*. The repair work in Jerusalem was threatened and opposed from the moment it started. At one point, armed bodyguards had to accompany the builders while they worked (Nehemiah 4:15–23). But Nehemiah simply refused to be intimidated. When we do the right thing, we shouldn't be surprised if we face opposition. You may even attract subtle forms of sabotage from those threatened by the changes. Decide to stop drinking and a so-called friend will offer to buy you a pint. The right thing is often the tough thing. If it requires imagination to start the work, it will take gritty determination to finish it. But it's so worth it.

Be encouraged, the gracious hand of God is upon us. The rubble is raw material. The small actions we take over the long haul can restore *shalom*. The returning exiles transformed Jerusalem in record time because their God was – and still is – in the business of restoration. So take heart, rubble-dwellers. Whatever challenges we face, no matter how insurmountable they seem, the story of Nehemiah is a promise we can take hold of, one brick at a time.

READ: Nehemiah 1:1–4; 2:11–20; 4:12–23.

REFLECT: Where in your life have you settled for too much rubble and dysfunction? Make a practical plan to work for change. Share it with a wise friend and get going!

# 21

# Peace and the Prince

*The end of the Old Testament*

Confession time. I recently watched the Disney film *Tangled*, a modern take on the German fairy tale of Rapunzel. In fairness, it was my daughter's idea and it provided a timely reminder that epic stories, from Rapunzel to Mary Poppins, James Bond to Harry Potter, all share a basic plotline. After setting the scene and introducing the cast, the narrative descends to a *low point* or crisis (Rapunzel trapped in a tower), then there's a *turning point* or intervention (the prince climbs into the tower) before reaching a *high point* (they live happily ever after). Specific details will vary and there may be stories within the story but the essential features are the same; a turning point must be reached and a prince must be found if the story is to reach a happy ending. Some of the most loved authors believe stories are shaped like this because they echo something deeper – what J. R. R. Tolkien called the 'story of a larger kind'.[17] He was referring to the Christian story, the Bible. Its plotline is the original or archetypal story and the likes of Tolkien, Fleming, Rowling and Disney have been drawing inspiration from it ever since, whether they realise it or not.

Consider the plotline we have covered so far. Genesis set the scene and introduced the cast with early humans setting up home in a garden of *shalom*. However, the snake in the grass brought crisis into the story. Tempted by the serpent, Adam and Eve rebelled against their maker and were expelled. The human story has played out East of Eden ever since in a state of exile. So now we need a hero-figure to defeat evil and bring us home. Noah and the ark seemed promising but ended in drunken chaos. Then God called Abraham and promised that through his descendants 'all peoples on earth will be blessed' (Genesis 12). Sure enough, Israel emerged but soon found themselves enslaved in Egypt . . . the rescue team now needed to be rescued. So God stepped in through the Exodus. Moses brought them out of Egypt and Joshua led them into the Promised Land. But then it was hardly 'happily ever after'. Even King David, the closest approximation to a prince-hero in the Old Testament, went on to commit adultery and murder. Soon Israel's compromise brought another crisis. If *Exodus* brought them into their homeland, *exile* saw them driven out again.

Despite seemingly endless cycles of crisis–intervention–crisis, God never gave up on Israel. As the prophets foretold, after seventy years of captivity in Babylon the exiles were allowed to return home and rebuild. Alongside Nehemiah and the physical reconstruction work, God also called Ezra who initiated a spiritual detox programme. He led the people in a ceremony of rededication, taught the law of Moses (or Torah) and celebrated the Passover festival for the first time in a long time. So by the end of the Old Testament Israel were back in their homeland, with Jerusalem and the temple restored.

However, it's still not the happy ending everyone was hoping for. The book of Nehemiah closes on a disappointing note as the people cry to God for help: 'See, we are slaves today, slaves in the land you gave our ancestors . . . We are in great distress' (Nehemiah 9:36–7). Although their physical exile was over, it was hardly *shalom*; instead, they felt like captives in their own land. They had a roof over their heads but it was not the home they dreamt of. Israel's experience echoes the larger human story. It's Russian dolls again. We are living in the right place – earth was always intended to be our home – but clearly all is not well. We experience evil, suffering and death as continual reminders that we too are exiles-in-our-own-home, strangers in our own skin. No matter where we dwell on this beautiful planet, we experience 'the desire for a far-off country'.[18] As we've seen, it's the deep longing of those made for one reality (Eden) but who are experiencing the opposite (exile).

In Israel's case, their post-exile disappointment was exacerbated by the grandeur of the promises they had received. While still in exile, the prophet Ezekiel had seen dramatic visions that totally eclipsed their present reality. In Ezekiel 40–1 he saw a vast new temple with dimensions far exceeding anything Solomon built. Then in Ezekiel's vision, the glory cloud of God's presence, which had vacated Solomon's temple during the exile, returned in greater measure. Finally, a river of life poured out of the temple and flowed down the mountain that Jerusalem was perched on. When it reached the infamous Dead Sea, it transformed it into a place of life and beauty (Ezekiel 47). The vision was a dramatic restatement of the promise made to Abraham: 'all peoples on earth will be blessed through you' (Genesis 12:3). Out of this nation, Israel, hope will spring forth for all nations.

By the close of the Old Testament, these visions seemed to be the mindless hallucinations of a prophet who had taken something illegal. The rebuilt temple was nothing compared to the one in Ezekiel's vision and, either way, the glory of God never filled it again. It was an empty shell. Israel was pregnant with prophecies she could not deliver on. The Old Testament is a catalogue of unfulfilled promises and loose ends that raise a crucial question: Where is the Prince?

In Israel's case, there would be a 400-year interval before the answer came. This interlude is known as the Intertestamental period, between the close of the Old Testament and the start of the New. It was a difficult time as Israel was overrun by a series of world empires – the Persians, Greeks and then the Romans. Despite several revolts and bloody uprisings, the period was largely one of defeat and oppression. Israel learned the hard way that taking things into our own hands and forcing a solution ends in heartache. Surrounded by super-powers, they had to hold on in hope that their day would finally come. For now they were left sitting in the waiting room. A tough place to stay. But sometimes it's where God wants us: waiting for a partner, waiting for promotion, waiting for pregnancy, waiting for retirement. Of course, there are alternative 'Prince Charmings' who offer short-cuts and instant gratification, but if you read the reviews from others who tried them, the feedback is pretty unanimous: 'I wish I'd waited.' Would you agree from your experience?

There is only one Prince who can answer our human cry for peace. Long before he came, the prophet Isaiah promised Israel he would be worth the wait:

For to us a child is born,
to us a son is given . . .
And he will be called
Wonderful Counsellor, Mighty God,
Everlasting Father, *Prince of Peace*.

*Isaiah 9:6*

Jesus Christ is the long-awaited Prince who fulfils Israel's plotline and provides the turning point in our human story. The *shalom* he brings is much more than mere ceasefire. Even in the storms of life there is a harbour for the soul. Even when the bottom falls out, the peace of God will guard your heart and mind in Christ Jesus. I've seen people experience this time and again. I think of recent conversations with friends facing daunting challenges yet still knowing God's presence in the furnace:

> Despite being made redundant, Richard told me: 'I've not lost my peace. I don't ultimately rely on people to provide for me but God.'
>
> Despite economic recession, Jenny told me: 'As CEO, I said to the company we won't panic or cut corners. We will trust in God and weather the storm.'
>
> Despite test results showing the lump is malignant, Bob told me: 'We've got peace to face this challenge. God is faithful and we trust him.'

*Shalom* is robust. It keeps us buoyant in the storms of life and brings us out the other side. As we reach the end of the Old Testament, it's time to prepare ourselves for the arrival of the Prince. As we sit in the waiting room, what are we hoping for? What is your cry for peace?

READ: Ezekiel 47:1–12; Isaiah 9:1–7.

REFLECT: How does the story of Israel's long wait resonate with you? Bring to God any disappointments and unfulfilled promises.

# INTERLUDE

O come, O come, Emmanuel,
and ransom captive Israel,
that mourns in lonely exile here,
until the Son of God appear.
Rejoice! Rejoice! Emmanuel
shall come to thee, O Israel.

O come, Thou Dayspring, from on high,
and cheer us by Thy drawing nigh;
disperse the gloomy clouds of night,
and death's dark shadows put to flight.
Rejoice! Rejoice! Emmanuel
shall come to thee, O Israel[1]

# INTERLUDE

[illegible]

[illegible]

PART 4

# MESSIAH

## Our human need for love

# Introducing love

Karaoke has never been my favourite pastime (understatement). However, at university it was an obligatory part of our rugby team's Wednesday night shenanigans. While I've tried hard to erase the memories, I do recall that by the end of each evening the song choice became slower and more romantic. Pete was one of our more good-looking teammates and he never failed to impress at this point. Dancing and smooching with the latest girl, his dulcet, drunken tones would sing Whitney Houston's classic 'I will always love you!' Through trial and error, Pete had identified this as his song of choice for clinching the romantic deal. One sober morning-after-the-night-before, I tried to point out to him that singing the same lyrics of undying love to a different girl each week had a certain irony to it. My point seemed lost on a guy who was busy living the modern dream.

In the Shakespeare play *As You Like It*, one of the characters exclaims: 'Good shepherd, tell this youth what 'tis to love!'[1] What a profound line for our times. When it comes to love, we seem to have lost our way in a fog of Hollywood romance and oversexualised fantasies. Nothing demonstrates this more clearly than the reality TV show, *Love Island*. However, true love is a powerful and intoxicating force – beautiful when you experience it and heart-breaking when you lose it. So *what 'tis to love?*

Part of the reason for our confusion between karaoke lyrics and true love is that, in English, we only have one umbrella term. 'Love' has to encompass such a range of settings and emotions – from a father telling his daughter 'I *love* you' to the enjoyment of tucking into a breakfast: 'I *love* pancakes with syrup.' However, the New Testament was originally written in Greek and this ancient language had a far more sophisticated vocabulary for love. The Greek word *eros* referred to sexual or romantic love. In the right context, this love can be fully affirmed and enjoyed. After all, the Bible began with a naked couple in a garden and part way through there's a whole book, the Song of Songs, celebrating sexual love. However, *eros* alone is never enough to satisfy our human need.

There's also *philia*, which referred to loving friendships and family relationships. Again, these are gifts to be cherished. But when the early Christians wanted to speak of God's love, they drew on a different word and filled it with new meaning: *agape*. It conveys a unique quality of love, way beyond human forms. As we will see in this section, *agape* love serves and sacrifices, bleeds and dies. It has power to resurrect the fallen and mend the broken. All other loves, *eros* and *philia*, are but a faint echo.[2]

Our human need for love is vital. The Bible affirms it from start to finish. However, when we fail to direct this good desire towards its ultimate source, we fall for substitutes that let us down. Perhaps this explains why modern romance myths become so prominent in secular cultures that have distanced themselves from religion. We are seeking to find in human relationships what is ultimately found only in God – true love, acceptance and fulfilment. Maybe this is why contemporary love songs still draw heavily on sacred imagery, with lyrics referring to 'angels', 'heaven', 'stars' and the 'divine'. An American cultural anthropologist called Ernest Becker, though not a Christian, captured this modern trend with extraordinary insight:

> The love relationship of modern humans is a religious problem . . . After all, what is it that we want when we elevate the love partner to the position of God? We want redemption – nothing less. We want to be rid of our faults, of our feeling of nothingness. We want to be justified, to know that our creation has not been in vain. We turn to the love partner for the experience of the heroic, for perfect validation; we expect them to 'make us good through love'. Needless to say, human partners can't do this.[3]

Becker's brilliant analysis exposes a modern myth that underpins pretty much the entire Hollywood industry. It goes something like this:

> If I could only find the perfect lover, I would escape the 'me' that I'm not happy with (redemption) and experience true acceptance (validation).

This plotline manifests itself in films, novels, box sets and theatres the world over. And what's more, it's absolutely true. If we could find the one who would always love us and never fail us, it would bring redemption and fulfilment. There's just one snag: 'human partners can't do this'. If we fail to appreciate Becker's killer line, we risk bouncing around from one relationship to another, never finding what we're looking for. Desiring the right thing, we look for it in the wrong places and experience break-ups, betrayals, shame and regret. Or we might live a morally conservative version of the same myth – though remaining outwardly faithful to our marriage we nevertheless become inwardly resentful and critical of our flawed partner who cannot meet our deepest needs. What we are actually searching for is not a marriage but a messiah, not mere romance but redemption.

When our desire for perfect love becomes misdirected, we end up becoming less human and more broken. The Bible is therefore one long story that redirects our desire for *agape* love back to the source. Our human need will only be satisfied if perfect love from beyond our fallen world should come looking for us. And this is precisely what we discover as we enter the New Testament:

> For God so loved [*agape*] the world that he gave his one and only Son, that whoever believes in him shall not perish but have eternal life.
>
> *John 3:16*

Jesus Christ is God's love in person. He is the source of our desire and the fulfilment of our deepest need. The life of Jesus recorded in the four Gospels is love in action, love incarnate: the broken healed, the guilty forgiven, outcasts embraced and the marginalised welcomed home. Set in the context of a Roman Empire in love with power, Jesus displayed the power of love – bleeding and dying for his enemies. The seismic claim of the New Testament is that through his perfect life, bloody death and bodily resurrection the Messiah has launched an *agape* revolution. Now we are invited to be part of it by receiving God's love, allowing it to permeate us and sharing it with others.

From a young age, our daughter was very intuitive when it

came to expressing her emotions. Whenever she felt sad or upset she would reach her arms up and say: 'I've got a pain in my heart. I need a hug!' As adults, our emotions become less obvious. But I'm not sure we really move on from the basic need for a higher love that lifts us up. The Bible from start to finish is a love song – not a meaningless karaoke number but a serenade from heaven to earth. As we consider the central character in the whole plotline, we are invited not only to learn from his example but to reach out and embrace the love that can meet our deepest need.

22

# Messiah is a new beginning

## *The Gospels and the big story*

Jesus of Nazareth was a historic human being who in many ways experienced life like the rest of us: squeezed down the birth canal into a dangerous world of bullies, family tensions, taxes and death. In his case, it all took place within a relatively small geographical footprint that was off the beaten track. Jesus grew up in Nazareth. Today it's a small town in Northern Israel. I happened to be there recently on the same day that England were playing in the Rugby World Cup final and, to my horror, there was nowhere showing the match. Nazareth seemed completely cut off from it all. It would have felt similar in Jesus' day. Back then, his hometown was the butt of jokes: 'Nazareth! Can anything good come from there?' (John 1:46). From the age of thirty, Jesus relocated to the region of Galilee where over the next three years he conducted the majority of his public ministry. Lake Galilee is certainly a scenic spot with some nice fish restaurants, but the region is not particularly influential. Jesus spent most of his time within a small triangle of communities on the northern shore of the lake – Capernaum, Bethsaida and Chorazin.

Given such obscurity, the fact that two thousand years later we've even heard of Jesus of Nazareth should surprise us. In a world of powerful empires his life could easily have been forgotten: a former tradesman wandering around a small patch of Palestine teaching a handful of rural communities, before suffering an early death in Jerusalem.

End of story.

Instead, an extraordinary Jesus-movement emerged, which today includes approximately one third of the world's population – that's roughly 2,400,000,000 followers of Jesus of Nazareth. I was reading a book last night by the explorer Bear Grylls, in which he confessed: 'I am slowly learning that Jesus is the key to everything.'[4] Afterwards, I scrolled through Twitter and saw a feed from Roberto Firmino, a famous football player. He posted a video of himself being baptised as a Christian. How improbable that global celebrities who have thousands of followers of their own still recognise their need to follow *Jesus of Nazareth*. The English literary genius, H. G. Wells, summed up the paradox of Jesus' ordinary but extraordinary life: 'I am an historian, I am not a believer. But, this penniless preacher from Galilee is irresistibly the centre of history.'[5]

The structure of the Bible (OT and NT) along with the division in our Western calendar (BC and AD) bear witness to the remarkable impact that Jesus has had on our world. The arrival of the Messiah was D-Day in our human story, a small hinge upon which the entire narrative turns. In order to appreciate the short life of Jesus (just thirty-three years) we must therefore step back and see it in the light of the whole Bible. The backstory helps us appreciate the significance of the Jesus chapter. To draw an analogy from a favourite childhood film, only when we realise that the family of Jane and Michael Banks are so dysfunctional can we appreciate that the arrival of Mary Poppins is so much more than just a nanny to help tidy up the

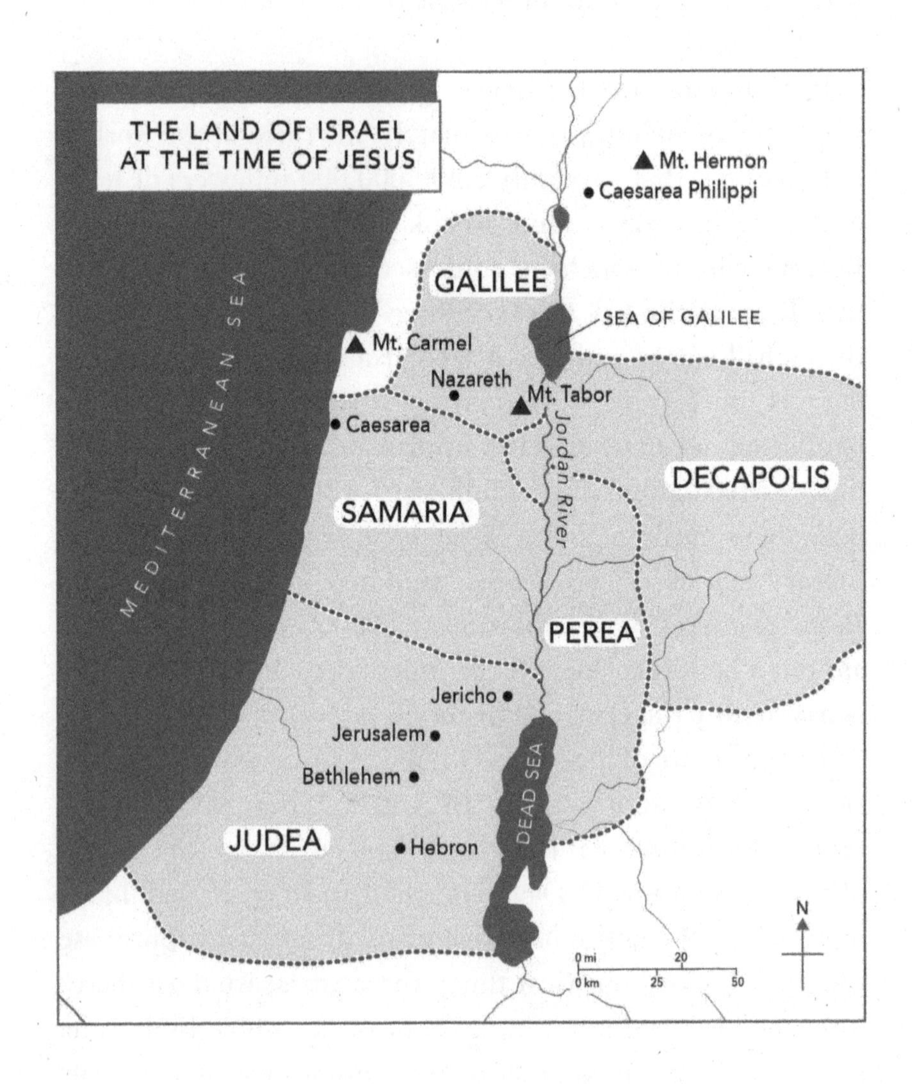
THE LAND OF ISRAEL
AT THE TIME OF JESUS
Mt. Hermon
Caesarea Philippi
GALILEE
SEA OF GALILEE
MEDITERRANEAN SEA
Mt. Carmel
Nazareth
Mt. Tabor
Caesarea
Jordan River
DECAPOLIS
SAMARIA
PEREA
Jericho
Jerusalem
Bethlehem
DEAD SEA
JUDEA
Hebron
N
0 mi
20
0 km
25
50

nursery. In a similar way, the four Gospels (Matthew, Mark, Luke, John) situate the arrival of Jesus within a failing story that needs a messiah to secure a happy ending. The Gospels go out of their way to ensure that we don't wander into the New Testament and miss what's at stake. The Messiah is not a mere moral nanny to help tidy up our lives; he is the fulfilment of a divine plan that meets our deepest need. Or as J. R. R. Tolkien put it: 'The Birth of Christ is the eucatastrophe of Man's history . . . There is no tale ever told that men would rather find was true.'[6]

This is why at first sight the Gospel of Matthew seems to get the New Testament off to such a disappointing start:

> This is the genealogy of Jesus the Messiah the son of David, the son of Abraham.
>
> *Matthew 1:1*

A genealogy is hardly a page-turner. In the ancient world, though, these lists provided a shorthand way to summon up a much larger story. Matthew's genealogy zooms out over centuries of Israel's history. He gives carefully edited highlights of the Messiah's family tree in order to reveal Jesus' identity through his ancestry. Jesus is 'son of David' – remember that Goliath-slaying king? Well, David was merely the warm-up act, pointing to the ultimate Messiah. Then even further back, Jesus is 'son of Abraham' – remember those global promises: 'all peoples on earth will be blessed' (Genesis 12)? Well it's game-on. The time has come. Finally, Israel's vocation will be fulfilled so the whole world can experience the end of exile and the freedom of a new Exodus.

However, look carefully and the Messiah's family tree is not as straightforward as we might expect. Along with iconic males like Abraham and David, Matthew deliberately highlights some bold and controversial females:

> Salmon the father of Boaz, whose mother was *Rahab* . . .
> David was the father of Solomon, whose mother had been *Uriah's wife*.
>
> *Matthew 1:5-6*

'Rahab' was a foreign prostitute who worked with Canaanite soldiers in the ancient fort of Jericho (Joshua 2). She got caught up in Israel's story when they conquered the Promised Land in the time of Joshua. But as providence would have it, she ended up being David's great-great grandmother (roughly). 'Uriah's wife' was Bathsheba, with whom David committed adultery (2 Samuel 11). Matthew doesn't airbrush out these awkward realities but showcases fractured stories within the genealogy of Jesus. The point is clear: Jesus didn't come from a sorted, religious, Ned-Flanders-from-the-Simpsons kind of family. His backstory was like ours . . . complicated, awkward and yet deeply loved by God.

If Matthew's Gospel frames Jesus within Israel's story, the opening line of John's Gospel situates him within a larger cosmic story:

> In the beginning was the Word, and the Word was with God, and the Word was God. He was with God in the beginning . . . The light shines in the darkness, and the darkness has not overcome it.
>
> *John 1:1–2, 5*

John takes us back before the dawn of time and reveals the one behind it all: 'the Word [*logos*] was with God in the beginning'.

In Greek, the term *logos* meant 'word' but it's also where we get the English word 'logic' from – the idea that rhyme and reason underpin all things. John's Gospel steps right back to the dawn of time and frames Jesus as the Logos, the cosmic author who can bring coherence and meaning to our story.

The phrase 'in the beginning' (John 1:1) is of course a deliberate echo back to Genesis 1:1 and the opening line of the Bible. It's a dramatic statement that just as Genesis was about creation, the arrival of Jesus is in some way the beginning of a new creation. Jesus is our way back to that unspoilt world of glory and *shalom*. As we've seen, when humanity turned away from God, darkness invaded. By the end of the Old Testament, Israel's exile captured the despair and brokenness we all face as a result. However, the opening line of John's Gospel heralds the dawn of a new day. Jesus Christ is a cosmic sunrise over our fallen world. Or as verse 5 puts it: 'The light shines in the darkness.'

Whenever I hear that phrase, I think of someone I know called Des. After a difficult upbringing he experienced a relationship betrayal that broke him completely. One Christmas, he was in such a dark place he decided to drink himself into a stupor and end it all. On his way to the off-licence he heard the sound of singing and wandered into the back of our church's carol service. As he stood there, a lady got up and read from John 1: 'In the beginning was the Word . . . The light shines in the darkness and the darkness has not overcome it.' Des later told me how these words struck him like rays of hope: 'For the first time I felt loved.' In Jesus Christ, Des discovered that his tired old story could have a new 'beginning'.

Through the arrival of the Messiah, the whole Bible story gets a fresh start or second *genesis* part way through. The same can be true for our story today. No matter how broken life may feel, through Jesus we can experience God's love breaking in like rays of morning sunshine.

READ: John 1:1–18.

REFLECT: Get up early and watch the sunrise or stay up late and light a candle. See God's love breaking into our world through Jesus. Invite him to shine into your darkness.

23

# Messiah puts a face to the name

*The birth of Jesus*

Choosing a name for a baby can be challenging. You're trying to avoid potential banana skins, like unfortunate initials. More positively, you want a name that means something, a name they can live up to. When our third child was born, we initially went for 'Jamie'. But having seen him, we began to like 'Toby'. In the end we couldn't decide so rather unconventionally we asked our Facebook friends to settle the matter in a vote. Apologies if you are a Jamie but our third child is very much Toby. In the ancient world, the pressure must have felt even greater. To name a person was to declare something prophetically over their lives. Their name was intimately connected to their spiritual *identity* (who I am) and their sense of *destiny* (what I will become).

Fortunately for Joseph and Mary, when it came to naming the Messiah, the pressure was taken off. An angelic visitation removed any need for a vote:

> An angel of the Lord appeared to [Joseph] in a dream and said . . . '[Mary] will give birth to a son, and you are to give him the name Jesus, because he will save his people from their sins.'

> All this took place to fulfil what the Lord had said through the prophet: 'The virgin will conceive and give birth to a son, and they will call him Immanuel' (which means 'God with us').
>
> *Matthew 1:20–3*

The appearance of angels in the Bible is always significant. The Greek word *angelos* means 'messenger'. They are sent from heaven when there is major news to announce to earth. In the nativity accounts, heaven's special agents appear to a most unlikely collection of individuals: a teenage virgin Mary, her rather bruised fiancé Joseph, a gang of rough shepherds and Zechariah, a dumbstruck priest in the temple. The unprecedented flurry of angelic activity is a sure sign that the most decisive moment in the entire Bible is unfolding. And the clue is in two crucial names that the angel declared over the Bethlehem babe.

First, 'Immanuel', which means 'God with us'. In some mysterious way, Jesus is the ultimate revelation of God's divine presence. In the Old Testament, there were plenty of temporary manifestations – the burning bush for Moses, the glory cloud that engulfed Solomon's temple for instance. But how much of God can you really know from a bush or a cloud? These dramatic manifestations were still *God above us*, several steps removed. However, the angel's message is that a woman is about to give birth to the very presence that had animated the bush and the cloud.

John's Gospel captures the idea in an iconic phrase: 'The Word became flesh and made his dwelling among us' (John 1:14). Or as *The Message* version puts it: 'The Word became flesh and blood, and moved into the neighborhood.' The staggering claim is that if you want to know what God is like, look no further. No better way could be imagined for humans to know God than for God to become a human. *Immanuel* is our way to experience God up close and personal. He is not whatever we've imagined him to be. God is like Jesus – pure and simple. At the burning bush, God revealed his name to Moses. Now Jesus puts a face to the name. As America pastor Bill Johnson says: 'Jesus Christ is perfect theology.'[7] Everything there is to know about God has been revealed in him.

Theologians refer to this as the 'incarnation'. The Latin word *carne* means 'meat' or 'flesh' – like chilli-*con-carne*, chilli with meat. So God *in-carne* means 'God in the flesh', 'God in human form'. My favourite carol puts it this way:

> Veiled in flesh the Godhead see,
> hail th' incarnate Deity!
> Pleased as man with man to dwell,
> Jesus our Immanuel.

As an inexperienced parent, when our children woke scared in the night I used to try and reason with them: 'Look under the bed, there are no monsters . . . check the wardrobe if you don't believe me.' I soon learned that it wasn't logic they needed; I just had to sit on the bed and be *with* them. My presence was enough to restore peace. The Messiah is not an abstract philosophy that stays in the realm of ideas. He's Immanuel. God *with* us.

'Immanuel' was a prophetic title but the name that stuck for this boy from Nazareth was 'Jesus'. It's derived from an ancient Hebrew root pronounced *Yeshua*. As the angel said, it means 'the Lord saves'. The Hebrew verb to save (*yasha*) conveys the beautiful idea of being delivered from oppression and led into a wide open place. When you appreciate that *Yeshua* is the same as the name 'Joshua', it all falls into place. When Israel was oppressed in Egypt, Moses delivered them from under Pharaoh but Joshua led them into the Promised Land. So Jesus is the new Joshua. He will break the power of oppression and lead us home to a spacious place. Jesus – what a beautiful name!

The promise of salvation through the Messiah was summed up in perhaps the most dramatic appearance of angels in the entire Bible:

> And there were shepherds living out in the fields near by, keeping watch over their flocks at night. An angel of the Lord appeared to them . . . [and said] 'Today in the town of David a Saviour has been born to you; he is the Messiah, the Lord' . . . Suddenly a great company of the heavenly host appeared . . . saying,
>
> 'Glory to God in the highest heaven,
> and on earth peace to those on whom his favour rests.'
>
> *Luke 2:8–9, 11, 13–14*

The arrival of a 'Saviour' and 'Lord' who brings peace sounds like religious language to us. But at that time the Romans ruled the world with an iron fist and Caesar Augustus called the shots. When he was born (*c*. 63 BC), Rome announced that he was the world's true 'Saviour' and 'Lord' who would secure that most prized possession – peace. They referred to this as '*pax Romana*' (the peace of Rome). The idea was simple: pay homage to Caesar, pay taxes to Rome, and you will be left in peace. Now listen to the angels' announcement: right under the emperor's nose the true 'Saviour' has been born. The one lying in the animal's trough is in fact the world's rightful 'Lord' who alone can bring 'peace on earth'.

In this political context, the message of the angels was controversial. But who they announced it to was even more shocking. If you've ever been chosen to don a tea-towel and play the part of a shepherd in your school nativity, I'm afraid it wasn't a compliment. In biblical times, shepherds were considered to be spiritually unclean and socially disreputable. And yet this group of undesirables was given the most dazzling display of angelic glory in the entire Bible. The message is clear: 'Jesus' means 'the Lord saves' and that means he can save anyone. In fact, Jesus became a magnet for those who would never consider themselves 'religious' – tax collectors, fishermen, soldiers and prostitutes. Those the religious leaders wrote off, Jesus welcomed in. Those who assumed they were beyond the pale, found God knocking at their door and those who assumed they had no need, missed out.

A few years ago, a famous historic mansion near where we lived opened its doors to the public on Christmas morning – a gesture of goodwill to those not normally allowed in. Afterwards, I got talking to a lady who turned out to be the Lady of the Manor. When she heard that I was minister of a church nearby she asked in a rather posh voice: 'Is it a church for the down-and-outs?' I was initially thrown by the premise of the question, but then a feeling of indignation rose up and I blurted out: 'Yes it is. And you would be very welcome too!' Before God, we are all down-and-outs. Because of Jesus, we are all invited in. He is *Immanuel,* God with us. He is *Jesus*, who delivers us into a spacious place.

READ: Matthew 1:18–25 and Luke 2:8–20.

REFLECT: Listen to the song 'What a Beautiful Name' (Hillsong Worship) or walk in a wide open space. Meditate on the significance for you of the Messiah's names: *Immanuel – God with us; Jesus – the Lord saves.*

# 24

# Messiah launches a new humanity

*The baptism and temptation of Jesus*

After an extraordinary start to life – angelic appearances, exotic gifts from mysterious Magi – Jesus' first thirty years were pretty average for a first-century Jewish male. So ordinary, in fact, that very little information has survived. Like every Hebrew boy he was circumcised after eight days and dedicated to God in the temple (Luke 2:21–4). Jesus then grew up in Nazareth, learning his stepfather's trade as a carpenter/builder. The eldest of at least six children, Jesus would have experienced all the joys and complexities of siblings, parents and friendships (Mark 6:3). Apart from the time when his parents accidentally left him behind in Jerusalem for three days (oops!), all we know about the next couple of decades is that: 'Jesus grew in wisdom and stature, and in favour with God and man' (Luke 2:41–52).

Then, around 27 AD, Jesus' slightly maverick cousin, John, made his way out into the Judean wilderness to a spot down by the Jordan River. Not any old spot. This was the precise location where centuries earlier Israel had crossed the Jordan after the Exodus and entered the Promised Land. As crowds came out to John in the wilderness, he started baptising or dunking (that's what *baptizo* means) them into the river as if they were crossing over again. For someone immersed in the Jewish Scriptures, these prophetic actions were carefully choreographed to create a sensational headline, which John bellowed to the crowds:

> 'Repent, for the kingdom of heaven has come near!' . . . 'Prepare the way for the Lord, make straight paths for him.'
>
> *Matthew 3:1–3*

John's announcement shattered 400 years of silence since the close of the Old Testament. He deliberately drew directly on a high-octane prophecy from Isaiah who centuries earlier imagined a day when God would return to rule as King (Isaiah 40:3–5). Now remember, Israel still felt like they were in a state of exile; they had a roof over their heads but it didn't feel like home. They were under the heel of Roman oppression. So John's dramatic announcement conveyed a clear message. It was time for exile to end. 'The day of the LORD', which the prophets had dreamt of, was finally dawning.

Before the King himself arrived Isaiah's prophecy envisaged a messenger bringing advance warning. Before modern communications, this was the job of a herald – to run on ahead and serve notice so the people could fill in potholes, tidy themselves up and get ready to welcome royalty. John understood himself to be that herald, preparing the way for the Messiah. So on that basis, the next character to arrive on the scene would be the One . . . 'Then Jesus came from Galilee to the Jordan' (Matthew 3:13). According to the Gospels, the arrival of Jesus *is* the arrival of Israel's King and the relaunch of God's kingdom. Into a world ruled by emperors and masters who abuse power and cause oppression, God is setting up an alternative, centred on Jesus Christ. We've seen how the world was originally entrusted to human beings but we fell for the voice of temptation and pulled the ceiling down on our own heads. Now, John the Baptist announces the arrival of a new character, a pivotal human who will crush the ancient serpent and restore hope to humanity. The next two events in the life of Jesus – baptism in the river and temptation in the wilderness – should therefore be understood as nothing less than the Messiah launching a new humanity out of the old.

> As soon as Jesus was baptised, he went up out of the water. At that moment heaven was opened, and he saw the Spirit of God descending like a dove and alighting on him. And a voice from heaven said, 'This is my Son, whom I love; with him I am well pleased.'
>
> *Matthew 3:16–17*

When Jesus was baptised he experienced something unique: 'heaven was opened' or literally it was 'torn' open. This was far more than sunshine breaking through clouds. It was a dramatic, almost apocalyptic moment as the fabric of our fallen reality tore open, revealing a new proximity to God. The experience of heaven being open and God coming close wasn't exactly new, more a recovery of something we lost way back when. Exiled from Eden, we humans have got used to heaven being closed and God feeling remote. But in Jesus things are changing. God is breaking back in and rupturing our fallen world with his glorious presence. The Holy Spirit then descends upon this human like a dove. The scene takes us back to the dawn of creation when 'the Spirit of God was hovering over the waters' (Genesis 1:2). The baptism of Jesus is the restoration of God's original design for humanity – a people baptised or drenched in the presence of God.

A voice from heaven then announces: 'This is my Son, whom I love [*agape*]; with him I am well pleased.' Crucially, this fatherly affirmation of love and pleasure comes *before* the ministry of Jesus has really got going. He's not yet performed a miracle or preached a sermon. But God's love for us humans is more basic and beautiful than a rewards system. It's the voice of a father who deeply loves his son regardless of output or achievement.

Through faith in the Messiah, we also can be immersed in the perfect love of a heavenly Father. We can know that we are truly accepted even *before* we've done the work. Without this experience, large swathes of our existence can be spent trying to impress others. But when we experience the unconditional love of God, we function from a secure place. Instead of living *for* acceptance we can live *from* acceptance. There's nothing to prove, and no need to impress. Recently, my daughter had a geography exam. Over breakfast, I could see she was nervous. So I put my arm around her and reminded her: 'You're my girl. I love you. And the result can't change that. So enjoy the challenge.' At the baptism of Jesus we witness something similar: through the love of God our Father, we can be freed from the fear of failure and given confidence to face life's challenges.

For Jesus, the beautiful experience of baptism was quickly followed by forty brutal days of testing:

> Then Jesus was led by the Spirit into the wilderness to be tempted by the devil. After fasting for forty days and forty nights, he was hungry. The tempter came to him and said, 'If you are the Son of God, tell these stones to become bread.'
>
> *Matthew 4:1–3*

Life can be like that sometimes. Sublime moments and breakthroughs are followed by periods of severe testing. Why? Because when we live in the freedom of the *agape* love of God, we arouse a spiritual opponent who otherwise lurks in the shadows. Have you ever sensed this kind of opposition personally? According to the Bible, Satan is a real spiritual being, very powerful and highly insecure when his tyrannical rule is threatened. Temptation, deceit and outright lies are his way of hitting back. Out in the Judean wilderness, Jesus got the full force of it.

However, notice Jesus was 'led by the Spirit' into this confrontation. It was actually God not Satan who initiated these rounds of temptation. Why would God put his 'beloved Son' through this? Think about the backstory. In the garden of Eden, Adam and Eve were called to trust the voice of God, but instead they ate the forbidden fruit. So God delivered Israel through the waters of Exodus and called them to be a new humanity, restoring blessing to the world. But Israel also gave in to temptation. Out in the wilderness, they worshipped a golden calf and ended up wandering aimlessly for *forty* years. The Gospels therefore present Jesus as a one-man-Israel. After passing through the waters of baptism he endured *forty* days in the wilderness but never gave in. Equally, Jesus is the new Adam. Despite weeks of fasting, he refused Satan's temptation to turn stone into bread and tuck into forbidden food. Jesus also rebutted two other temptations, each time quoting Scripture to silence the dark voice. That's worth noting.

Up to this point, the Bible has been a sad story of humans giving in to evil and facing the consequences. But now, out in the Judean wilderness, the tide is turning and a new humanity is emerging. Empowered by God's love, Jesus stood toe to toe with our archenemy and refused to back down. Though Satan questioned his identity three times, '*If* you are the Son of

God . . .', Jesus remained secure and won a decisive victory. For the first time in our entire human story, the result went conclusively the other way: 'Then the devil left him' (Matthew 4:11). This time Satan gave in. Jesus had successfully launched a new humanity, breaking patterns of defeat and restoring hope. Now we can be part of this story, as we centre our lives on the Messiah and receive the love of our Father in heaven.

READ: Matthew 3:13–4:11.

REFLECT: Can you identify specific areas of weakness and temptation for you (lust, greed, laziness, lying)? Jesus knows what it's like to be tempted so ask him for help to resist.

25

# Messiah brings Jubilee

*The kingdom of God*

If you are familiar with *The Lion King*, you know a Disney film that echoes the Bible's plotline. When the rightful king (Simba) gets evicted from his homeland by his evil uncle Scar, the fertile plains become a dust bowl and the animals begin to starve. The turning point comes when the true Lion King returns from exile to lay claim to the throne. The animals know what's at stake. If the kingdom is to flourish again, the good king must rule the kingdom. Needless to say, after a scary fight with Scar and a gang of hyenas, Simba is made king and the land flourishes once more.

In the Gospels, the arrival of Jesus Christ is nothing less than the return of the world's rightful King. We've seen that *Messiah* literally means the 'one anointed to rule', so no surprise that talk of 'the kingdom' was absolutely central to the ministry of Jesus. At stake is the flourishing of the entire cosmos. Jesus cannot be reduced to a moral nanny or a religious studies teacher. Humans, hyenas, dust and Disney – everything is impacted when the Good King rules again.

So after winning a decisive victory in the wilderness, Jesus began his public ministry by announcing the arrival of a new era:

> 'The time has come . . . The kingdom of God has come near. Repent and believe the good news!'
>
> *Mark 1:15*

Unlike the United Kingdom, the kingdom of God is not a political state with physical borders. As Jesus would later say to the Roman ruler, Pontius Pilate: 'My kingdom is not of this world' (John 18:36). Imagine God's kingdom less as a geographical *region* and more like a spiritual *realm*, a realm in which all things are as they should be – a perfect state of *shalom*. Now dare to believe it could be like that here on earth. Or as Jesus taught us to pray: 'Thy kingdom come . . . on *earth* as it is in *heaven.*' This gets to the heart of the mission of Jesus. He has come to destroy all that vandalises and to restore planet earth to the way it was supposed to be.

Now we can appreciate why the arrival of the kingdom is such 'good news' or 'gospel'. In the ancient world, the Greek word *euangelion*, which means 'good news', was reserved for the sort of announcements that bring great joy – 'It's a girl!' 'He passed!' 'We won!' The gospel is the news that this world's rightful King is back on the scene. He has come to kick out evil uncle Scar and re-establish *shalom*.

What might that look like in practice? One Sabbath, Jesus went to the synagogue in his hometown of Nazareth. There he asked for the scroll of the prophet Isaiah to be handed to him. This would have got the crowd going. Isaiah anticipated more than any other prophet the moment when God would return to rule as King (e.g. Isaiah 52:7–10). So to help reimagine what God's kingdom looks like, Jesus read from Isaiah 61:

> 'The Spirit of the Lord is on me,
> because he has anointed me

> to proclaim good news to the poor.
> He has sent me to proclaim freedom for the prisoners
> and recovery of sight for the blind,
> to set the oppressed free,
> to proclaim the year of the Lord's favour.'
>
> *Luke 4:18–19*

In a world of oppressive empires and tyrannical rulers, imagine the shock of this kingdom manifesto. Instead of the rich getting richer, it's the poor who get good news for a change; instead of the powerful consolidating their powerbase, it's the enslaved and oppressed who are led into a wide open space.

Jesus deliberately ended his manifesto on a phrase pregnant with significance: 'to proclaim the year of the Lord's favour'. In the Old Testament, once every fifty years a year of Jubilee was announced. In order to break cycles of poverty and inequality, during the year of Jubilee the nation of Israel hit the reset button: all debts were cancelled, slaves emancipated, prisoners released. Poverty, injustice and inequality ended overnight. Jubilee was therefore a prophetic foretaste of life under the 'Lord's favour', when the kingdom of God came on earth as in heaven. No wonder as Jesus rolled up the scroll, 'the eyes of everyone in the synagogue were fastened on him'. Then he gave the killer line that set the course for his entire ministry: 'Today this scripture is fulfilled in your hearing' (v. 21). Jesus is the rightful king. He is the Jubilee that our world so desperately needs.

Throughout the rest of his ministry, Jesus demonstrated the kingdom in concrete ways, healing the sick, driving out evil and embracing the marginalised. In this sense, his miracles were not magic shows. Quite the opposite. When Jesus touched lepers, healed paralytics and raised the dead back to life he was revealing what should be 'normal'. Sickness, evil and death are not original. We get so used to them that we can't imagine a world without them. But as the Messiah steps in, these intruders are forced to flee and whole communities get a taste of life in God's kingdom.

Jesus also taught about the kingdom. His most famous message, the Sermon on the Hill (if you've been to Galilee, you'll know it's not a mountain), has become arguably the single most influential teaching in history. Yet precisely because it's familiar, we miss how radical it was. When Jesus finished, there was a stunned silence. The original hearers were 'amazed' (Matthew 7:28). His sermon completely reimagined what success looked like. Consider Jesus' Beatitudes, short sayings that launched his sermon. *Beatitude* means 'supremely blessed'. They reveal a radical new vision for human flourishing:

> You're blessed when you're at the end of your rope. With less of you there is more of God and his rule.
>
> You're blessed when you feel you've lost what is most dear to you. Only then can you be embraced by the One most dear to you . . .
>
> You're blessed when your commitment to God provokes persecution. The persecution drives you even deeper into God's kingdom.
>
> *Matthew 5:3–4, 10 (The Message)*

This is topsy-turvy teaching. It's just as subversive today as it was back then. When a university lecturer put these sayings before her philosophy class, without revealing who they were from, her class quickly became adamant that such teaching was neither desirable nor practical. Instead, it was downright dangerous. Precisely! Jesus' kingdom will not politely sit alongside modern values nor will it accommodate our proclivity to greed, selfishness and individualism. That's why Jesus called his hearers to 'Repent!' The word literally means 'change your mind'. It implies rethinking life and making a U-turn. To experience the blessed life is to embrace a radically alternative way of being human.

In the Gospels, we encounter several examples of those who made the U-turn and experienced Jubilee for themselves. These are not fictional characters. We're told their names, jobs, locations and other unnecessary information. It all serves as a reminder that the Gospels are not fabricated myths but trustworthy accounts.[8] For example, the reason we know about Zacchaeus, the vertically challenged tax collector is because Luke's Gospel relied heavily on eyewitnesses who saw what really happened. When Jesus passed through Jericho, crowds lined the streets and jostled for position. Zacchaeus didn't stand a chance. Not only was he short, he was also hated. He worked for the Romans, collecting taxes, exploiting his own community and lining his pockets. But despite acquiring power, status and wealth, on the inside Zacchaeus was desperate for a change. So, in a shocking moment of self-abandon he hitched up his robes and climbed a sycamore tree to glimpse the Messiah. However, Jesus wasn't content to be a mere celebrity admired from a distance. So he singled out Zacchaeus, the most disreputable person in town, and invited himself round for dinner.

In that culture, to eat with someone was a sign of true acceptance. Over dinner, the lonely tax collector encountered God's *agape* love and it totally transformed him. Meeting the Messiah redefined what success looked like. To the amazement of all his enemies, the greedy little man spontaneously announced: 'Look, Lord! Here and now I give half of my possessions to the poor, and if I have cheated anybody out of anything, I will pay back four times the amount' (Luke 19:8). This is what happens when the Messiah's kingdom comes. It so gets hold of a man that his passion for life is turned upside down. As a result, Jericho got a taste of Jubilee – debts repaid, oppression ended and enemies transformed into friends. All because the Messiah brought in a kingdom more powerful than social stigma and more desirable than Roman gold. The power of *agape* love.

READ: Luke 4:14–22; 19:1–10.

REFLECT: Is there a specific area of your life where you need to make a U-turn? In the words of Zacchaeus, declare to Jesus how things will change:

'Look, Lord! Here and now I ______________________________
______________________________.'

26

# Messiah gathers a team

*The call to discipleship*

A few years ago while climbing in Scotland, I had to call for help from Mountain Rescue because of injuries sustained by another climber. They quickly arrived on the scene but had to cross a fast-flowing river to reach us. Unfortunately, one of the Mountain Rescue team slipped and dropped their kit bag in the river. His colleague ran along the bank to retrieve it but then he also slipped and fell in. All of a sudden, we faced an unexpected scenario: the Mountain Rescue team needed rescuing before they could attend to the injured climber!

Israel was originally chosen to be God's rescue team, called to deliver his saving mission to the world. Unfortunately, the Old Testament is largely a story of Israel falling in and needing to be rescued themselves. So, a major part of the Messiah's task was to mobilise a new team that could start a revolution of *agape* love. To achieve this, Jesus formed a small group of close followers to embody his kingdom values. By the shores of Lake Galilee, he began to assemble a motley crew, including fishermen, tax collectors and violent extremists (Zealots). At first, he chose twelve disciples who later became known as Apostles. Of course, in the Bible, twelve is a highly significant number: it represents the twelve tribes that formed the nation of Israel. Jesus was making a clear statement that his followers would fulfil the global promises that stretched all the way back to Abraham (Genesis 12).

Given the raw material Jesus had to work with, a rigorous formation process was required to create a robust kingdom team. Fortunately, Jewish culture already had a highly effective *Rabbi–disciple* model for training. The Rabbi was a respected teacher of the law who would call young disciples (we might say apprentices) to follow him and even live with him. By a process of osmosis, the disciples soon began to think and act like the Rabbi. In fact one of the Greek words translated as 'disciple' is *mimetes* from which we get our word 'mimicry'. To be a disciple or follower of Jesus is not about memorising facts or verses. It's about achieving such proximity to the master that we mimic his entire way of life. We are not called to be adoring fans, cheering Jesus on from the sidelines. The goal of the disciple was to become like the Rabbi and do what the Rabbi did. That's why when Peter saw Jesus walking on water, his disciple-instinct was: 'Master, can I walk on water too!' If this leaves you feeling inadequate, don't despair. After months on the road with Jesus, his disciples were still putting their foot in it: Peter had a sinking episode; James and John wanted to firebomb a town (Matthew 14:29–30; Luke 9:54). But Jesus refused to give up on them. How reassuring is that?

One of the most famous interactions between Jesus and his disciples took place in a town called Caesarea Philippi way up north. It's a crucial turning point in the Gospels as Jesus' identity and mission got clarified on a whole new level. By this stage, the disciples had witnessed some remarkable moments – instantaneous storm-calming, mass catering from a kid's lunch-box, the sort of health care that empties entire hospitals. By now an obvious thought must have been bubbling in their minds. But before they had time to compare notes, Jesus confronted them head on with a question that every human must answer:

> 'But what about you?' he asked. 'Who do *you* say I am?'
>
> *Matthew 16:15*

One of Jesus' followers, Simon Peter, who had the subtlety of a bulldozer, spoke up on behalf of the twelve: 'You are the Messiah, the Son of the living God' (v. 16). Others at the time were trying to explain away the phenomenon of Jesus, reducing him to an enlightened teacher or prophet. But Peter dramatically raised the stakes, declaring him to be God's anointed King and eternal Son. It takes guts to say that to a human being standing in front of you who grew up down the road from you. But those who got closest to Jesus simply couldn't find a better explanation.

Crucially, far from rejecting Peter's claim, Jesus endorsed it: 'Blessed are you . . . for this was not revealed to you by flesh and blood, but by my Father in heaven' (v. 17). This wasn't the first time Jesus had embraced huge claims about his identity. Indeed, given the sort of things Jesus said about himself, he could not have been just a nice religious figure or good moral teacher. As C. S. Lewis noted, either he was a deluded lunatic 'on a level with the man who says he is a poached egg' or he was indeed the Messiah, the Son of God.[9] Which do you think is more plausible?

After clarifying his identity, Jesus went on to answer a related question: *What had the Messiah come to do?* His answer involved some strange new ideas that didn't go down well:

> From that time on Jesus began to explain to his disciples that he must go to Jerusalem and suffer many things . . . and that he must be killed.
>
> *Matthew 16:21*

Having just accepted the title of Messiah, it made no sense for Jesus to start talking about defeat. Surely God's anointed King would destroy Israel's enemies not suffer at their hands? The disciples must have wondered whether the poached egg option might in fact be the case. To help resolve matters, the fisherman once again waded in:

> Peter took him aside and began to rebuke him. 'Never, Lord!' he said. 'This shall never happen to you!' Jesus turned and said to Peter, 'Get behind me, Satan!'
>
> *Matthew 16:22–3*

The force of Jesus' rebuttal suggests something major is at stake. Through the voice of Peter, Satan has slipped back on to the scene to tempt the Messiah away from his mission. But Jesus remained adamant: he 'must' suffer and die. The Greek word for 'must' is *dei*. It's emphatic, carrying a sense of divine necessity. This is the only way for the kingdom to come on earth as it is in heaven. To mess with this is to interfere with the most determined plan in the universe. As Peter learned the hard way, it's not our job to coach or manage the Messiah. We are invited to follow him ('get behind me'), not to lead him. Point taken.

One week later, bruised egos still recovering, Jesus led three of his closest disciples (Peter, James and John) up a high mountain. Suddenly, he began to shine with ethereal radiance and beauty. His clothes became translucent as if glory was emanating from within. This event is known as the transfiguration, a term that refers to the change in Jesus' form or appearence. As the drama unfolded, two guests suddenly appeared on the mountain with Jesus – Moses and Elijah. These men represented Israel's entire history. The Old Testament was often referred to as the Law and the Prophets. Moses represented the former and Elijah was considered to be Israel's greatest prophet. It's as if the Old Testament is meeting with the Messiah for a round-table discussion. Wouldn't you have loved to eavesdrop on their conversation? What we are told is that Moses and Elijah spoke about 'his departure' (Luke 9:30–1). The Greek word used here is *exodus*. For humanity to be truly set free and brought into a spacious place, the Messiah must embody the plotline of the Exodus story. The crux of it all was the sacrifice of the Passover lamb.

High up on the Mount of Transfiguration, the mission of the Messiah was becoming clear. If the rescue team were to be rescued and salvation brought to the world, it would require the ultimate display of love by the Messiah himself. After descending from the mountain, 'Jesus resolutely set out for Jerusalem' (Luke 9:51), where our entire human story would come to a head in one dramatic week. The Messiah had refused satanic temptation and bravely chosen to suffer and die for us:

> Greater love [*agape*] has no one than this: to lay down one's life for one's friends.
>
> *John 15:13*

READ: Luke 9:18–36.

REFLECT: Write down a one-line response to Jesus' probing question: 'Who do you say I am?' In the light of your answer, take some time to hand in your resignation as head coach and to follow Jesus as Lord.

27

# Messiah launches an *agape* revolution

*The crucifixion*

If you were a marketing consultant developing a brand logo for a global movement, it would be strange to choose an icon of torture and execution. Nevertheless, the cross has become one of the world's most recognised symbols. And millions choose to wear it around their necks every day. Even Coca-Cola can't achieve that kind of brand ownership.[10] However, given that the cross has become a fashion accessory, it's easy to forget what it symbolises. Crucifixion on a wooden frame was a mechanism for brutal execution and total humiliation. The Romans deployed it only for seditious criminals who threatened the stability of the Empire (pax Romana). The terrifying spectacle was intended as a deterrent, a public warning of what happens if you mess with the powers-that-be. However, despite the shame and repulsion associated with crucifixion, the Gospel writers were not tempted to gloss over what happened: all four accounts go into slow motion for the end of Jesus' life. John, for instance, spends ten out of his twenty-one chapters on Jesus' final week. For the early Christians, the cross was not a premature end or meaningless tragedy. Quite the opposite. It was the climax of the Messiah's mission and the launch of an *agape* revolution.

To grasp how this works, we need to rewind to the start of Jesus' final week. It's April *c.* AD 30. The population of Jerusalem had swelled with pilgrims celebrating the Passover festival with family and friends. The atmosphere was charged with anticipation, as Passover celebrated the old Exodus but also held out hope of a new one – a fresh act of deliverance from Roman oppression. At the start of the week, Jesus raised expectations by riding down the Mount of Olives on a donkey, a direct fulfilment of an ancient prophecy:

> See, your king comes to you,
> righteous and victorious,
> lowly and riding on a donkey.
>
> *Zechariah 9:9*

The crowds got the message and started waving palm branches and shouting '*Hosanna!*', which means 'Save us!' or 'Rescue us!' As far as they were concerned, it was game-on. However, by Monday Jesus began to disappoint. Instead of attacking the Roman barracks, he entered the Jewish temple. There he became angry and turned over the tables where money changed hands and goods were sold. It was an act of judgement on the greed and hypocrisy of the religious leaders. Jesus had come to Jerusalem for a fight, but not with the Romans. He had a much darker and more pervasive enemy in his sights.

Thursday was officially the day to celebrate Passover through a symbolic meal. So Jesus had his disciples book an upper room on the outskirts of Jerusalem, where they shared the Last Supper. This meal was famously portrayed in Leonardo da

Vinci's painting, which has since been the subject of numerous conspiracy theories, including Dan Brown's *Da Vinci Code*. However, only the Gospels accurately relay what really went on behind closed doors. Part way through the meal, Jesus as host took the *matzoh* bread in his hands. This flat bread symbolised the Israelites' rushed departure from Egypt without time for the dough to rise:

> Jesus took bread, and when he had given thanks, he broke it and gave it to his disciples, saying, 'Take and eat; this is my body.'
>
> *Matthew 26:26*

In an audacious moment, Jesus reoriented the whole meaning of the meal towards himself. A new way of Exodus would be opened up through his broken body. But that was not all. After supper, Jesus tore up the Passover script once again:

> He took a cup . . . 'Drink from it, all of you. This is my blood of the covenant, which is poured out for many for the forgiveness of sins.'
>
> *Matthew 26:27–8*

Just the sight of blood is too much for some people; drinking blood definitely crosses a line. While Jesus wasn't being literal, he was alluding to the Passover lamb, whose blood was daubed on Israel's doorposts with a hyssop branch (Exodus 12:22). Now the blood of Jesus would provide forgiveness and a whole new way for humans to experience God.

Jesus then led his disciples across the Kidron Valley and retreated into a grove of olive trees known as the Garden of Gethsemane. Here the full horror of what lay ahead seemed to descend on him. Falling to his knees, he imagined himself holding a cup in his hands. In the Old Testament, this cup represented God's judgement upon the sins of Israel and other nations. But now the cup was in the Messiah's hands. Having just offered a cup of forgiveness to his disciples, Jesus must take their cup of judgement and drink it as his own. Just the thought of it was too much:

> Being in anguish, he prayed more earnestly, and his sweat was like drops of blood falling to the ground.
>
> *Luke 22:44*

Someone with anything less than *agape* love would have turned back at this point. But Jesus stepped forward and chose the cross. In order to redeem all the negatives that stemmed from the choice Adam and Eve made in the *Garden of Eden*, Jesus made the ultimate choice of love in the *Garden of Gethsemane*. He went out to meet Judas, one of his closest disciples, who for some extra cash betrayed Jesus with a kiss. Extraordinary. Only a few hours earlier, knowing full well what Judas would do, Jesus had got down on his knees and washed his filthy feet. What kind of love is this?

Jesus' arrest was followed by a series of mock trials. During Thursday night, he was passed around from pillar to post, as everyone from Herod Antipas (Jewish ruler) to Pontius Pilate (Roman ruler) tried to avoid condemning a clearly innocent man. But by now the crowd were baying for blood. Eventually Pilate caved in and handed Jesus over to be flogged and crucified. Flogging alone could kill a man. A whip made up of leather cords and bits of bone was lashed against the victim's back, tearing out chunks of flesh. Already brutalised, Jesus was forced to carry his cross through a mocking crowd until he

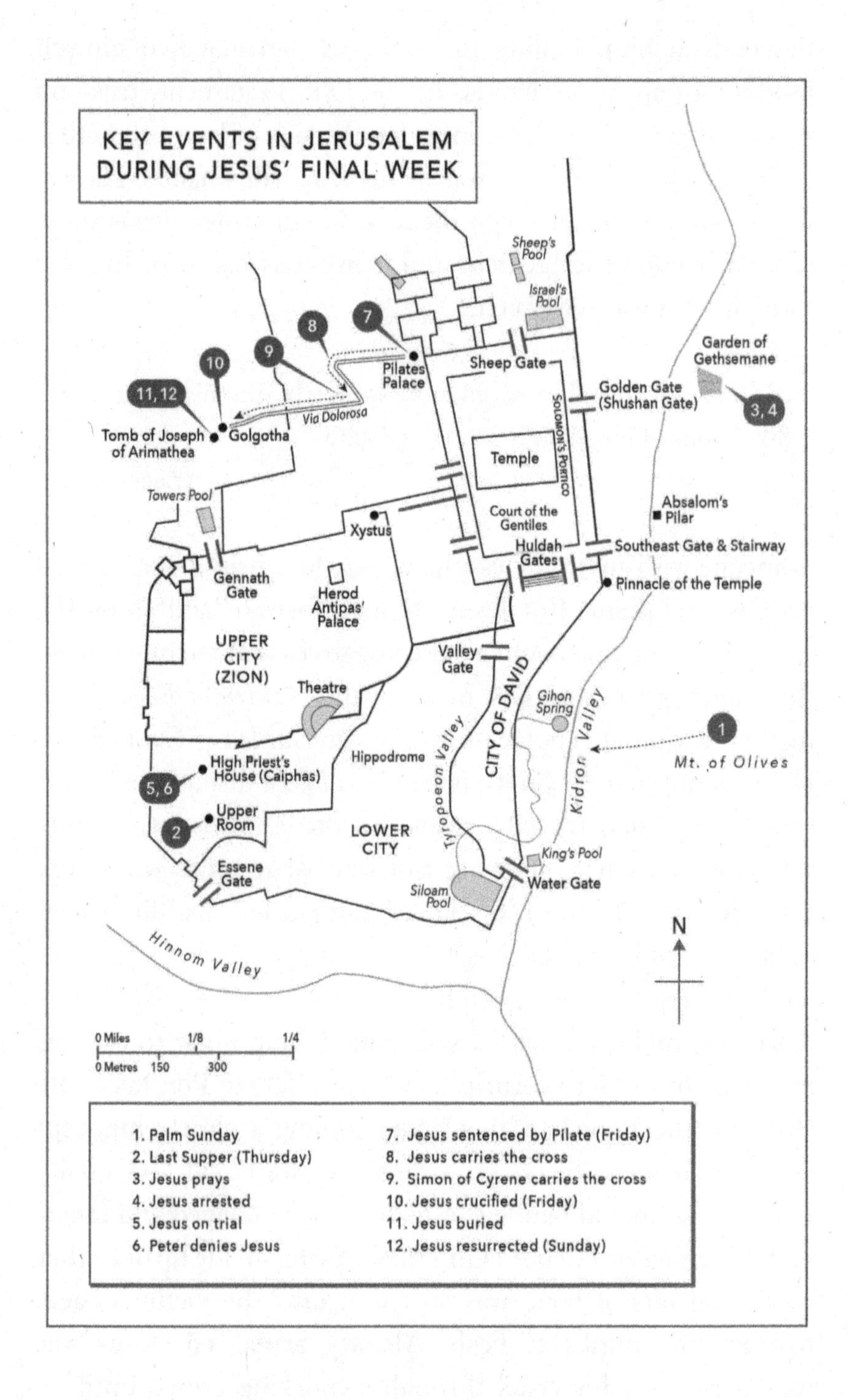
KEY EVENTS IN JERUSALEM DURING JESUS' FINAL WEEK
Sheep's Pool
Israel's Pool
Pilates Palace
Sheep Gate
Golden Gate (Shushan Gate)
Garden of Gethsemane
3, 4
7
8
9
10
11, 12
Via Dolorosa
Tomb of Joseph of Arimathea
Golgotha
SOLOMON'S PORTICO
Temple
Court of the Gentiles
Towers Pool
Xystus
Absalom's Pilar
Huldah Gates
Southeast Gate & Stairway
Pinnacle of the Temple
Gennath Gate
Herod Antipas' Palace
UPPER CITY (ZION)
Valley Gate
CITY OF DAVID
Theatre
Gihon Spring
Kidron Valley
1
Mt. of Olives
Tyropoeon Valley
Hippodrome
High Priest's House (Caiphas)
5, 6
Upper Room
2
LOWER CITY
Essene Gate
King's Pool
Water Gate
Siloam Pool
N
Hinnom Valley
0 Miles 1/8 1/4
0 Metres 150 300
1. Palm Sunday
2. Last Supper (Thursday)
3. Jesus prays
4. Jesus arrested
5. Jesus on trial
6. Peter denies Jesus
7. Jesus sentenced by Pilate (Friday)
8. Jesus carries the cross
9. Simon of Cyrene carries the cross
10. Jesus crucified (Friday)
11. Jesus buried
12. Jesus resurrected (Sunday)

collapsed under its weight. Finally, they arrived at a rocky outcrop called Golgotha, just outside the city walls. There, six-inch nails were smashed through his wrists and ankles and he was lifted up to hang naked in public, through the heat of the day (9.00 a.m.–3.00 p.m.). From midday, an eerie darkness descended as the Messiah entered the eye of the storm.

> About three in the afternoon Jesus cried out in a loud voice . . . 'My God, my God, why have you forsaken me?'
>
> *Matthew 27:46*

Now the Son of God was banished into deepest, darkest exile, drinking to the dregs the cup of divine judgement. On the cross, the innocent Son of God took the place of the guilty. An ancient prophecy by Isaiah foresaw this moment centuries earlier:

> He was pierced for our transgressions,
> he was crushed for our iniquities;
> the punishment that brought us peace was on him,
> and by his wounds we are healed.
>
> *Isaiah 53:5*

Finally, Jesus asked for a drink. Wine vinegar was lifted to him on a hyssop branch – remember that? Here is the ultimate Passover lamb, sacrificed to open up a new way of Exodus freedom for all humanity. Jesus therefore saved his final breath for a cry of victory in the midst of apparent defeat: 'It is finished!' (John 19:30). Notice, he didn't say 'I'm finished!' but 'It is finished!' The curses that ruin creation, the Pharaohs that dominate our world, the sins that enslave our hearts, the exile that shuts us out – *It is finished!* The cross was the ultimate act of self-substitution. Jesus willingly stepped into our predicament and took our dark terrors – sin, judgement and hell. The Son of God got nailed for us. But precisely because of this, the cross is also a great exchange: because Jesus got what we deserve, we can have what he deserves. He was forsaken so we can be forgiven. He was cursed so we can be blessed. He was shut out so we can come home.

If we want to know how God feels about us, we need look no further. At the foot of the cross we encounter a perfect love that forgives sins, heals wounds and restores peace. The bloody and brutal crucifixion of the Messiah has launched a revolution:

> God demonstrates his own love [*agape*] for us in this: while we were still sinners, Christ died for us.
>
> *Romans 5:8*

READ: John 19:1–30.

REFLECT: Imagine yourself standing with the crowd at the foot of the cross. What do you see? What do you feel? What do you want to say or do? Make a prayerful response to Jesus.

28

# Messiah triumphs over death

*The resurrection*

After the brutal crucifixion of Jesus on Good Friday, it seemed that all hope was lost. The mighty Romans had crushed yet another would-be messiah and restored the status quo. However, something so dramatic unfolded in Jerusalem over the course of the weekend that by Monday morning the world was not the same place anymore. The resurrection of Jesus on Easter Sunday proved to be a defining moment in world history. Indeed, the whole Bible is shaped like an hourglass. It all funnels down to this narrow point. As the Messiah was crucified, thick darkness descended. But the resurrection of Jesus has released a cosmic sunrise of hope over our entire human story.

How so? Well, the claim of the resurrection is not that a sick person at death's door staged a remarkable recovery, nor that a heart briefly flat-lined on the ECG monitor before being resuscitated. Jesus was not revived from death; he broke through it. He triumphed over it and now lives and reigns on the other side. So the resurrection of Jesus is not freakish paranormal activity. It's the redefining of what 'normal' looks like for human beings. The drama of the moment is captured by key sounds. As Jesus died there was *tearing* in the temple as the wall of curtain that separated people from God was ripped open. When Jesus rose again there was the sound of *cracking* as the seal on the grave broke open and the stone-cold reign of death was rolled away. Whole new possibilities now appear, which the old order of things cannot contain. A real human being, Jesus of Nazareth, is enjoying eternal life on the other side of death. The resurrection, if true, is a game-changer for all of us. So, what is the *evidence* for the resurrection of Jesus and how might we *experience* its power today?

**Looking at the evidence**

Surprisingly, even non-believing historians accept several pieces of evidence that make it hard to come up with an alternative explanation.[11] In particular:

- The tomb was found to be empty.
- The disciples claimed Jesus appeared to them on several occasions.
- Christianity exploded in the decades that followed.

At dawn on Sunday morning, several women hurried to the tomb where Jesus had been buried late on the Friday. They would have wanted to embalm the body straightaway but Sabbath restrictions meant they had to wait. However, upon arrival they discovered that the tomb was open and empty. They reported this to some of the male followers of Jesus who wanted to see for themselves. So Peter and John raced to the tomb and when they entered: 'saw the strips of linen lying there, as well as the cloth that had been wrapped round Jesus' head' (John 20:6–7). Since the disciples did not believe resurrection was possible, they initially looked for alternative explanations – perhaps grave robbers had broken into the tomb and taken the body. But why would they have left the expensive linen behind? And why were the grave clothes lying there like an empty cocoon after the creature had emerged? With more questions than answers, the disciples headed home.

Over the next six weeks, there followed a series of remarkable appearances. Each one demonstrated that Jesus is not just a memory or artefact of history. He is the risen Messiah whom we can personally encounter. Here are some highlights:

*John 20:11–18*

The first person to encounter the risen Jesus was Mary Magdalene. This is significant because in the ancient world she would have been considered an unreliable witness. Even a respectable woman was not permitted to give testimony in a court of law. But Mary had a chequered history. We don't know all the detail but Jesus had cast seven demons out of her (Mark 16:9). If you were making this whole resurrection thing up, Mary Magdalene would be the last witness you would call. So perhaps it actually happened this way? When Mary saw Jesus, she initially mistook him for the gardener. But then he spoke her name and the darkness lifted. That's the thing about the resurrection: because Jesus is alive, he calls us by name and has the power to set us free.

*Luke 24:13–35*

Two disciples were heading out of Jerusalem utterly despondent. As far as they knew, Jesus was dead and buried. But in a moment of comedy, Jesus drew alongside them like a fellow traveller. They slowly began to recognise him as he led an extraordinary Bible study, showing why the Messiah had to suffer and then rise again. They later reflected: 'Were not our hearts burning within us while he talked with us on the road?' (v. 32). And that's another thing about the resurrection: Jesus can breathe fresh fire into cold, depressed hearts. He gives us back our passion.

*John 20:19–23*
Back in Jerusalem, some of the other disciples were experiencing a lot of anxiety. They had locked themselves in a room, too afraid to go out. Suddenly, Jesus stood among them and said: 'Peace be with you!' (v. 19). The risen Jesus can enter places nothing else can reach, bringing peace. His perfect love drives out fear and gives us back our confidence for life.

*John 21:1–19*
Sometime later, Jesus appeared to the disciples by the shores of Lake Galilee, their old stomping ground. He cooked breakfast on a fire and ate fish with them like old times. Clearly, this was no ghostlike phantom but a real person living on the other side of death and enjoying the good things of life. Jesus then had a one-to-one with his closest disciple, Simon Peter. This burly fisherman had caved in during the trial of Jesus and denied knowing him three times. Now he was given an opportunity to reaffirm his love for Jesus and to experience total forgiveness. As Peter discovered, the risen Jesus offers failures a brand new start.

The growth of Christianity is the final piece of evidence for the resurrection. After all, there were several other failed messiahs at the time of Jesus. Judas of Galilee, for example, was a self-proclaimed messiah who gathered followers before being executed by the Romans, *c.* AD 6. His movement died with him and I don't think anyone is worshipping Judas of

Galilee today. On that basis, Christianity was dead and buried when Jesus of Nazareth lay stone cold in a sealed tomb, *c.* AD 30. The magnet had been switched off and his ex-disciples were scattering in defeat. So how do we explain the way Christianity exploded in the first century to become a global phenomenon with 2.4 billion followers today? The only satisfactory explanation is that the magnet turned back on again. As biblical scholar N. T. Wright concludes: 'I cannot explain the rise of early Christianity unless Jesus rose again, leaving an empty tomb behind him.'[12]

**Experiencing the victory**

One noteworthy feature of the risen Jesus is that the scars and wounds of his crucifixion remained visible even after the resurrection. Doubting Thomas even got to touch them:

> [Jesus] said to Thomas, 'Put your finger here; see my hands. Reach out your hand and put it into my side. Stop doubting and believe.'
>
> *John 20:27*

These wounds not only provide visible proof of the victory of Jesus but also point to how we might experience that victory today. The scars tell the story of God's love in action. Because the One who was mortally wounded is now alive and whole, he can heal our brokenness and restore our fractured world. As Thomas Aquinas (1225–74) wrote: '[Christ] kept His scars not from inability to heal them, but to wear them as an everlasting trophy of His victory.'[13]

There is an old Japanese art of mending broken pottery called *Kintsugi*. The name means 'golden joinery' and the process involves using a resin, mixed with gold, to reassemble broken pieces. The result is a pot or vase that is arguably more valuable than the original piece. Instead of hiding the repair, the brokenness becomes part of the aesthetic beauty. The golden scars tell a story.[14]

This provides a powerful illustration of the way true healing works. The risen Jesus is the master of *Kintsugi*. His sacrifical love is the golden resin. As the lives of Zacchaeus, Mary, Peter and Thomas all testify, Jesus takes what's broken and puts it back together again in such a way that it becomes more beautiful and valuable than before. So let's not hide our brokenness from him. Instead, let's hand the pieces to the risen Jesus and see what he can do. Imagine if our brokenness could be restored into a masterpiece by the golden resin of his love.

READ: John 20:1–31.

REFLECT: Why not search '*Kintsugi*' and look at some images for yourself. Perhaps it's time, like Thomas, to 'stop doubting and believe'? In prayer, offer Jesus your brokenness and receive the healing power of his love.

PART 5

# SPIRIT

## Our human thirst for community

# Introducing community

Several years ago, I took on the noble task of looking after my sister's children for a full half-hour all on my own. By the time she returned from the shop, the situation had spiralled out of control. The kids were crying inconsolably and I was frantically trying to distract them, making funny faces and rude noises. My sister waltzed in, took one look at their rosy cheeks and poured them each a drink. Within moments, calm was restored and I was annoyed: 'Why didn't they just tell me if they were thirsty?' With a note of sarcasm, my sister explained that you can't expect a toddler to attribute their emotional distress to an underlying thirst. That's supposed to be our job.

As toddlers need juice, as bodies need $H_2O$, we humans have an innate thirst for community. And when we don't experience it, we act up in strange ways that to the untrained eye may seem unrelated. Research has uncovered a whole host of negative symptoms that trace back to an unmet thirst for community. A *New York Times* article summarised the impact of social isolation on health and wellbeing like this:

> Individuals with less social connection have disrupted sleep patterns, altered immune systems, more inflammation and

> higher levels of stress hormones . . . All told, loneliness is as important a risk factor for early death as obesity and smoking.[1]

In our times, a combination of expressive individualism and digital consumerism is exacerbating the situation, causing a loneliness epidemic on an unprecedented scale. And it's not just a late-in-life problem for the elderly; a recent survey of young adults discovered that in Western countries over a third described themselves as 'lonely and isolated'.[2] We've probably all experienced moments like this. The great paradox of our hyper-connected age is that we feel more alone than ever. Our headphones and mobile devices are turning us into isolated consumer units, watching sitcoms about relationships, tuning in to online conversations, but all the while wilting for lack of meaningful community. We are relationally dehydrated, and no amount of cheap entertainment will console us.

The Bible makes good sense of this cultural crisis. Remember right back at the beginning, before anything went wrong, a fundamental principle was declared:

> It's not good for the Man to be alone; I'll make him a helper, a companion.
>
> *Genesis 2:18 (The Messsage)*

The only thing not good in a perfect world was a human being on their own. As it was for Adam so it is for us. No number of pets or hobbies can distract us from the intrinsic need for human companionship. After all, we were made in the 'image' and 'likeness' of a God who is not a loner in the skies but a divine community of love: Father, Son and Holy Spirit. Without getting confused by the complexities of the doctrine of the Trinity, we must grasp the beauty of this. God is richly relational. Therefore, we also flourish when rooted in loving families and communities.

However, as we've seen, we have been exiled from Eden. The original harmony of one human family has experienced major disruption and fragmentation. Our loneliness could therefore be described as homesickness, a desire to return to a world without the pain of rejection, divorce and estrangement. In a brilliant essay entitled 'The Inner Ring', C. S. Lewis argued that one of the most dominant human emotions is a disordered desire to gain entrance into the inner ring or circle. This is not about a formal position or title. It's a more basic desire to be truly accepted and not to feel left out. Crucially, regardless of how many friendship circles we acquire, no matter how many parties we get invited to, the thirst is never quenched:

> Unless you take measures to prevent it, this desire is going to be one of the chief motives of your life . . . As long as you are governed by [it] you will never get what you want. You are trying to peel an onion; if you succeed there will be nothing left. Until you conquer the fear of being an outsider, an outsider you will remain.[3]

This is precisely why the next chapter of the Bible story is so vital. The life, death and resurrection of the Messiah was all about overcoming rejection and enabling reconciliation. Jesus came to restore our ruptured relationship with God so we could experience *agape* love. With this accomplished in Jerusalem, six weeks later at a festival known as Pentecost, the Spirit of God dramatically filled the Messiah's followers. As a result, a new community sprang up in Jerusalem, unlike anything humans could engineer – marked by transparent trust and unbridled generosity. Though far from perfect, this new community provided a setting in which human beings flourished. Ordinary people discovered a new sense of *belonging* in a community of love and a new sense of *purpose* on mission together.

When our horizons shrink to self-centred interests we become superficial, isolated and depressed. In order to flourish, we need to feel part of something bigger than ourselves. On the cross, Jesus took upon himself our sin and rejection in order that through the Spirit we might be reconciled to God and become part of a new community where we belong and discover our purpose. During a rugby match several years ago, one of our teammates deliberately hurt an opposition player at the bottom of a pile of bodies. The referee couldn't identify the guilty person but refused to let the game continue until the situation was resolved. In the end our captain, who definitely had not committed the offence, volunteered to be sent off instead. So, in a strange moment of exchange, the game got going again with the guilty person still on the pitch and very much part of the team. The death of Jesus was an act of extraordinary substitution, the innocent taking the place of the guilty. As a result, despite all our faults and failings, we are invited to be part of the Messiah's team. The Holy Spirit bonds together flawed disciples into a close-knit community to fulfil God's mission in the world.

This section will trace the remarkable impact that Christians made during the decades following the earthly ministry of Jesus. From a handful of Jewish men and women, Christianity quickly became a multicultural movement spreading across the known world. Devoid of elite celebrities or financial backing, this movement was fuelled by the presence of the Spirit who signals a new era in our human story. Though Jesus is no longer physically present on earth, the work of the Messiah continues through small communities empowered by the Spirit (i.e. churches). Finally, we have arrived at our own chapter in the Bible story: this is where we fit in. Now we ourselves are called on to the pitch with a part to play. In an age marked by loneliness and isolation, our thirst can be quenched by the Spirit who gives us a *family to belong* to and a *mission to serve*.

29

# The Spirit empowers ordinary people

*Continuing the Messiah's mission*

Have you ever met a celebrity or someone famous? With hindsight, I have, but I failed to realise it at the time. Our school rugby team played a match against a team with a brilliant player, known simply as 'Jonny'. They won the match largely because of him and afterwards I offered my personal congratulations: 'You're really good. You'll go far!' I like to think those words of encouragement inspired Jonny Wilkinson all the way to winning the Rugby World Cup in 2003! With the benefit of hindsight, the disciples must have cringed at some of the things they said to Jesus before they realised his true identity. But after his death and resurrection, their eyes were fully opened. Even doubting Thomas worshipped Jesus as 'My Lord and my God!' (John 20:28).

But now what? Having reversed defeat and conquered death, no doubt they expected the Messiah himself to dismantle his rivals, establish his kingdom and convert the world within a few months. Meanwhile, they would carry Jesus' bags and hold back the adoring fans. So imagine their shock when the Messiah turned round and said in effect: 'Well chaps, my work here is done. Now it's over to you!' The Bible story has many surprising twists and turns but arguably this is the best of them. The next chapter of the story will not feature the Messiah in person but a community of transformed people, known individually as Christians or collectively as the church. Christianity is not a celebrity cult of screaming fans; it's a global movement of restored humans empowered to change the world.

To further establish the point, the next book in the New Testament (after the four Gospels) is simply called 'Acts'. But it's not about the acts of Jesus. It's a record of what ordinary Christians got up to over the next thirty years as they took the world by storm. Acts was written by Dr Luke who also wrote Luke's Gospel. It opens with these intriguing words:

> In my former book . . . I wrote about all that Jesus *began* to do and to teach until the day he was taken up to heaven.
>
> *Acts 1:1–2*

Luke's Gospel was just the beginning of what Jesus intends to do on planet earth. But now instead of operating *in person* he will work *by proxy*. The clue is in the symmetry. In Luke's Gospel, Jesus got rid of evil, healed the sick and preached the good news. Now in Acts, Jesus' followers get rid of evil, heal the sick and share good news. Whereas in Luke's Gospel, Jesus was physically present on earth, now the Messiah's followers are his hands and feet in the world. In a beautiful poem, Gerard Manley Hopkins captured the idea:

> . . . for Christ plays in ten thousand places,
> lovely in limbs, and lovely in eyes not his
> to the Father through the features of men's faces.[4]

*But how is that possible?* I hear you ask. *How can flawed people like us pick up where the Messiah left off?* It's one thing to watch Jonny Wilkinson play rugby, it's quite another to be substituted on to the pitch to play in his position. I admire Usain Bolt but I can't run like him. I listen to Pavarotti but I can't sing like him. I enjoy reading Shakespeare but I can't write like him. I can worship Jesus but I can't minister like him, surely? And yet if you read Luke's Gospel and Acts in quick succession you get a strange feeling of déjà vu. Of course there are differences and the early Christians were far from perfect, but to cut a long story short, they went off and did it! A small community of Jesus' followers stepped into the Messiah's sandals and expanded his ministry on a global scale. And today the story continues. Jesus' followers all over the world provide practical help and spiritual hope on a staggering scale. The Messiah continues to establish his kingdom of good news – not *in person* but *by proxy* – through ordinary people like you and me.

To be prepared for the task, we must grasp two vital principles that fuelled early Christianity. First, Jesus is now in heaven, enthroned as King of the universe. After his resurrection, Jesus appeared to his disciples over a period of six weeks. Then Luke describes in two different accounts the moment when Jesus said *au revoir*:

> [Jesus] led them out to the vicinity of Bethany . . . While he was blessing them, he left them and was taken up into heaven.
>
> *Luke 24:50–1*

> He was taken up before their very eyes, and a cloud hid him from their sight.
>
> *Acts 1:9*

This may all sound a bit NASA – Jesus the astronaut launching into outer space – but that's not what's going on. Notice carefully 'a *cloud* hid him'. If you're used to a British climate this probably sounds like normal weather. But to Jewish ears, the cloud was an iconic symbol of heavenly glory. In the Old Testament, a cloud guided the Israelites through the wilderness and flooded Solomon's temple. So think of this glory cloud as a heavenly portal. The cloud transferred Jesus from our earthly realm into heaven.

This event is known as the ascension of Jesus. But think of it like a coronation. Having accomplished his mission on earth, it's the moment when Jesus is declared King of heaven. That means the Messiah is now ruling over our world from a position of supreme authority – seated on God's throne, installed in the Oval Office, top of the control tower. As he said to his disciples, moments before departure: 'All authority in heaven and on earth has been given to me' (Matthew 28:18). Now can you see where the early Christians got their confidence? They went out and changed the world because their leader was Lord of heaven and earth. Talk about friends in high places.

Around age five, our daughter went through a cute phase of asking, 'Who's the boss?' In her new school, at our church. One time over dinner she asked, 'Who's the boss of our family?' Awkward. Then at bedtime one evening she said: 'So, who's the boss of the world?' I replied: 'Jesus. Jesus is the boss.' She smiled, put her head on the pillow and fell asleep. It was as if she made the simple connection that has inspired Christians down through the centuries: *Jesus is the boss of the world and we're his people.* On that basis, we can sleep soundly and live boldly.

The second key to continuing the ministry of Jesus is to be empowered by the Holy Spirit. Before Jesus physically left, he made this crystal clear:

> I will ask the Father, and he will give you another advocate to help you and be with you for ever – the Spirit of truth . . . I will *come to you.*
>
> *John 14:16–18*

We struggle to grasp how this can work because we're so used to our limitations. We get stressed and shout: 'I can't be in two places at once!' But don't put that on Jesus. While ruling in heaven, through the Holy Spirit he is able to be with us on earth. Jesus described the Holy Spirit as our 'advocate' or in some translations, 'comforter' and 'helper'. The Greek word is *parakletos*, which means one who 'stands beside' (as a lawyer defending you) or 'walks alongside' (as a friend). The Spirit is not an impersonal force like *Star Wars*' or magic power like Harry Potter's. The Holy Spirit brings the personal presence of Jesus to his people.

Jesus also promised that we would receive 'power' when the Holy Spirit fills us (Acts 1:8). The Greek word is *dunamis* from which we get words like 'dynamic' and 'dynamite'. So it's time to reimagine what's possible. Let me break it gently: we're never going to sing like Pavarotti or write like Shakespeare or kick like Jonny Wilkinson. However, because Jesus is the boss of the world and the mighty Holy Spirit is here to help us, we can continue the ministry of the Messiah in our backyard. Just read the book of Acts. When the Holy Spirit filled ordinary people, they were *empowered* to bring hope to the world. Christianity is not a spectator sport; we are invited on to the pitch. So let's quit hiding behind our excuses and limitations. Let's believe the promise of Jesus:

> You will receive power [*dunamis*] when the Holy Spirit comes on you; and you will be my witnesses . . . to the ends of the earth.
>
> *Acts 1:8*

READ: John 14:15–19; Acts 1:1–11.

REFLECT: If Jesus lived in your neighbourhood or had your job, what might he do? Invite the Spirit to help you imagine what it could look like to take up the ministry of Jesus right where you are.

30

# The Spirit fires up the fearful

*Becoming who we were made to be*

As a family, we love lighting fires. We have a log-burning stove inside, a fire-pit outside and we enjoy campfires in the wild. Whenever you get a good fire going, magical things happen. Flames dancing in the hearth and the injection of warmth and light create a special atmosphere. Cold hearts warm up and even wild places begin to feel safe. Fire is like a magnet that draws everyone closer. Distracted individuals gather together and start sharing stories and making memories. That's why I love fire. In fact, if I ever become Prime Minister, a weekly communal fire would be mandatory.

Fire fighters, relax. That isn't going to happen.

On the day of Pentecost, the Holy Spirit lit a fire in the hearth of our human story that has been burning ever since. Six weeks after the Messiah's resurrection and ten days after Jesus ascended into heaven, the Holy Spirit came down like 'tongues' or flames of fire. This symbolism represented the holy presence of God now inhabiting humans with new proximity. In Jerusalem, a growing and close-knit community quickly gathered around the enchanting warmth. Soon Christianity spread like wildfire across the known world, transforming cold hearts and wild places wherever it went. The day of Pentecost was therefore an epoch-shaping moment, the birthday of a new community of hope.

Pentecost was an annual Jewish festival, celebrating the beginning of harvest time, so the streets of Jerusalem would have been packed with pilgrims from many nations. Among them was a small remnant of Jesus' followers, 120 in total. As they were meeting together:

> Suddenly a sound like the blowing of a violent wind came from heaven and filled the whole house where they were sitting. They saw what seemed to be tongues of fire that separated and came to rest on each of them. All of them were filled with the Holy Spirit and began to speak in other tongues as the Spirit enabled them.
>
> *Acts 2:2–4*

The symbolism of wind and fire captures the primal nature of what happened on the day of Pentecost. Though the Spirit is truly personal, these metaphors convey his untameable power. Wind echoes back to the dawn of creation when the *spirit* or *wind* of God (it's the same Hebrew word: *ruach*) hovered over a dark, watery chaos. Then God breathed his *spirit* or *breath* into human nostrils to animate them as 'living beings' (Genesis 2:7). At Pentecost, the original gift of God's presence, which was lost through the fall, is now being restored to humanity. In *The Lion, the Witch and the Wardrobe*, the evil queen turns creatures into stone with a wave of her wand. But as the mighty Aslan enters her palace, he stands before the stone statues she has frozen and breathes over them. One by one the statue figures begin to ripple and shimmer with new life. C. S. Lewis' fiction beautifully conveys what happened at Pentecost. Jesus the Messiah breathed his resurrection life into human beings. Frozen hearts and fearful souls experienced the warm animating breath of God once again. The Spirit makes us alive in a whole new way.

Along with wind, in the Bible fire is a powerful symbol of God's presence. Moses encountered a burning bush, Israel witnessed pyrotechnic eruptions on Mount Sinai, Elijah called down fire on Mount Carmel. On each occasion, fire conveyed the holy, unapproachable presence of God. During the Old Testament, this presence dwelt in the inner recesses of the temple (the Holy of Holies) and very occasionally settled on VIPs (prophets, priests and kings). But for an ordinary Jew, the idea of experiencing this fiery presence up close and personal would have been unimaginable. However, on the day of Pentecost, the fire came to rest on the Messiah's people. In fact, the flames separated out so that each got their own personalised experience: '*all* of them were filled with the Holy Spirit' (v. 4). Those who witnessed the scene put two and two together and concluded that ancient prophecies were finally being fulfilled. Peter even quotes directly from the prophet Joel (active around the ninth century BC):

> In the last days, God says,
> I will pour out my Spirit on all people . . .
> Even on my servants, both men and women,
> I will pour out my Spirit.
>
> *Acts 2:17–18*

While Pontius Pilate reclined in his palace and Jewish priests busied themselves in the temple, the Holy Spirit came upon poor slaves, teenagers and blue-collar workers. Remember, when Jesus died, the curtain in the temple that separated people from God was ripped open. Now on the day of Pentecost, it's as if God's presence burst out of the physical building and took up residence in ordinary people. Now every human being can play host to the Holy Spirit. A letter in the New Testament put it in shocking terms:

> Don't you know that you yourselves are God's temple and that God's Spirit lives among you?
>
> *1 Corinthians 3:16*

A friend of ours used to live in Scotland near Balmoral Castle, the Queen's favourite place to holiday. One year her family received an invitation to the annual Balmoral ball. There they met the Queen and the royal family and, as it turned out, they got on rather well. Then to her surprise, our friend received a message at short notice that the royal family would like to come to their house for tea. Can you imagine how you would react? Spring-cleaning, cooking, polishing . . . finally she went outside to pick some flowers for the table. She was shaking like a leaf when the Holy Spirit whispered to her: 'I, the King of kings, live with you every day. It's only the Queen!' That thought instantly dispelled the anxiety and they enjoyed a wonderful time hosting the royal family. The Queen may never visit your home, but as temples of the Holy Spirit, we are hosting God's presence on a daily basis. What a privilege.

On the day of Pentecost, the disciples also began to speak in a multitude of languages they had never learned. A crowd soon gathered, amazed by the spectacle. Uneducated peasants were suddenly fluent linguists, broadcasting the good news of Jesus in European, African and Asian dialects. The crowd accused them of being drunk. But Peter argued that couldn't be the case as it was only nine in the morning (he'd obviously never been to university). This strange linguistic phenomenon wasn't a result of alcoholic spirits but it was a glimpse of the Holy Spirit's ultimate purpose. Think back to the Tower of Babel in Genesis. As humans gathered in pride to build their empire, God confused their speech until all they could do was babble at each other (hence the name). But now, the Spirit temporarily reversed this confusion and division. Pentecost gave an early glimpse of a truly united nations, centred on the Messiah. Ultimately, the Spirit's fiery intent is to reunite our fractured human race into one harmonious family.

The key spokesperson addressing the crowds on the day of Pentecost was none other than Simon Peter. Extraordinary. Just fifty days previously, Peter had publicly denied knowing Jesus three times. Now in the same streets and to many of the same people, he confidently shared the good news. A new fire was burning in Peter's soul. It expelled fear and gave new boldness to live an authentic life. That's what the Spirit can do. I've experienced it myself. Despite growing up in a Christian family, during my teenage years I tried to hide my faith from my peers. On one occasion I was coming home on the school bus and the driver gave out invitations to a Christian event. My friends screwed them up, threw them on the floor and said 'Christian ***'. Then they looked at me. What will Ollerton do? I screwed it up, threw it on the floor and said exactly the same. Inside I hated myself. I was a Janus-faced coward. Fast-forward two years and I found myself standing in front of my entire class, explaining why I believed in Jesus. What had changed? To cut a long story short, I was filled with the Holy Spirit. Like Peter, his fiery presence drove out fear and gave me a new confidence to live for Jesus.

To be filled with the Holy Spirit is not a spooky thing. It's what we humans were made for. The Spirit is not a surprise guest appearance at the end of the play but a central character from the very beginning. Only his presence burning in the hearth makes us truly human. He does not come to possess us or control us. Far from threatening who we are, the Spirit enables us fully to become the person we were made to be. His presence burns away the dross and restores what we've lost – the warmth of God's love and the joy of true community. So if you love a good fire, why not invite the Holy Spirit into the very core of your being?

READ: Acts 2:1–36.

REFLECT: 'As temples of the Holy Spirit, we are hosting God's presence on a daily basis.' How could you become more aware of this? Do you need to adjust or change anything in the light of it?

# 31

# The Spirit forms a new community

*The fellowship of believers*

No sooner was the Spirit poured out on the day of Pentecost than a close-knit community began to form. In fact, a special Greek word captured the depth of their relationships: *koinonia*. It's the warm, intimate atmosphere of friends around a bonfire. The word comes from a root meaning 'common' or 'communal' but it's often translated 'fellowship'. When you hear that word, don't imagine parish fêtes and church picnics. Try *Lord of the Rings* and Samwise Gamgee instead. The first volume of Tolkien's trilogy is entitled *The Fellowship of the Ring*. It features a young hobbit, Frodo Baggins, journeying from Middle-earth to Mount Doom on a mission to destroy the lethal Ring. A small team of brave companions agree to accompany Frodo on the dangerous pilgrimage. Together they face many dangers, toils and snares. But among them, Samwise Gamgee stands out as a faithful friend. Even when Frodo passed through the land of darkness, Sam went with him. Even when Frodo falsely accused Sam of betrayal, he stuck by him. And when Frodo could walk no further, Sam carried him.

Samwise Gamgee is a fictional character who embodies what true *koinonia* looks like. He helps us appreciate the loyal love of the Holy Spirit. The New Testament goes as far as to say that we humans can enjoy 'the *fellowship* [*koinonia*] of the Holy Spirit' (2 Corinthians 13:14). The Spirit is the ultimate companion, who guides us and defends us through every challenge. Even if we fail him, he will never desert us. There's a famous poem called 'Footprints', in which two pairs of prints are seen in the sand side by side. But when the going gets tough they reduce to one pair. However, the point of the poem is that we are not abandoned but *carried* through these times of trouble. So it is with the Holy Spirit. He is the *paraclete*, 'advocate', 'comforter' and 'helper'. The Spirit is our Samwise Gamgee, with us every step of the way.

However, Frodo was also accompanied by a larger group of hobbits. Though far from perfect and less dependable, they also proved vital to the mission. When Tolkien wrote *The Fellowship of the Ring* he didn't have just Frodo and Sam in mind but the whole troop. In the same way, the fellowship we have with the Holy Spirit brings us into fellowship with other Christians. In fact, everyone who receives the Spirit automatically becomes part of the Messiah's people, the church. As we are born into a nuclear family, so we are born again into the family of God. Like any family, this is by no means perfect. In fact at times it can be quite painful. But it is none the less vital if we are to flourish in our faith and succeed in our mission.

On the day of Pentecost, Peter wrapped up his bold message to the crowd with these challenging words: 'Repent and be baptised, every one of you, in the name of Jesus Christ for the forgiveness of your sins. And you will receive the gift of the Holy Spirit' (Acts 2:38). Peter invited everyone to experience the fellowship of the Spirit by trusting in the Messiah. Those who chose to believe demonstrated their commitment in a surprisingly public way. Baptism quickly became a process of initiation. It involved being dipped briefly underwater as a sign of full identification with Jesus Christ, his life, death and resurrection. But in the book of Acts, Dr Luke makes clear that baptism also symbolised full immersion into the new community that the Spirit was forming:

> Those who accepted [Peter's] message were baptised, and about three thousand were added to their number that day. They devoted themselves to the apostles' teaching and to *fellowship*, to the breaking of bread and to prayer . . . All the believers were together and had everything in common . . . They broke bread in their homes and ate together with glad and sincere hearts.
>
> *Acts 2:41–6*

Pentecost was the birthday of the church and from day one Christianity was communal. In Acts 2, Luke provides a window through which we can see what they got up to. Notice the passion: 'they *devoted* themselves'. Being together was not a duty but a delight. Like dehydrated hikers finding a bubbling stream, like old friends gathering at their favourite watering hole, the fellowship quenched a deep thirst. But unlike other social settings, offices, sports clubs, nightclubs, it was devoid of rivalries, showboating and cliques. Instead, they met 'together with glad and sincere hearts' (Acts 2:46). Sincerity is the opposite of hypocrisy. *Hypokrites* was a Greek word used for an actor who put on a show by hiding behind masks. Throughout the performance you never got to see the real person. So much human socialising is merely a mask. But the Spirit gives such a deep experience of true acceptance that the masks can come down. Instead of feeling the need to perform, we are free to be vulnerable, which is how real community is formed.[5]

*Koinonia* also means sharing life together: 'they had everything in common . . . They broke bread in their homes'. The early church was not an institution or a religious building; it was a place to belong. In our age of individualism and isolation, we desperately need to recover this simple truth: 'we are not ourselves by ourselves'.[6] To flourish, our lives must be rooted and cultivated in community. We can't make it on our own; we were never meant to. We are to journey through life as part of a troop, a band of brothers and sisters. The early Christians leaned on each other for mutual support. In their homes they ate together, worshipped, studied Scripture and prayed. As they did so, their lives became deeply interwoven.

Sequoias are the largest and oldest trees in the world. They can live for up to 3,000 years and grow over 80 metres tall. What's the secret to their success? The answer lies deep underground where their root systems interlock. They may look like individual trees but in fact the forest grows together as one giant organism, each part secured by the whole. That's the Spirit. That's *koinonia*. That's true Christianity.

However, that's not always our experience of formal religion today. Perhaps like me you've slept your way through some pretty tedious church services? Or maybe you've witnessed Christians squabbling and dividing? Worse still, you may have experienced ugly forms of control or abuse? If so, you might be tempted to think that true *koinonia* is a thing of the past. However, we must not read the book of Acts through rose-tinted spectacles. The early church had its problems too. By chapter 5, two of its members are caught red-handed swindling cash and lying. By chapter 6, tensions surface over a benefits scheme and claims of unfair treatment. Even when the Spirit is powerfully at work, church can be messy. That shouldn't surprise us if it's made up of people like you and me! But for all the letdowns, the Spirit hasn't given up on the church. Neither should we.

Instead, we need to recover the original vision of *koinonia* that we glimpse in the book of Acts. Right now our thirsty, lonely society needs it more than ever. Sadly, over the centuries, church has become institutionalised and weighed down by unnecessary traditions. Like barnacles that gather on the hull of a boat, these layers need to be scraped off so the original shape can be restored. To help strip it back to something simple, it's helpful to note that the original Greek word for 'church', *ekklesia*, was not a religious term; it simply referred to those who were 'called out'. The core idea traced back to the city of Athens where democracy was born. Around the sixth century BC, in a revolutionary move, the city invited all free men to attend a prestigious gathering known as the *ekklesia*. Those who turned up formed a political body that took responsibility for the city as a whole. It was considered to be a great honour to belong to the *ekklesia*. And that's the metaphor early Christians used for the church. The Spirit calls us out of our loneliness and invites us to belong to a privileged gathering. Therefore, according to American pastor Rick Warren:

> Being included in God's family is the highest honor and the greatest privilege you will ever receive. Nothing ever comes close. Whenever you feel unimportant, unloved, or insecure, remember to whom you belong.[7]

The fellowship of believers is the context in which humans can flourish. Here we effectively become part of a troop of hobbits on a vital mission, accompanied by the ever-faithful Samwise Gamgee.

READ: Acts 2:36–47.

REFLECT: Like sequoia trees, our lives need to be rooted in authentic Christian community. What holds us back? List some practical ways you can become more connected.

## 32

# The Spirit forges unity under fire

*Persecution and expansion*

A few years ago, I saw the Irish band U2 perform live in concert. The whole event was stunning but the highlight was their song 'One'. Eighty thousand fans joined in and sang in unison despite their incredible diversity – it was an emotional experience. Deep down we're all tired of wars, hierarchies and cliques. We all want there to be more *one* and less *two*, more unity and less division. The good news is that's where our human story is ultimately heading. In the Old Testament, the prophet Isaiah heralded a future day when all conflict will finally cease:

> They will beat their swords into ploughshares
> and their spears into pruning hooks.
> Nation will not take up sword against nation,
> nor will they train for war any more.
>
> *Isaiah 2:4*

In New York, outside the United Nations headquarters, this prophecy is depicted through the sculpture of a muscular man bending a violent weapon (a sword) into a tool for harvest (a plough). It signifies the hope of a world flourishing again in peace. The Messiah paid the ultimate price to secure this: 'making peace through his blood, shed on the cross' (Colossians 1:20). Now the community of the Spirit is called to embody this hope by being *one* even though we're not the *same*. In the New Testament, unity is not a nice-to-have but a prophetic statement to a fractured world. When God's people transcend culture, gender, race and class it's like the first rays of dawn breaking the horizon. A new day is coming when we will be *one*.

However, throughout the book of Acts the unity of this newly formed fellowship was severely tested in several ways. First, they faced persecution from Jewish and Roman authorities. Then as Christianity expanded into new territories, tensions surfaced regarding who should be included in the fellowship. Unity is such a powerful statement of hope; it should be no surprise that it's fiercely contested.

**Persecution forges unity**

After the day of Pentecost, the early Christians boldly shared their faith. In one sensational moment, a well-known paralytic who used to beg outside the temple was prayed for and instantly healed in the name of Jesus. He stood up on atrophied legs and began dancing around the temple courts. A vast crowd soon gathered and the Apostle Peter took the opportunity to preach to them. Soon the Messiah's followers grew to over 5,000. This caused panic among the Jewish authorities and they had the ringleaders arrested.

By chapter 4 of Acts, the honeymoon period was well and truly over. Christianity's two most important leaders, Peter and John, sat in chains and the authorities plotted how to crush this uprising once and for all. However, as promised, the Spirit gave them extraordinary boldness, even under extreme pressure:

> When they [the authorities] saw the courage of Peter and John and realised that they were unschooled, ordinary men, they were astonished.
>
> *Acts 4:13*

After a severe warning, the authorities let them go. Upon their release, Peter and John quickly gathered the community and reported what had happened. Their instinctive response is revealing: 'When they heard this, they raised their voices together in prayer to God' (Acts 4:24). Too often prayer can be a last resort, something we try once we've exhausted other options. Perhaps that's why we get so stressed at times? But for the early Christians, prayer was their first response not a last resort. I find it particularly challenging to hear what they prayed for:

> Now, Lord, consider their threats and enable your servants to speak your word with great boldness.
>
> *Acts 4:29*

Despite getting into trouble for speaking about Jesus, they pray for boldness to speak about Jesus. Extraordinary. A few years ago, I got to know a young man from a devout Muslim family in Pakistan. He had come to the UK as a student and during his time here, he had converted to Christianity. However, by the time I got to know him his visa was about to expire and it was time for him to return home to Pakistan. 'What would you like me to pray for?' I asked, expecting a request for personal safety. Instead, he replied: 'Pray that God will help me tell my family about Jesus.' He knew the risks were very real. But the Holy Spirit can give people extraordinary courage under fire.

Ironically, throughout the book of Acts persecution actually served to strengthen the Christian community. They joined together passionately in prayer and were even more united in mission. If you've seen *Band of Brothers*, or other wartime stories of comrades in arms, you will know that risk and danger can have a powerful bonding effect. In the same way, the unity of the early church was forged under fire and their impact grew as a consequence. Tertullian, a Christian leader in the second century AD (*c.* 155–240), summed up the paradox: 'The blood of the martyrs is the seed of the church.'[8]

**Expansion brings cross-cultural unity**

The first Christian martyr to have his blood spilled was a man named Stephen. A few months after Pentecost, he was arrested and brought before a Jewish council known as the Sanhedrin. There he gave a controversial speech that got him stoned to death (Acts 7:1–59). This triggered a new wave of attacks that drove Christians out of Jerusalem. However, as a gust of wind scatters the seed of a dandelion, Christianity spread further afield: 'Those who had been scattered preached the word wherever they went' (Acts 8:4).

A believer called Philip went to Samaria, a region otherwise out of bounds to Jews. As he preached about Jesus, huge numbers responded and were filled with the Spirit (Acts 8:4–8). Then he shared the message with a black Ethiopian eunuch (Acts 8:26–40). He had travelled all the way to Israel's temple in Jerusalem (2,500 km). As Ethiopia's chief economist, he was clearly a wealthy and successful VIP. But he still hadn't found what he was looking for (U2 again). Philip met him while he was on his way home and shared the good news. By evening this African businessman found what he was searching for in Jesus the Messiah. This beautiful story of a Jewish man and a

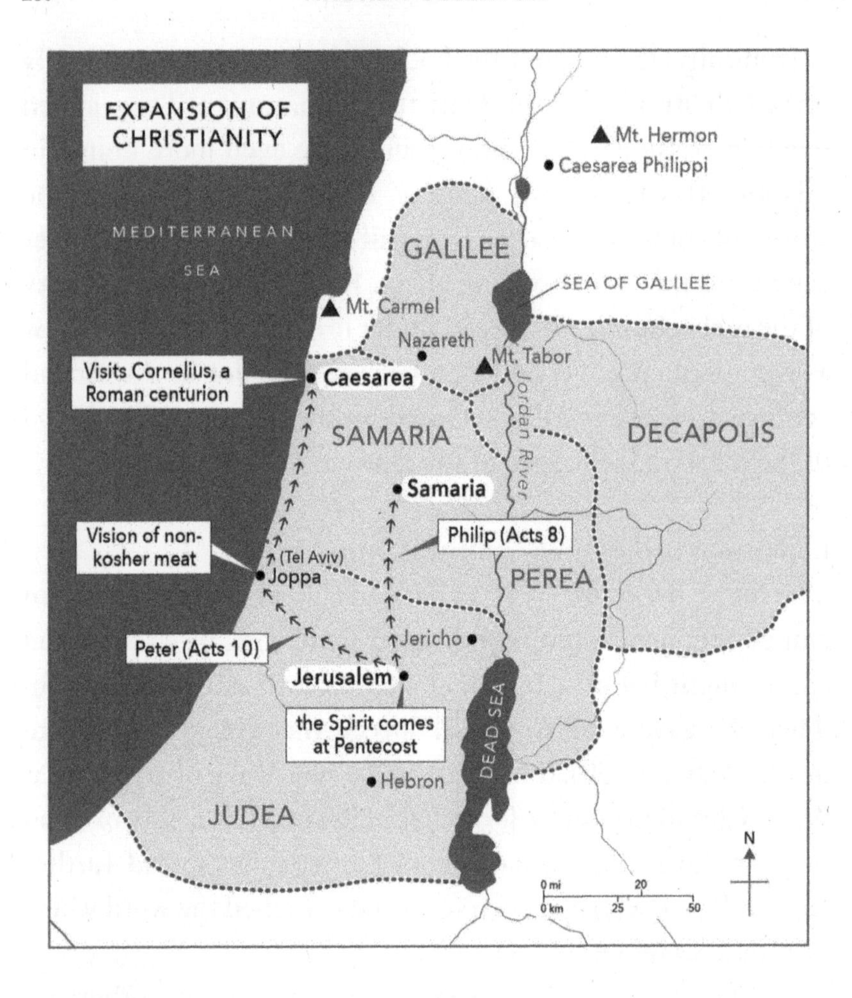


Black Ethiopian embracing each other continues to challenge our attitudes to diversity and inclusion today.

Meanwhile, the Apostle Peter was feeling hungry on a rooftop near modern-day Tel Aviv. Suddenly he fell into a trance and saw a vision of unclean or non-kosher meat being offered to him. When he refused, a shocking message came back: 'Do not call anything impure that God has made clean' (Acts 10:15). Something seismic was shifting and it took three episodes of the vision before Peter grasped it. The community of the Messiah was no longer just a Jewish thing; it was opening up to embrace those considered 'unclean' – Gentiles or non-Jews. Soon Peter found himself preaching in the home of a Roman centurion called Cornelius. While Peter was explaining the message of Jesus, the Holy Spirit fell upon the household of Cornelius. The experience of Pentecost was clearly available for Gentiles too. This small Jewish sect was quickly becoming a global movement, embracing Samaritans, Africans and Europeans.[9]

From this moment on, Christianity transcended any particular culture or race. It started as a Jewish thing. Soon it became influenced by North African leaders. Only later did it become associated with Europe and the West. Now the centre of global Christianity has shifted south to Sub-Saharan Africa and Latin America. Sociologists have predicted that by 2030 the largest Christian population will be in China.[10] The point is simple. Christianity embraces all languages, races and cultures because it's not the property of any of them. Instead, the Spirit forms a truly global humanity characterised by deep unity and remarkable diversity. As the New Testament puts it:

> There is neither Jew nor Gentile, neither slave nor free, nor is there male and female, for you are all *one* in Christ Jesus.
>
> *Galatians 3:28*

If you'd had the chance to visit the temple in Jerusalem during New Testament times, you would have quickly encountered several walls or barriers. The first divided Jews from Gentiles, the next segregated males and females, then priests from non-priests and finally a curtain separated God from everyone else. For many people today, this is what organised religion does: it erects unnecessary barriers, causing division and exclusion. But true Christianity should be different. The death of the

Messiah not only ripped open the curtain to give *open access* to God, it also broke down the dividing walls, forming an *open-planned* community. Now the Spirit unites people from every race and culture into one global family. In our local church, people from sixty different nationalities worship together. One Sunday, I got to meet Bibi from the Congo and Gordon from Glasgow, Scotland. In both cases, we struggled because of communication challenges! Nevertheless, through Jesus we have so much in common. So we can celebrate our differences and not feel threatened by them. In the Messiah, we're one even though we're not the same.

READ: Acts 4:18–31; 11:1–18.

REFLECT: What imaginary walls do we erect around who is included and 'acceptable'? If I'm honest, what are my prejudices? Make a promise before God to resist discrimination and to welcome the stranger.

# 33

# The Spirit changes what he touches

*Paul and the Damascus road*

Have you ever had a Damascus road experience? Done a one-eighty and completely changed your mind about something? I used to hate Jaffa Cakes. My only experience had been packet versions and I found the orange jelly decidedly off-putting. After many years of avoiding them, I finally encountered the real thing. I was attending a formal dinner at university and the food was delicious: a fish starter, pork scallops main course. I couldn't wait for dessert. I glanced at the menu. To my horror: *Jaffa Cake*. I had visions of a Michelin-star chef dishing them out from a packet. But a few minutes later, the waiters emerged carrying the most amazing dessert I had ever seen – a magnificent orange sponge layered with fresh cream, coated in rich dark chocolate with orange syrup. It dawned on me that I had never actually tasted real Jaffa Cake. The moment I did, I was converted on the spot.

Around AD 36 a short Jewish man was heading to the city of Damascus, determined to rid the world of Christianity. En route, Saul of Tarsus had the original Damascus road experience, which changed the entire course of his life. For the first time he encountered the *real* Jesus and was converted on the spot. The change was so dramatic that he began to be known by a new name. The Apostle Paul (formerly Saul) became the most important Christian leader of all time, second only to the Messiah himself. Whereas the first part of the book of Acts focuses on Peter, from Acts 9 Paul takes centre stage. The journeys he undertook and the letters he wrote account for almost half the New Testament. In this section we will consider Paul the person and his travels as recorded in Acts. In the next section, we will explore Paul's letters and the radical ideas they contain.

Saul was brought up in Tarsus, a cosmopolitan city located on the coast in modern-day Turkey. As a Roman citizen, he would have been immersed in Greek literature and Roman culture from an early age. However, he was also part of the Jewish diaspora who retained a strong sense of identity while living away from their homeland. Saul was educated by the famous Rabbi Gamaliel and would have known the Hebrew Scriptures backwards. He was proud of his Jewish roots and later let slip that he was even a member of the Pharisees, the religious party that orchestrated the crucifixion of Jesus. True to form, when Stephen was stoned to death, Saul was there, cheering them on (Acts 7:58).

This all begs the question, why did Saul hate Christians so much? A piece of first-century graffiti provides part of the answer.

A Christian stands gazing at a crucified figure, who has a human body and the head of a donkey. The caption reads: 'Alexamenos worships his god.' In the ancient world, the idea of a crucified hero was a joke. For a Pharisee like Saul, the suggestion that Israel's Messiah would end up on a Roman cross was downright offensive. Worse still, the early Christians worshipped this failed Messiah as if he was God. Blasphemy! They must be stopped at all costs.

On his way to hunt them down, a light appeared over Saul, brighter than the noonday sun, which in the Mediterranean is quite something. The glory of Jesus knocked Saul off his horse and left him temporarily blinded. But to quote British rapper Stormzy, it was a 'blinded by your grace' moment. Finally, Saul glimpsed the Truth. Though crucified in defeat, Jesus had been raised in power. The carpenter from Nazareth was indeed God's Messiah King. System overload. Saul's entire worldview would need a complete rewiring in the light of Jesus.

His attitude to Christians also had to change. As he lay prostrate in the dust, Jesus asked a revealing question: 'Saul, Saul, why do you persecute *me*?' When Saul was attacking Stephen and others like him, he was inflicting pain on the Messiah himself. Perhaps this was the origin of Paul's famous metaphor: *Christ is the head and the church is his body*. The Messiah and his people are one organic whole. From this moment on, Jesus Christ became his new Lord and the Christian community his new home. Saul was converted to the Apostle Paul.

How stressful and disruptive must this have been. You think you know how the world works, then suddenly a new reality stops you in your tracks and forces you to rethink everything. To some degree, this is what *conversion* means for all of us. Christianity is not about giving assent to a set of beliefs or practising a religious hobby on Sundays. Conversion is about rethinking the entire purpose of our lives in the light of Jesus. In the world of DIY projects, we refer to barn conversions or loft conversions, by which we mean taking an existing space and completely transforming it. Christianity is a whole life conversion. It means taking our existing selves – our talents, relationships, careers, and possessions – and repurposing them in service of the Messiah.

Over the course of the next two decades, Paul embarked on several mission trips that took him to a remarkable number of places. He preached about Jesus and planted new Christian communities in multiple locations throughout modern-day Turkey, Greece and Italy.

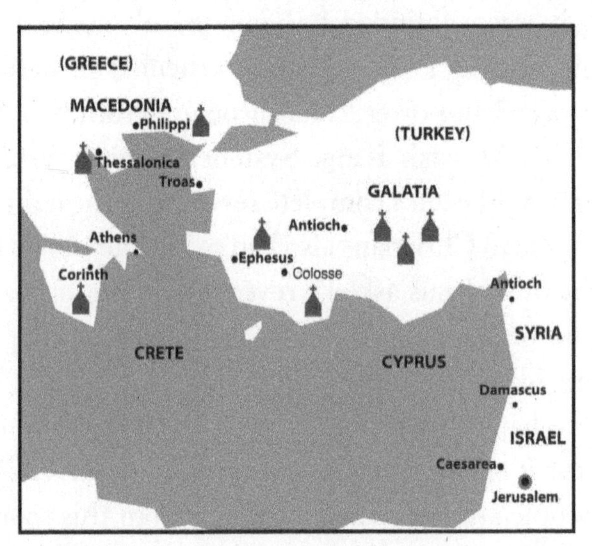


*Cities where Paul and his team planted churches*

Given the lack of support and relentless opposition, Paul's impact was nothing short of miraculous. I recently visited the ruined city of Ephesus in Turkey. It used to be the second most prestigious city in the world, behind Rome, with a quarter of a million residents. It was known for its wealth and luxurious living – terraced houses, central heating systems, expensive boutiques and an entertainment centre that could seat 25,000 people. In AD 52 Paul arrived in Ephesus as a lone figure dwarfed by this vast urban centre. But as he began to preach the good news, hundreds of people turned from idols to Jesus. On one occasion, they gathered up all their magic and occult materials and burned them. That bonfire alone was worth 50,000 pieces of silver, the equivalent of around five million dollars today (Acts 19:19). The impact on the economy soon caused a riot and Paul had to flee for his life. But he left behind him a thriving Christian community that spread across the whole region of Asia Minor. Despite their material luxuries, Paul brought something better to Ephesus. Once they tasted the new life of the Spirit, there was no going back to cheap packet versions.

Paul's extraordinary success is plain to see. But what's less obvious is the quality of friendship that he enjoyed along the way. Paul is often caricatured as a strict and heavy-handed figure who liked to be the boss. But those who knew him well experienced a different side. In one of his earliest letters, Paul wrote with daring affection in the context of a Roman society that prized masculine strength:

> Just as a nursing mother cares for her children, so we cared for you. Because we loved you so much . . .
>
> *1 Thessalonians 2:7–8*

Paul became the leader of a band of brothers and sisters who would take a bullet for each other. On my recent trip to Turkey, after visiting Ephesus, I travelled 150 kilometres south to the ancient port of Miletus. Around AD 57 Paul passed through this seaport and arranged a rendezvous with some of his friends from Ephesus. They travelled all the way to see Paul, fearing it might be the last time. Acts 20 records their emotional encounter:

> When Paul had finished speaking, he knelt down with all of them and prayed. They all wept as they embraced him and kissed him.
>
> *Acts 20:36–7*

This rare depth of friendship is a beautiful thing. But it's not something you can manufacture. Instead it's a by-product that we experience when we become fully invested in God's mission. We will not escape loneliness and isolation simply by trying to. Making friends is not a sufficient goal in itself. We need to discover a greater purpose in life. Only then will close bonds develop with those who share the same passion. As Paul began living for something greater than his own personal comfort he experienced the richest *koinonia*. When Jesus Christ becomes our true Lord, when personal happiness is nothing compared to him, then we will be free to enjoy the sort of community that quenches our thirst and transforms the world.

READ: Acts 9:1–19; 19:1–20.

REFLECT: Paul regularly shared the story of how God changed his life. What's your story or testimony? Could you write it down and share it with someone this week?

# 34

# The Spirit transforms society

*The power of the gospel*

The most intriguing site within the ancient ruins of Ephesus in modern-day Turkey is undoubtedly the public toilets. Here, male citizens would have sat next to each other on a long line of stone seats and done their business in every sense of the word. In winter, they would send their slave ahead of them to sit on the stone seat to warm it up ready for their arrival. Some traditions indicate that slaves also took responsibility for wiping their master's backside with a sponge on a stick, known as a *xylospongium*. Perhaps that's where the saying comes from: 'Don't get the wrong end of the stick'?

End of toilet humour.

The Apostle Paul spent eighteen months in Ephesus so at some point he must have visited the toilets and no doubt shared the message of Jesus with those sitting next to him. If they listened carefully, they would soon have realised the groundbreaking implications of Paul's message. Christianity was no mere religion or philosophy. It was a new way of being human, impacting all areas of life. Consider how ingrained Roman hierarchy was in a city like Ephesus. The ancient world was a social pyramid, with a few rich and powerful at the top but many poor and vulnerable at the bottom. Up to half the population were slaves. This imbalance made many at the top nervous of a revolt from below. Consequently, any hint of subversion was stamped on. A clear pecking order was maintained through everyday practices, including who warmed the seat and held the stick.

Now consider a single verse from Paul's letter to a Christian community near Ephesus:

> Here there is no Gentile or Jew, circumcised or uncircumcised . . . *slave or free*, but Christ is all, and is in all.
>
> *Colossians 3:11*

Inside the *ekklesia* a whole new society was forming that operated on completely different terms. The moment you came in, deeply ingrained social markers became irrelevant. In here, Paul says, you can forget slave versus free, Jew versus Gentile, male versus female. 'Christ is all' (the only thing that matters) and Christ is 'in all' (the common denominator). Begin to grasp the implications and it should be no surprise that Paul sparked riots and spent years of his life in prison. Christianity was simply not compatible with the old order. It was the arrival of something new and ground-breaking.

The social implications of Paul's message were deeply rooted in his theology (*Theo-logos*, words or ideas about God). He used the communication networks of his day, Roman roads and formal letters (or epistles), to spread his radical ideas. There are thirteen letters attributed to Paul in the New Testament. Each one has unique elements, depending on the particular city or context it addresses (e.g., Epistle to Ephesians for Ephesus). However, a core message pulsates through them all and captures the heart of what made Paul tick. He refers to it as the 'gospel' and considers it the most transformative truth on earth:

> I am not ashamed of the gospel, because it is the power of God that brings salvation to everyone who believes.
>
> *Romans 1:16*

For Paul, what makes the gospel good news is that it is first and foremost about what God has already accomplished for us. Paul's letters are therefore structured by a crucial dynamic:

**WHAT GOD HAS DONE (THEOLOGY) ➔ WHAT WE DO (PRACTICE)**

Consider Paul's most famous letter to the church in Rome (Romans). The first eleven chapters contain almost no instructions about what we must do. Instead they describe what God has done through Jesus on our behalf. Initially, Paul argues that all humanity is by nature in a hopeless predicament. Sin is a social leveller: 'There is no difference between Jew and Gentile, for all have sinned and fall short of the glory of God' (Romans 3:22–3). However, God stepped in to provide salvation. The Son of God died on a Roman cross as our substitute. He took the punishment for our failure (sin) so that we may enjoy his status and privileges. So instead of needing to keep our distance from God as if he were an angry headmaster, we can know him as our loving Father. For Paul, this is the gospel – not what we can do for God but what God has done for us: 'Therefore, since we *have been justified* through faith, we have peace with God through our Lord Jesus Christ' (Romans 5:1).

Notice Paul's deliberate use of the past tense. To be justified means to be declared righteous. It's to pass the ultimate exam and be granted eternal favour with God. Religion assumes this verdict is left hanging until the end of our lives, when we find out if we were good enough. No wonder we experience high levels of stress and anxiety. But according to the gospel, the results are already in: through faith in Jesus, we can be justified up front, not based on *our* flawed attempts but *his* complete performance. Salvation is also a social leveller. It works the same, whether you are the master or the one warming the seat: 'Christ is all, and is in all.'

A couple of years ago I completed a PhD. In the British system, this involves writing an 80,000-word thesis, which is then submitted to academic experts for review. A few weeks later, you attend a *viva voce* examination to defend your work. The academics grill you for several hours before conferring to reach a decision. They then call you back in to tell you whether you've passed or not. Years of hard work come down to one nerve-racking meeting. But in my case something unusual happened. After exchanging pleasantries, the lead examiner got up and came over to me: 'We've decided to tell you in advance that you've passed. Well done, Dr Ollerton!' With that he thrust out his hand and we shook on it. Before answering a single question, I was declared 'Dr Ollerton'. As their decision sank in, I experienced a deep sense of peace. Over the next couple of hours, we went on to discuss all the ways I could improve my work. But now I could embrace their feedback, secure in the knowledge that I had already passed.

For Paul, this is how the gospel works. God gives us a new identity up front. Our Father in heaven makes us his children and that's not going to change. Secure in this new status, we can embrace all the feedback and make some necessary changes.

In other words, the Spirit comes alongside to help turn our *new identity* into a *new lifestyle*. As Paul put it: 'You were once darkness, but now you are light in the Lord. Live as children of light' (Ephesians 5:8). This is how the gospel works. It gives us a new identity and then calls us to live up to it: *You're a child of God now, so act like it!*

As the early Christians applied Paul's teachings, they modelled a different way of being human. In Roman culture, males were dominant and females were considered second rate. The men were typically loose with their bodies and tight with their wallets. A slave girl was considered a suitable object for the master to relieve his sexual urge with whenever he pleased. But the gospel brought a whole new vision. Every female is to be honoured as a 'sister' in Christ and the male must practise self-control. As several historians have noted, these values caused a sexual revolution that still underpins our assumptions about what is acceptable behaviour today.[11] Recent revelations of men exploiting women (#metoo), along with the pervasive influence of pornography and sexual objectification, show how much we still need the values of the gospel today.

Paul's theology gave rise to a radical new community founded on principles that rocked the ancient world. Imagine witnessing a first-century gathering of the *ekklesia* (church) in the home of a wealthy patron in Ephesus. The atmosphere would have been one of unity and laughter as this spiritual family ate a meal together and worshipped Jesus as their Lord and Saviour. To do this, they broke every social convention going: slave and master, male and female dining at the same table in order to be 'one in Christ'. Welcome to the fellowship! Only the gospel can do this. More than a religion, it's a new way of being human. No aspect of life is beyond its reach.

From the meal table to the public toilets, the gospel changes everything.

READ: Romans 1:1–17; 5:1–11.

REFLECT: How might the gospel push us beyond our comfort zones? Take a step to build a bridge of friendship with someone who is significantly different from you today.

35

# The Spirit gives us a part to play

*Joining the mission*

Late in life, my father got into family history in a big way. He produced several homemade volumes, telling the Ollerton story from the seventeenth century right through to the present day. Soon after he died, I sat down to read them. I became engrossed in the history as I read about ancestors who built their own houses, travelled with the Merchant Navy and fought in two World Wars. Inspiring stuff. But as I turned the final page a surprise awaited me: a picture of myself staring back. I am now part of the next generation of the Ollertons, bearing the family name and writing a chapter in the story. That realisation was inspiring and sobering at the same time.

This is precisely how the end of the book of Acts should leave us feeling. It finishes with Paul imprisoned in Rome, awaiting sentence by the emperor. On death row, guess what he's doing? Sharing the gospel with his guards (a captive audience) and anyone else who visited (Acts 28:31). Then Acts just stops, abruptly, without any sense of what happened next. It's the opposite of a neat ending. Instead, it gives the reader a subliminal message: this story must be continued. Now we are caught up in the narrative. The Bible is an unfolding drama, a real-life story, and we all have a part to play.

With this in mind, British theologian Tom Wright helps us understand the way the Bible enables us to play our part in God's story.[12] Imagine a company of actors who discover a long-lost Shakespeare play. It originally had six acts but only five have survived – the first four and the final act. So the actors must perform the missing fifth one in order for the play to be brought to completion. How would they do this? By immersing themselves in the rest of the narrative, they would enter the mind of the playwright and sense the inner logic and heartbeat. Then through *faithful improvisation* they could perform the missing fifth act in keeping with the whole.

The Bible is a divine account of our human story, stretching back to the dawn of time and forwards into eternity. By immersing ourselves in the story, we can faithfully live it out in our modern context. Though the Bible does not directly address genetic engineering, gender dysphoria or Artificial Intelligence, we can confidently respond to contemporary scenarios through a process of faithful improvisation.

In our family, the word 'improvise' has become synonymous with the drama teacher in David Walliams' book *Demon Dentist*. This eccentric character tries to awaken creativity by getting his bored pupils to improvise as he shouts out random scenarios: 'A meteorite is about to hit the earth. Impro!' Whenever they transgress his theatrical rules he exclaims: 'That is an impro no no!' It's worth buying the book just to experience the scene when the main character, Alfie, is chased through the school by his social worker on a moped and interrupts the drama lesson: 'an absolute impro no no!'

We are real-life actors called to continue the story of Acts. So how can we be faithful to the task and avoid some common 'impro no nos'?

**Follow Scripture rather than culture**

Key to faithful improvisation is pleasing God and fulfilling his purpose. We are not at liberty to make things up based on what feels good or what culture wants to hear. Instead, the actors must trust that the director holds the key to human flourishing. Take, for instance, challenging instructions contained in Paul's writings. Even the Apostle Peter described Paul's letters as 'hard to understand', so take heart if you also struggle. But Peter still considered them part of the 'Scriptures' and warned against rejecting them (2 Peter 3:16). They are not merely Paul's ideas but divinely inspired truths. Of course, some cultural practices require a bit of improvisation. As we've already noted, 'Greet one another with a holy kiss' (Romans 16:16) may have a different manifestation in our social context. However, once minor adjustments have been made, Paul's letters remain an authoritative guide for every culture.

Before we got married, my wife used to live in a quaint old cottage. One day, she asked me to hang a painting for her. Eager to impress, I got out my spirit level and fixed the painting so the bubble was smack in the centre. Perfect. But when I stepped back, the painting looked crooked. I checked again. It was definitely level. Charlotte came in: 'That's not straight!' I quickly responded 'Oh yes it is'. As it turned out, the picture was straight but the rest of the cottage wasn't. The walls were bowed, the windows crooked, the doorframes warped. Framed in that context, the one thing that was straight looked like it was the problem. In our twenty-first-century culture, the teachings of the Bible may seem out of place. It can be tempting to adjust the message to make it fit in. Perhaps you've experienced this in discussions about science or human identity and ethics? But this is an 'impro no no'. Faithful improvisation means trusting that the Bible transcends cultural opinion. Let's immerse ourselves in Scripture, set it as our spirit level and apply it with courage.

**Go together, not alone**

The book of Acts provides historical description of the emergence of early Christianity. From day one it was all about community. The New Testament contains numerous letters written by the likes of Paul, Peter, James and John and addressed to Christian communities scattered across the ancient world. It's easy to read them as if they were addressed to 'me'. But when Paul says '*you* are light in the Lord', the 'you' is plural. The church is to be the light in this dark world, a new humanity that overthrows oppression and brings hope. Only together can we take on the needs of the world and make a lasting difference. I remember on my gap year becoming a passionate activist and leading numerous initiatives to help the needy and share the gospel. However, in the process I became isolated and quickly burnt out. Lesson learned. As the old African proverb goes: 'If you want to go fast, go alone. If you want to go far, go together.'

While I've been writing this chapter on community, Covid-19 has swept the globe and caused an extended period of social isolation. The full effects are yet to be seen but the coronavirus has already served to remind us of two humbling truths: we're not in control as much as we think we are and we need community more than we thought we did. As human beings we grow in family and mature in community. Isolation is not natural. So we must actively pursue meaningful relationships, even if that involves self-imposed limitations to become more rooted. In particular, we are invited to belong to a local church where the Spirit is at work to nurture true fellowship. Will we pluck up the courage to depend on each other for mutual support?

**Live with outward not inward focus**

The book of Acts is so dynamic. There's enough travel and movement to cause motion sickness just reading it. The early Christians had a fire in their bones that drove them to cross land and sea, take huge risks and pay the ultimate price. The coronavirus pandemic reminded me of a book by Rodney Stark, which argues that early Christianity spread rapidly during the plagues. When disease swept through cities and people fled in fear, it was the Christians who moved in to serve. A fifth-century church leader described their counter-intuitive response: 'Heedless of danger, they took charge of the sick, attending to their needs even though they became infected by others with the disease.'[13] What bravery. These early Christians understood that their small lives were part of a much bigger story. The mission of sharing the good news of Jesus with a lost and dying world gave them something to live for, even to die for.

Western culture has made humans the centre of reality instead of God. The self has become the end in itself. While this may sound like freedom, we have forfeited a deeper sense of meaning and purpose. Life has been reduced to gaining temporary achievements, while 'amusing ourselves to death'.[14] The book of Acts calls us beyond these small horizons. It's an invitation to lose ourselves in a grander mission, bringing hope and truth to the world. As Andy Crouch puts it:

> Find a community, a small group who can lovingly fuel your dreams and puncture your illusions. Find friends and form a family who are willing to see grace at work in one another's lives . . . then go make something of the world together.[15]

We are actors in a divine drama, called to improvise faithfully. The Bible reveals what our spiritual ancestors got up to. Now it's our turn to bear the family name and take on the mission. Empowered by the same Spirit who filled Jesus, Peter, Stephen and Paul, we can write the next chapter of this remarkable story. So why not take a mug shot of yourself and use it as a bookmark in your Bible. Read the history with a picture of yourself staring back. It's a continual reminder that we now have a vital part to play in how this story develops.

READ: Acts 28:11–31; Romans 12:1–8.

REFLECT: Are you 'amusing yourself to death' or playing your part in God's story? It's time for some faithful 'impro'! What might that mean for you?

PART 6

# HOPE

## Our human longing for home

# Introducing hope

A few years ago, our family decided to climb Mount Snowdon, the highest peak in England and Wales. It was a hot August day and our children were only five and seven years old. By the time we reached halfway, they had a meltdown. What made things worse was the passenger train that ran alongside the path; as we tried to talk our kids out of their tantrum, another train would chug past with happy people waving. In the end, we negotiated a peace deal. They agreed to walk another ten minutes to the nearest horizon if we promised to let them turn back. However, when we got there, the view opened up and we could see the summit for the first time. I pointed to the peak and said: 'Look, there's Snowdon!' They nodded. 'Can you see the building just beneath the summit?' They nodded again. 'That's a café selling enormous ice creams and there's a train waiting to take you back down. So what do you want to do?' That's hope. It puts something glorious on the far horizon that's worth striving for. And it's a powerful force. Hope can motivate a five-year-old all the way to the summit of Mount Snowdon!

The Bible concludes with stunning visions of a far horizon that lies ahead of us. If you're tempted to read the last page of a novel upfront, try Revelation 21–2. These chapters depict a vast community of people populating a pristine earth, purged of all evil and pain. The *shalom* that we forfeited at the beginning will be fully restored by the end. This hope is a powerful thing; it can motivate us to keep going even when life is tough. Whatever challenges you are facing right now, the final pages of the Bible invite us to look up and see what's coming. One day, we exiles will finally arrive *home*.

'Home' is such an evocative word. It conjures up deep longings. More than a roof-over-the-head, home is where we truly belong, feel safe and find purpose. For me, home is my mother's music and my father's books. It's family banter over dinner and a board game by the fire. To be separated from this haven causes an inner disturbance that we describe as *homesickness*. Whether we grew up in a safe, loving environment or not, there remains in all of us a deep longing for home. As a heavy bowling ball rolls around in its own weight, seeking a place to rest, so our hearts long for an ultimate resting place. The pleasures of this life only point forwards, towards something beyond. As Randy Alcorn says:

> The best things in life are souvenirs from Eden, appetizers of the New Earth. There's just enough of them to keep us going, but never enough to make us satisfied with the world as it is, or ourselves as we are . . . Desire is a signpost pointing to heaven. Every longing for better health is a longing for the New Earth . . . Every taste of joy is but a foretaste of a greater more vibrant joy than can be found on Earth as it is now.[1]

In this sense, the whole Bible tells the story of home. In the beginning, it was *home, sweet home*. The world was a shared living space, in which God and humanity lived together. But as sin and evil invaded and proliferated, humanity was driven out into a state of exile. We've been living in a *broken home* ever since. Throughout the Old Testament, Israel acted as custodians of hope through symbols such as the Sabbath, which anticipated the recovery of ultimate rest, and the temple, which gave a glimpse of heaven on earth. Then finally, the *homeowner* himself stepped in. The Messiah came to heal the broken and forgive the guilty by paying the ultimate price. Now the Spirit is at work, renewing our humanity until, one day, it will be *home time.* Finally, our deepest longings will be satisfied as we experience the uninterrupted joy of *home, sweet home* for eternity.

This story provides us with something certain to look forward to in a fragile world where hopes are so easily dashed. Back to Mount Snowdon. Unfortunately, by the time our exhausted family arrived at the summit, the café had sold out of ice creams and the return train was fully booked for the rest of the day. The long march back down the mountain provided an opportunity to explain to our children that all hopes in this life will ultimately disappoint us!

We live in a culture that has largely rejected the Bible's vision of a future hope beyond this life. Instead, modern living is built on the assumption that this is all we've got. As the old saying goes: 'Eat, drink and be merry. For tomorrow we die.' Perhaps the modern equivalent would be YOLO – *You Only Live Once*. This secular philosophy not only removes hope from the far horizon, in doing so it places extra pressure on life here and now. Consider the rise of mental-health issues related to the *Fear Of Missing Out* (FOMO). This anxiety manifests itself in a range of ways that I can identify with:

- The choices we make regarding careers, lovers, holidays, clothes become incredibly stressful because they are loaded up with a need for ultimate fulfilment. This pressure can leave us paralysed, unable to make even simple decisions and stick to them: *I'll keep my options open and triple book myself instead.*

- Fear of failure can also become overwhelming. If this life is all we've got, then there's huge pressure to succeed. Ironically, this can prevent us from living bold and adventurous lives. A common deathbed regret: *I wish I'd taken more risks.*
- Consumer greed, unmanageable debt, cheating on loved ones can all seem justifiable given the pressure to get happy before it's too late: *I need a cruise, a hot tub, a puppy and a new relationship this year.*
- The threat of incurable diseases, random accidents and death itself can induce a mild state of paranoia and the feeling that everything is about to be snatched away: *What if it's something serious this time?*

Ironically, the very philosophy that emphasises the need for immediate satisfaction actually generates a crushing weight of psychological pressure. More than ever, in our fragile and anxious culture, we need to discover a robust and glorious hope that we can count on. In the Bible we glimpse it: a future that is so solid and certain no accident or disease can snatch it away. Once we are part of God's story, we need not fear missing out. No matter what suffering or pain we encounter in this life, if the Bible is true, our best days lie ahead of us.

In this final section, we will explore the theme of hope by delving into the last book of the Bible, Revelation. At this point you may be thinking: *But isn't Revelation full of weird visions that only wacky people are into*? Not quite. For all its complexities, Revelation provides a beautiful crescendo to our human story. It takes us higher than we've been before, to see visions of the ultimate summit ahead of us. And as we glimpse our final destination on the far horizon, it gives us the *hope* we need to keep going, all the way *home*.

36

# Hope is rooted in history

*The resurrection of Jesus*

In colloquial speech, hope means little more than wishful thinking: *I hope it doesn't rain; I hope our team wins; I hope the kids are OK*. We insert the word precisely because something seems uncertain and might not happen. This is the polar opposite of the way hope is used in Christian theology. The Bible speaks of hope as a solid, beautiful thing that is already on the far horizon, waiting for us to catch up with it. We have been reborn:

> . . . into a *living hope* through the resurrection of Jesus Christ from the dead, and into an inheritance that can never perish, spoil or fade . . . kept in heaven for you.
>
> *1 Peter 1:3–4*

This passage encourages us to think of hope like an inheritance, which becomes ours as soon as we enter God's family. On the day I was born, my grandfather transferred a substantial amount of money into a child inheritance bond in my name. Once I reached the age of twenty-one, it would all become mine. I can still remember how it felt when my parents first told me about it. Suddenly, an eleven-year-old Andrew Ollerton had a whole new reason for living! All I had to do was get to twenty-one and it was mine. That's the way Christian hope works. It's an eternal inheritance already deposited in our name, which gives a whole new motivation to life.

That all sounds encouraging. But let's play devil's advocate for a moment: how can we know all this? No one who dies ever returns to report the facts. So how can we be certain about what lies on the other side? Surely the Bible is no more accurate than Dante's *Comedy* or a sitcom about the afterlife – it's all just speculation. The Bible's response is to point backwards to an event in the past that reveals our future. Unlike other religions and philosophies, Christianity is a historical faith. It all boils down to the presence or absence of a body in a tomb in Jerusalem, around April AD 30. If the bones of Jesus of Nazareth are still there, rotting away, then our hopes are dashed. As the Apostle Paul put it: 'If Christ has not been raised, our preaching is useless and so is your faith' (1 Corinthians 15:14). However, if the resurrection of Jesus is true, the decisive victory over death has already occurred. The risen Jesus is therefore living proof that our hope is well placed. If he is already reigning on the far horizon then perhaps our future is more certain than we've dared to imagine? A historic event behind us guarantees what lies ahead of us.

This, by the way, was not what anyone expected at the time. According to Jewish theology, resurrection would happen at the end of history, not part way through it. That's why even Jesus' own disciples needed to be persuaded that he had risen from the dead. When he appeared to them, they were caught off-guard, like someone still in their pyjamas when the front doorbell goes unexpectedly.[2] To everyone's great surprise, our future hope as humans has already begun. The resurrection of Jesus therefore revises the way we think about the end times or what theologians call 'eschatology'. *Eschatos* is Greek for 'goal' or 'end'. The term implies a timetable or sequence of events associated with the end of the world. We will consider this in more detail but, for now, here are two implications for the way hope works.

First, *we already have one foot in the future.* The moment Jesus rose again, a future age was launched ahead of time. As Tom Wright puts it: 'The new age has burst upon the scene while the present age is still rumbling on.'[3] The fresh flowers of spring are already breaking through the decayed concrete of this world. Our ultimate future hope is up and running in the body of Jesus of Nazareth. There's no going back now. It's completely irreversible. The ascended Messiah has already secured our final outcome. He is our 'living hope', if by faith we are connected to him.

Imagine a team of rock climbers, arriving at the foot of an imposing cliff face. The lead climber is the key to everyone's success. He sets off alone up the cliff to pioneer a route. If he makes it to the top, he sets up an anchor or belay point by fastening the rope to the rock. Now the rest of the team can scale the cliff secure in the knowledge that they are roped to him. They may slip, but he will not let them fall. He will draw them up to his position. This is how Christian hope works. Jesus has already made it, and we are roped to him just as the New Testament says:

> We have this hope as an anchor for the soul, firm and secure . . . where our forerunner, Jesus, has entered *on our behalf.*
>
> *Hebrews 6:19–20*

I recently visited my Aunt Shirley when she was in the final stages of breast cancer. Her body was a withered wreck, a picture of the old creation that's on its way out. But as a Christian, Shirley faced death with living hope. Her eyes sparkled with confidence as she paraphrased a verse from the Bible: 'I'm not losing heart. This old body might be wasting away. But I'm getting closer to home every day.' When the chips are down, Aunt Shirley had a robust eschatology. Because Christ is risen, she already had one foot in the future. Roped to Jesus, she knew where she was going.

Second, *the resurrection of Jesus gurantees the final outcome.* With history still very much in play, God raised Jesus from death. The resurrection therefore announced ahead of time the victory of God over all our enemies – sickness, sin, evil, Satan and death. The cosmic battle of good and evil that was expected to be decided at the end has been resolved upfront. Because Jesus died under the weight of our sin, his resurrection proves that our debt has been fully paid. Death couldn't hold him down any longer. To put this in sporting terms, we might say that the final score was secured long before the final whistle had been blown. So the game may continue but the victory is never in doubt. Take this on board and our lives begin to feel a bit less vulnerable.

I sometimes watch *Match of the Day*, which shows football highlights from games that have already finished. Recently, I watched with a friend who supports the same team but I'd already had a look online at the final score. I knew our team won 2:1 in the end. That completely changed my experience of watching the match. My friend became visibly nervous when our team went behind and started shouting at the referee. But I had peace because I knew in the end it would turn out well. The resurrection of Jesus is the final score – not only for world history but also for our story. It will turn out well for Aunt Shirley and all who trust in Jesus. So there's no need for nervous anger or fretful anxiety. We have a 'living hope' that gives peace to those who are dying and a whole new reason for living.

READ: 1 Peter 1:1–12.

REFLECT: Write this verse on a piece of card or make it your screen saver: 'In his great mercy [God] has given us a new birth into a living hope through the resurrection of Jesus Christ' (1 Peter 1:3). Reflect on this throughout the day.

# 37

# Hope is based on Revelation

*The throne and the Lamb*

If the option were available, would you choose to know the future? It could be fascinating to visit the year 3000 and see if they live under water (a prediction by the boy-band Busted). Equally, you could make a lot of money at the bookies if you knew all the winners. But imagine knowing in advance the fate of loved ones or the date of your own death. When it comes to the future, we are caught in a conundrum. Knowing would be hugely unsettling but not knowing causes stress and anxiety. Ultimately, we need some reassurances that the future is worth striving for. Well, instead of reading horoscopes, why not try the book of Revelation? It provides more accurate insights into *what the future holds* but most importantly it reveals the one *who holds the future*.

The Greek for 'revelation' is *apokalupsis* from which we get 'apocalypse'. While this may sound like a film about war and destruction, the word literally means 'unveiling' or 'disclosure'. So the book of Revelation is like a pair of curtains being drawn back so we can glimpse what is otherwise hidden on the other side. In particular, the book is made up of visions that address two questions:

> What *is* taking place in heaven right now? (Present)
> What *will* take place when Jesus returns? (Future)

The following sections will focus on visions that will only be fulfilled when Jesus returns (Revelation 18–22). However, this section explores earlier visions that peer through the keyhole into the heavenly realm right now. They reveal two vital truths that strengthen our hope in the face of life's uncertainties.

First, *Jesus is king*. Revelation may have been written around AD 90 in a context of persecution. The visions in the book are attributed to a man called 'John' (Rev 1:1). This may be the apostle John who had been exiled to an island called Patmos by the Roman authorities. Other Christians faced far worse; many were thrown to lions and bears in the amphitheatres where they were torn apart for sport. Emperor Nero allegedly poured tar over Christians and set them alight as human torches for his garden parties. In this context of severe persecution, John experienced apocalyptic visions that revealed who was really in charge: 'On the Lord's Day I was in the Spirit, and I heard behind me a loud voice like a trumpet' (Revelation 1:10). When John turned round he came face to face with the risen Jesus. He was dressed in a royal robe with a golden sash round his chest. His timeless purity was expressed through hair as white as snow and eyes like blazing fire. He spoke with such authority that his words came forth like a sword. Utterly overwhelmed, John fell flat on his face:

> Then he placed his right hand on me and said: 'Do not be afraid. I am the First and the Last. I am the Living One; I was dead, and now look, I am alive for ever and ever!'
>
> *Revelation 1:17–18*

This vision of Jesus would have been deeply reassuring for minority Christians, under the heel of Rome. Their master was now the majestic King of heaven who ruled over the emperor on earth, whether he realised it or not. Deep inside the Houses of Parliament in London is the Robing Room, where the British monarch puts on their regalia before an opening ceremony. On the opposite wall from where they would sit there is a large mural, an artistic impression of the majesty of Jesus Christ as depicted in Revelation. It is strategically positioned as a reminder to the monarch that they may rule on earth but Jesus is King of heaven. In a turbulent world of threats and intimidation, we still need John's visions. They remind us that over all earthly powers is King Jesus and he has his hand on our lives: 'Do not be afraid.'

Second, *God is the director*. The book of Revelation is written in a different style or genre from the rest of the Bible. It uses symbolism to convey realities that are quite literally out of this world:

> There before me was a throne in heaven with someone sitting on it . . . Surrounding the throne were twenty-four other thrones . . . round the throne, were four living creatures . . . Day and night they never stop saying:
>
> 'Holy, holy, holy is the Lord God Almighty.'
>
> *Revelation 4:2, 4, 6, 8*

Orbiting around this great scene, John saw four living creatures, each with six wings. This means they are heavenly beings and yet each one also had a familiar face – a lion, an ox, a man, an eagle. These hybrid creatures symbolise a cosmic harmony between heaven and earth as they join together and worship 'God Almighty'. Closer in, John saw twenty-four thrones.

This number symbolises the entire people of God – twelve tribes from the Old Testament and twelve Apostles in the New Testament. Then, at the very centre, John saw a heavenly throne, symbolising divine power and authority. It's the ultimate control centre, where the supreme ruler sits to conduct the affairs of their realm.

A couple of years ago, I was given a tour of the White House in Washington, DC. When we reached the West Wing, we had to wait until the president left the Oval Office. Even then we were only permitted to stand in the doorway and gaze into the world's most powerful room. I tried to imagine the conversations and decisions that had taken place there over the years. But without a president at the desk, it seemed eerily empty. However, in John's vision, when he peered into the heavenly control room, the King was on the throne. Despite the chaos and evil we see on earth, there is a director of operations actively ruling and he never takes his eye off the ball: 'Holy, holy, holy is the Lord God Almighty.'

In chapters 5 and 6, John then gets to listen in on discussions taking place in heaven. It all focuses on a double-sided scroll bound with seven seals. The number seven symbolises perfection or completion. So the scroll represents God's perfect plan or script for world history. Crucially, in John's vision the only person who had the right to open the seals was the Lamb, Jesus Christ. His sacrifice on the cross provided the only key that can unlock God's perfect plan for the cosmos.

If you delve further into Revelation, the symbolism and imagery becomes hard to understand. But don't miss the big idea. Behind the scenes of human history, there is a supreme director. From heaven, God is working out his purpose on earth no matter what human rulers get up to. One of my friends at university became a Christian in our second year and began to read the book of Revelation. His response captured the complexities but also the clear headline of the book: 'I didn't have a clue about most of it. But one thing is certain, Jesus is going to win!' Though life on our side of the curtain is full of uncertainties, Revelation lifts our gaze to the throne of God, where King Jesus is ruling over all things. We may not know what the future holds but we can know the one who holds the future.

READ: Revelation 4:1–11.

REFLECT: Where do we see chaos and evil in our world today? Take some time to pray over specific situations. Be assured, nothing is too big for God to handle or too small for him to care about.

38

# Hope includes Judgement Day

*Justice is coming*

Our lives are structured like a story, with a beginning, middle and end. We are not looping round the circle of life but travelling through an arc of time. Scientists suggest this is also the case for the universe as a whole. It had a beginning and it will eventually have an end, what's been dubbed 'the heat death' of the universe. Rather more urgently, some are now predicting that the human race will soon face extinction as climate change reduces our beautiful blue planet to a scorched dust bowl. Activists are warning of a 'climate apocalypse' and Covid-19 also got *#apocalypse* trending on social media. Headlines about the 'end of the world' have become the new vogue.

The Bible agrees that our world will reach a definite end. However, this will not be imposed on us by environmental catastrophe or the forces of chance. The final chapters of Revelation depict a good and sovereign God, orchestrating a series of events that bring history to a carefully planned conclusion. Our human story is not a plastic bag blowing in the wind; there is a divine author, who knows the end from the beginning and has scripted the final outcome.

In this section, we consider dramatic events that will bring history to its conclusion: the destruction of evil, the return of Jesus Christ and a final Judgement Day (Revelation 18–20). These sobering realities are not easy to come to terms with and they raise questions: On what basis will people be judged? What are the penalties for non-compliance? However, those who witness these events in Revelation are moved to spontaneous applause, as if a great leader has taken a series of difficult decisions to ensure the right outcome. As God's judgements are passed, a great multitude starts singing the Hallelujah chorus:

> Hallelujah!
> Salvation and glory and power belong to our God,
> for *true and just are his judgments.*
>
> *Revelation 19:1–2*

Understood properly, the destruction of evil, the return of the King and the Day of Judgement bring the changes that our broken world so desperately needs.

**The destruction of evil (Revelation 18)**

Throughout the Bible, all that's wrong with this world was symbolised by one particular city: Babylon. It became synonymous with the 'Tower of Babel', which, as we've seen, was built by early humanity in a proud bid to 'make a name' for themselves (Genesis 11:4). Centuries later, the Babylonian Empire destroyed Jerusalem and took God's people hostage into exile. So Babylon therefore became associated with the forces of evil that ruin God's good world through violence, corruption and greed. Today, humans continue to build all sorts of 'Babylons' through the deadly cocktail of pride, technology and oppression. Indeed, modern urban centres and capitalist economies display all the hallmarks of 'Babylon' as described in the book of Revelation: material affluence, commercialisation, sexual promiscuity, huge inequality and an assumed invincibility. Sound familiar? Take a look at Revelation 18:1–10. However, in John's vision, all of a sudden Babylon is brought crashing down through an act of divine judgement. This icon of human arrogance is reduced to rubble in just one hour, leaving the merchants and traders distraught.

Although entirely different, the tragic destruction of the Twin Towers on 9/11 and the more recent coronavirus pandemic serve as reminders that this world is a fragile place. Things that seem invincible will not last. The mighty Roman Empire is now a history lesson after all. Revelation therefore provides a timely warning that this present world is passing away. Like the merchants of Babylon, if we invest all our energies in making money and acquiring possessions we will end up devastated. Instead, let's live for the things that last and 'seek first the kingdom of God' (Matthew 6:33).

**The return of the King (Revelation 19)**

A friend once bought me a T-shirt with the slogan 'Jesus is coming: look busy!' I politely refused to wear it for a couple of reasons. For a start, the motivation is all wrong. Serving Jesus is not like cross-country running at school: make an effort only when the teacher might be watching. Then the language of Jesus 'coming' isn't helpful either – it makes him sound like an absentee landlord on the other side of the universe, who will one day come to collect the rent. Instead, the New Testament uses the Greek verb *parousia*, 'appearing', to describe the end time moment when everyone will encounter Jesus. Remember, he ascended into the heavenly realm not into outer space. Jesus is currently out of sight to planet earth but that does not mean he is far away. Right now, we interact with him through our spiritual senses. But one day, the curtain will lift and Jesus will be revealed in plain sight. This is how John imagines the dramatic moment:

> I saw heaven standing open and there before me was a white horse, whose rider is called Faithful and True . . . On his robe and on his thigh he has this name written: KING OF KINGS AND LORD OF LORDS.
>
> *Revelation 19:11, 16*

In this apocalyptic vision, heaven finally is opened up so that everyone can see the truth. It's the moment when earth catches up with heaven and the realisation dawns that Jesus Christ is KING OF KINGS AND LORD OF LORDS. To remove any doubt, John sees this title tattooed down his thigh. Whereas his first appearance was in humility, a baby in a manger, his second will be a display of power, riding on a stallion and accompanied by the armies of heaven. On that final day, the majesty of Jesus will be broadcast live to the entire globe. From rainforest jungles in Brazil to urban jungles in China, every eye will see, every knee will bow and every tongue will confess that Jesus Christ is Lord.

**The Day of Judgement (Revelation 20)**

The return of Christ will bring about a final day of reckoning. This may sound like an old-fashioned idea. However, we all have a deep desire for justice, especially when we see bad people getting away with it. Who wouldn't want to call time on human trafficking, domestic abuse and scandalous waste? However, our challenge is one of perspective and consistency. We want justice but not when we are on the wrong side of it.

We want accountability but not when we're pulled up short. Right?

At the end of my final term at university, I received an email from the office of the Chancellor summoning me to a meeting. My mind immediately flashed back to a few days earlier. After my final exam, I had jumped into the city fountain to celebrate and had to be pulled out by a police officer. Now as the day of reckoning approached, I feared being expelled and losing everything I'd worked for. I felt a deep sense of dread. For those of us who are less than perfect, it's the sort of feeling that stirs when we read Revelation 20:

> Then I saw a great white throne and him who was seated on it . . . And I saw the dead, great and small, standing before the throne, and books were opened. Another book was opened, which is the book of life.
>
> *Revelation 20:11–12*

These heavenly books symbolise an exhaustive record of our actions, not only in public but also in private. The point is simple: in the end, no one will 'get away with it'. A *perfect Judge* will serve *perfect Justice*. Our courts of law and judicial systems echo on earth the ultimate justice that will one day be fulfilled. Deep down we know that justice and sentencing are good and necessary. And yet we also know that if everything hidden should be revealed, our thoughts as well as deeds, and if everyone we have sworn to secrecy were to divulge their secrets, we would be left blushing. In the light of such a full disclosure, who would back themselves to come out on the right side of God's justice?

However, before you suffer an end-times panic attack, did you notice the mention of another book, 'the book of life'? This is a clue that can bring hope to the guilty. It is possible to face

Judgement Day knowing that in spite of all our failings, our names are written in the book of life. How? Remember, when Jesus died on the cross, the sky turned black because he came under the judgement we deserve. So long before we arrive at Judgement Day, he's already been there on our behalf. That's why Jesus could promise: 'whoever hears my word and believes . . . has eternal life and *will not be judged*' (John 5:24). In the light of what Jesus has done for us, what otherise would be a fearful day can become a moment to look forward to.

To my surprise, when I entered the Chancellor's office, he smiled and shook my hand: 'Well done. You've won a prize,' handing me an envelope with a gift-voucher. Confused, I blurted out: 'But what about the fountain?' He looked blank and ushered me out of his office. Clearly, there was no record of my wrong. Just a promise of reward. I'd been given a small foretaste of what it might feel like when a day of reckoning becomes a day of grace. Ultimately, that's the difference Jesus will make on Judgement Day.

READ: Revelation 18:1–3; 19:1–16.

REFLECT: In the light of eternity, how might we need to reprioritise? What has become *too important* and what needs to become *more important*?

39

# Hope is new creation

*A physical future*

On the way home from church our son suddenly announced: 'I don't think I want to go to heaven anymore.' Concerned that he might have converted to the dark side, we began to investigate this change of heart. It turns out he got really bored during an extended time of singing in the church service. Then in the children's lesson he picked up the idea that heaven is basically a massive crowd singing endless songs to Jesus. He put two and two together and made his dramatic announcement. On that basis, who would blame an energetic kid for questioning whether our future hope is all it's cracked up to be?

The rest of this section provides an adult version of the response we gave to help reframe our son's understanding of our future hope. First and foremost, the Bible does not culminate with visions of people *going up to heaven* but with people coming *down to populate a restored earth*. Our ultimate home is not up in heaven. We belong in a pristine new creation, more physical and sociable than we would dare to imagine. Heaven is only a halfway house. Our ultimate destination is a beautiful new world. Only then will we sigh: 'Home, sweet home.'

To capture this, the final chapters of the Bible (Revelation 21–2) deliberately loop back to the opening chapters of creation (Genesis 1–2). As our human story began in a beautiful world, so our future hope returns us to it:

> Then I saw 'a new heaven and a new earth,' for the first heaven and the first earth had passed away, and there was no longer any sea . . . And I heard a loud voice from the throne . . . 'There will be no more death or mourning or crying or pain, for the old order of things has passed away.' He who was seated on the throne said, 'I am making everything new!'
>
> *Revelation 21:1–5*

In this section we will unpack the implications of this vision on a cosmic scale, then in the next we will consider what this means at a more personal level.

To begin with, notice the pristine nature of this new cosmos. The material world has been rid of everything toxic and destructive and restored to a state of perfection. In order for this to happen, our old decaying world will first experience a deep purge and clean. This is described in Revelation 20, where terrifying figures that symbolise evil – a beast representing worldly power and a dragon representing satanic power – are hurled into a lake of burning sulphur and destroyed (20:10). Equally, any collaborators whose names were not in the book of life were also thrown into the lake (20:15). This destructive process is necessary if the world is to be rid of all that corrupts. I recall difficult times when doctors injected chemotherapy into my father's body. It had such a weakening effect and yet its goal was to purge the cancer and restore life. God's judgement of evil is for a similar purpose but on a cosmic scale.

On the other side of this purge, the entire world will be

given the all-clear, and without any further risk of relapse. The cosmos will be beyond even the possibility of evil, disease and corruption, as its source will have been destroyed. Can you begin to imagine what that will feel like? We are so used to living in the presence of dark realities, we think they're normal and don't even notice them. But after the deep purge, we will experience true *shalom*, the way the world was always supposed to be. Soon after I started going out with Charlotte, she came for dinner to the flat that I shared with a friend. I thought we'd done a pretty good job of tidying up, but no sooner did Charlotte enter than she remarked, 'What's that smell?' Of course the two of us who lived there replied: 'What smell?' The next time we caught up she revisited her experience and concluded: 'I can't believe you live like that!' One day, in a new normal where all is pristine, we will look back with amazement at things that we now assume to be givens – plastic waste, abuse, injustice, anxiety – 'I can't believe we used to live like that!'

Second, notice how solid the new world will be. Our future is physical and material as surely as John sees a new earth. The Greek word used for 'new' is *kainos*, which implies not brand new (*neos*) but something restored to its former glory, even surpassing it. A renewed version of planet earth will be our permanent home, but upgraded to such an extent that we will hardly recognise the place. This defies every philosophy, reaching as far back as Plato, that assumes the material realm is inherently evil and to be escaped. Instead, from the beginning, Genesis affirmed that the physical world is 'very good'. Equally, the incarnation and resurrection of Jesus have provided salvation not just for every soul but also for every molecule and mammal. Our material world has a glorious future too.

The Apostle Paul therefore depicts the natural world in its

current state like a pregnant woman, groaning under the weight of the hope she carries. This metaphor restores a sense of perspective in the face of growing eco-anxiety. Despite very real challenges, the world will not end in cosmic disaster or human extinction. Instead, the metaphor of pregnancy suggests that current ecological tensions and natural disasters are agonising contractions before something new emerges:

> The created world itself can hardly wait for what's coming next . . . The difficult times of pain throughout the world are simply birth pangs.
>
> *Romans 8:19, 22 (The Message)*

The Bible helps us imagine a flourishing future world far more solid and beautiful than anything we can touch or taste here and now. John's visions include natural features such as rivers, trees, fruits and mountains. As a climber, I'm particularly excited to read about high mountains in the new world (21:10). I've also taken great delight in pointing out to my sailing friends that there will be 'no longer any sea' (21:1). Don't panic if you love surfing and beaches. John is alluding to a common assumption in the ancient world that the sea was a source of chaos. That's why a terrifying beast is seen emerging from the ocean in Revelation 13. But after the deep purge, there is no more chaos left, hence no more sea in the metaphorical sense. Properly interpreted, this means no more natural disasters, freak accidents or environmental degradation. Instead, divine beauty will radiate from every plant and shrub and be manifest on every mountain and beach. If in this life you don't make it to every destination on your bucket list, fear not. You will have ample opportunity to explore a physical world with levels of beauty that make our current experiences seem like an old black and white photo.

What will it be like for us to step into that new world, where everything radiates with divine glory? If you want to imagine the experience, try watching YouTube videos of people born colour-blind putting on corrective glasses for the first time. Their response of shock, disbelief, joy and tears gives a foretaste of what lies in store. We will enter a new world where all of life is vibrant with colour and beauty. Our future hope is more solid and physical than we've dared to imagine: a pristine new creation, with rivers, mountains, beaches and trees – more than enough to satisfy energetic kids and adventurous adults. This is our ultimate destination.

From our side of history, John's visions in Revelation enable us to peer through the keyhole and glimpse the beauty that lies ahead. As C. S. Lewis concluded:

> At present we are on the outside of the world, the wrong side of the door. We discern the freshness and purity of morning, but they do not make us fresh and pure. We cannot mingle with the splendours we see. But all the pages of the New Testament are rustling with the rumour that it will not always be so. Someday, God willing, we shall get in.[4]

READ: Revelation 21:1–27.

REFLECT: Type into a search engine 'People seeing colour for the first time'. Watch the video and imagine how it will feel when you enter a pristine new creation.

40

# Hope is a garden city

*A sociable future*

'Will we ever see Taid again?' sobbed one of our children at the graveside of their grandad. Heart-rending moments stir big existential questions. Often the response is vague and wishful: 'He's in the clouds looking down,' or 'She's a star in the sky watching over you.' But John's visions in Revelation give a more solid basis for hope. As we've seen, we are heading home to a final destination that will be far more physical and beautiful than this world. The glimpses we get in Revelation also suggest it will be more sociable than we've imagined. There will be familiar faces, now beautified in glory. We will inhabit a perfect society with more camaraderie than a TV sitcom. God our Father will be close, so close we will dwell in his eternal embrace. *Home, sweet home*. As well as beautiful landscapes, Revelation 21–22 also highlights some relational features to look forward to: *resurrection* bodies, a perfect *society* and a cosmic *temple* of glory.

**Resurrection Bodies**

First, before setting foot on this new creation, our frail, mortal bodies will experience a physical resurrection. This hope is rooted in history, when the corpse of Christ experienced resurrection power that reversed death. Every cell in his body was infused with eternal life. Remember, this was no mere resuscitation; the caterpillar was metamorphosed into a butterfly. Though clearly the same person, with crucifixion wounds to prove it, his friends struggled to recognise him. He walked through locked doors like we pass through mist or smoke. The fabric of this world seemed flimsy compared to his substantial body. He made a fire on the beach, cooked and ate fish with his friends. When they accused him of being a phantom, he retorted: 'Touch me and see; a ghost does not have flesh and bones, as you see I have' (Luke 24:39).

The risen Jesus shows us the future. Our resurrection bodies will be real 'flesh and bones' transfigured in glory, eating food with friends and enjoying the good things of life. The word 'glory' in Hebrew literally means 'heavy' or 'weighty'. It's a clue that suggests we are lightweights compared to the world to come. C. S. Lewis captured this brilliantly in *The Great Divorce*. He imagines one of us in our current state being shown round the solid realities of a new creation. Bending down to pluck a daisy, we discover that we can't. It's as hard as diamond to us:

> As I stood, recovering my breath . . . I noticed that I could see grass not only between my feet but also through them. I was a mere phantom compared to this real world.[5]

Lewis goes on to describe the moment when a dazzlingly glorious figure approaches over the horizon. Utterly overcome, we fall down exclaiming, 'Is this the one?', meaning the Messiah or some archangel. But our tour guide laughs: 'Not at all! This is someone you'll never have heard of. Her name on earth was Sarah Smith and she lived at Golders Green in London.' This alludes to a shocking New Testament promise: that when we *see* Jesus we will become *like* Jesus (1 John 3:2). The most ordinary person will be as glorious as the Messiah himself. *Will we see grandad in heaven?* Yes, but like we've never known him before!

This promise of physical resurrection gives ultimate hope in the face of pain, mental-health issues, disability and the creep of old age. We will one day enjoy perfect bodies – perhaps for you this can't come soon enough? Equally, if you're currently in great shape, don't forget: no matter what you can bench-press in the gym you couldn't pluck a daisy in the real world. Our future resurrection calls us out of fitness obsessions *and* lifts us out of melancholy or nostalgia. Whatever state we're in now, our best days lie ahead of us. As Tom Wright has argued, we are not *shadows of our former self.* Quite the contrary:

> A Christian in the present life is *a mere shadow of their future self*, the self they will be when the body which God has waiting in his heavenly storeroom is brought out, already made to measure and put on for ever.[6]

How exactly God will resurrect our mortal body remains a mystery. Clearly he won't need to salvage old molecules to make a new model. After all, we shed our skin and change our kit about every seven years as it is. What we do know is there will be continuity – it's really me – and yet radical change – it's the perfect version of me. Here's how the Apostle Paul summarises it. Cue Handel's *Messiah*:

> Listen, I tell you a mystery . . . in a flash, in the twinkling of an eye . . . the trumpet will sound, the dead will be raised imperishable, *and we will be changed*!
>
> *1 Corinthians 15:51–2*

**Perfect Society**

As resurrected people we will build a new society. This is portrayed in Revelation through the symbolic arrival of a 'New Jerusalem'. In the Bible, Jerusalem was the urban centre that represented the people of God. Now the entire population is seen descending from heaven to earth:

> [An angel] showed me the Holy City, Jerusalem, coming down out of heaven from God. It shone with the glory of God . . . On no day will its gates ever be shut, for there will be no night there.
>
> *Revelation 21:10–11, 25*

What do you think of when you imagine a city? They can often be epicentres of crime, poverty, overcrowding and injustice. But imagine an urban centre populated by perfect people. The gates never need to be shut because threat and danger are no more. In the ancient world, failure to shut the gates at night would be like sleeping with your front door open. We are so used to crime and security issues it's unthinkable. A high percentage of the world's population live in the shadow of bullies, scared to go out after dark and feeling threatened in their own home. What freedom we will enjoy when the world's population has been through the great purge. The whole city will feel safe, with no shady characters or dark alleys to worry about.

This new society will then get on with the original vocation that God gave to humans. In Genesis, God called humans to cultivate the world by exercising authority and creativity. The Bible ends with this vision finally coming to pass. Eternal life will not be a static existence but full of adventure, enterprise and grand designs. You may feel like you'd prefer an everlasting holiday. But after a while, that would begin to feel like the never-ending church service idea. Boring. Instead, we will enjoy the challenge of taking on new tasks. We will work without frustration and rest without interruption. Of course, if you are a lawyer, locksmith or police officer you will be out of a job! Together, we will live in safety and work in harmony. Human society and the natural world will form one sustainable ecosystem. Together, we will cultivate a beautiful world that we can call home.

**A Cosmic Temple**

Resurrection bodies, family reunions, fulfilling vocations . . . But according to John's vision what really brings heaven to earth is the presence of God: 'Look! God's dwelling-place is now among the people, and he will dwell with them . . .' (Revelation 21:3). In the new world there will be no physical temple (21:22). Instead, the whole world will be sacred space. In John's vision, an angel measured the dimensions of the New Jerusalem. The width, length and height of the city were 12,000 stadia or 2,220 kilometres. This symbolic number results in a perfect cube, which was the exact shape of the Holy of Holies in Solomon's temple. The whole world will be like entering the inner sanctuary of the temple, where God had his throne and living quarters. Can you imagine living in such close proximity to God? In the Old Testament, the high priest was allowed through the curtain into this space just once a year. But we will call it *home*.

Resurrection bodies, a perfect society, sacred space . . . How will it feel finally to enter in? The ending to C. S. Lewis' *Last Battle* captures something of the emotion:

> It was the Unicorn who summed up what everyone was feeling.

> He stamped his right fore-hoof on the ground and neighed, and then cried: 'I have come home at last! This is my real country! I belong here. This is the land I have been looking for all my life, though I never knew it till now. The reason why we loved the old Narnia is that it sometimes looked a little like this. Bree-heehee! Come further up, come further in![7]

READ: Revelation 22:1–21.

REFLECT: Of all that we've considered, what are you most looking forward to in the new creation? Thank God for it in advance!

41

# Hope beyond the grave

*Confidence to face death*

Biblical hope has two decisive reference points: behind us, the resurrection of Jesus and ahead of us, the new creation. *Home, sweet home*. So that leaves us somewhere in the middle. We know what has been accomplished through the *first* visitation of Jesus and we glimpse what lies in store at his *second* appearing. But what difference does all this make in the meantime? After all, the world keeps spinning, people keep dying and we are still hurting. So how does hope work here and now?

When I was a boy, one of my favourite movies was *Force 10 from Navarone*, a war film starring Harrison Ford. With the Nazis poised to cross a strategic bridge and invade Yugoslavia, a Special Forces team is sent to blow up a huge dam ten miles up the valley. However, when they plant the bomb deep inside and detonate the device, it hardly makes a sound. A few Nazis on top of the dam wall shrug their shoulders. One of the Special Forces team gasps with frustration: 'It didn't work. It didn't do a damn thing!' But the wise explosives expert calmly responds: 'Be patient. Just give it time!' Sure enough, the explosion had compromised the internal structure of the dam and slowly but surely cracks began to appear. Soon the dam broke open, releasing a torrent that destroyed the enemy further down the valley.

Christian hope works in a similar way. The impact of the first appearing of Jesus may seem small compared to the problems of the world. But don't miss the deeper significance. His resurrection broke the stronghold of evil and death and set in motion an irreversible chain of events. At his second appearing, the enemy will be decisively swept away and destroyed. In the meantime, we can live with the confidence of that explosives expert: we are on the right side of history. Though Satan, evil and death persist, the cracks are already appearing in their reign. So for the remainder of Part 6, we will consider how to live and die with confidence in the light of our hope. First up, death.

One of the Founding Fathers of the United States allegedly quipped, 'There are only two things certain in life, death and taxes' (Benjamin Franklin). Regardless of creed or culture, death remains the most inevitable fact of life. However, in the absence of any meaningful response, our society prefers to hide from this reality. Like an ostrich burying its head in the sand, we sing along with Robbie Williams, 'I hope I'm old before I die'. But death looms large on the horizon, mocking any sense of permanence and casting its fearful shadow over our lives. The prospect of suffering before death is no doubt part of this, but a deeper angst stems from the uncertainty of what lies beyond. Shakespeare's character Hamlet is famously caught on the horns of this dilemma: 'To be or not to be? That is the question.' Life's troubles make him want to end it all through suicide. But he is held back by the fear of what lies beyond in that 'undiscovered country'. Thus 'conscience does make cowards of us all'.

The Bible is nothing if not honest at this point. Far from pretending we are all sorted with a ticket to paradise, it is replete with warnings that a sharp divide awaits on the other side. Judgement Day will separate the wheat from the weeds. No one spoke more clearly about this than Jesus himself:

> If your eye causes you to stumble, pluck it out. It is better for you to enter the kingdom of God with one eye than to have two eyes and be thrown into hell [*gehenna*], where 'the worms that eat them do not die, and the fire is not quenched'.
>
> *Mark 9:47–8*

Just outside Jerusalem lies the Valley of Hinnom, formerly known as *Gehenna*. To this day it is a threatening place, overshadowed by rocky outcrops. In Jesus' day it was a huge landfill site with smouldering fires burning up the refuse of the city. Though strategically positioned downwind, everyone would have caught the occasional whiff and equated it with the worst place imaginable. When Jesus taught about hell, he used the word *Gehenna* to conjure up deep feelings of repulsion. Instinctively, you want to avoid going there. And that's the point. Beyond death there is a hellish reality to be avoided. It's what the book of Revelation refers to as 'the second death' (21:8). There's a first or physical death but then there is a darker, more permanent reality that is the real sting.

Of course, mystery shrouds these matters and many questions remain. In particular, how will God's judgement be reconciled with his love? Fortunately, our job is not to work this out or second-guess particular outcomes. Instead, we must trust God with the unknowns and take responsibility for our own response. Ultimately, the Bible gives us sober warnings out of kindness. God has personally intervened to redirect us from *Gehenna* to Eden, from the pit to paradise. When Jesus died outside the city walls of Jerusalem, he took our hellish darkness on himself so that we never have to go there. While hanging on the cross, Jesus ministered to a guilty thug who was crucified next to him. Simply on the basis of a cry for mercy, Jesus promised:

> Truly I tell you, today you will be with me in *paradise*.
>
> *Luke 23:43*

Avoiding hell is not about building up a resumé of charitable deeds. It's about personally calling out to Jesus Christ. Eternity will be an extension of the response we make to God's Son here and now. The warnings are therefore designed to disturb us out of any complacency. As the old hymn, 'Amazing Grace', puts it:

> 'Twas grace that taught my heart to fear
> and grace my fears relieved.
> How precious did that grace appear
> the hour I first believed.

When I was younger, I was plagued by a fear of death, even if a childlike version. I remember driving home with my family across the old Severn Bridge between England and Wales. It was swaying on a stormy night and I became convinced the end was nigh. The next morning, I went to church and was given the chance to win a chocolate bar by reciting a memory verse. It happened to be John 3:16, perhaps the most famous in the Bible: 'For God so loved the world that he gave his one and only Son, that whoever believes in him shall *not perish* but have eternal life.' All of a sudden, the truth struck home. I even lost awareness of the chocolate bar and turned aside to pray. From that moment, the fear of perishing departed and the hope of eternal life moved in. When it comes to facing death, whatever stage of life, personally trusting in Jesus Christ is the game-changer.

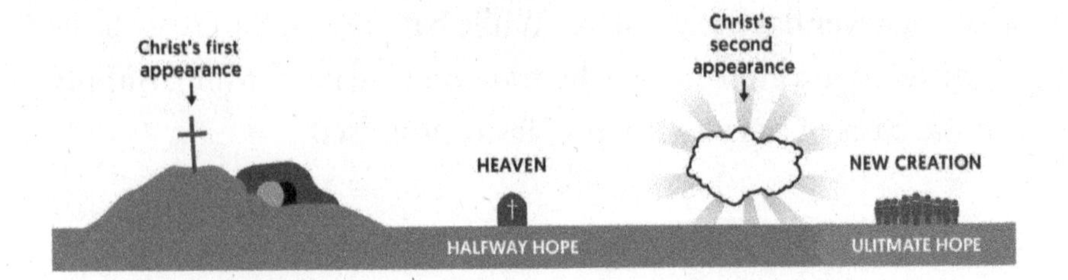


The specific hope Christians have beyond death reflects a two-stage timetable. Because we live after the resurrection of Jesus, the power of death has been broken. Therefore, when someone dies in Christ their soul departs from their body and enters heaven to enjoy paradise. As Paul put it: 'away from the body and at home with the Lord' (2 Corinthians 5:8).

That's why, at the point of death, there is a sense of departure. Though the body remains and decomposes, the person is no longer there. They are now enjoying rest in the heavenly realm. However, the waiting of souls in heaven is still only a halfway hope, not our final home. Remember, we belong in a physical new creation. When Christ appears a second time, he will bring this to completion. The New Testament therefore refers to death as 'sleep'. It's only a temporary state until the sun rises over a new creation, never to set again. With this in mind, as my father died the last thing I said to him was: 'Goodnight, Dad. See you in the morning.' It still hurts but we grieve with hope knowing it's not the end. As the seventeenth-century poet George Herbert put it in his poem 'Time', death used to be the 'executioner', but the gospel has made him into a 'gardener'.

Without Jesus Christ, death would taunt and intimidate us. But the resurrection of Jesus has won the decisive victory. So we can live and die with confidence. As a world-famous preacher once quipped: 'Someday you will read that Billy Graham is dead. Don't you believe a word of it. I shall be more alive than I am now. I will just have changed address!"[8] Or, as the Apostle Paul put it:

> 'Where, O death, is your victory?
> Where, O death, is your sting?'
> . . . thanks be to God! He gives us the victory through our Lord Jesus Christ!
>
> *1 Corinthians 15:55,57*

READ: 1 Corinthians 15:35–58.

REFLECT: Have you put your faith in Jesus as the only basis for eternal hope? Take time to turn from all that's wrong and receive the assurance of eternal life.

42

# Hope in the here and now

*Courage to face life's challenges*

Have you ever watched a drama or read a novel with a brilliant ending? All of a sudden, things fall into place. Previous events and characters that appeared to be random turn out to be vital clues and links in the chain. It makes you want to flick back and revisit all the things you missed. That's how the Bible works. From the vantage point of the end, the plotline reveals its full significance in reverse.

On the very last page of the Bible, a symbol of hope reappears that casts our minds right back to the beginning:

> On each side of the river stood *the tree of life*.
>
> *Revelation 22:2*

From an original Garden of Eden (Genesis) to a beautiful garden city (Revelation), the Bible has turned full circle – paradise lost has been regained. With the tree of life featuring at either end, the plotline in between now takes on new significance. In Genesis, when God called Abraham to leave his home and travel to another land, it wasn't a random relocation exercise; God was beginning a new humanity who would journey as exiles towards an ultimate home (Hebrews 11:8–10). Later in Exodus, when God delivered Israel and brought them into the land of Canaan, it was a prototype of a much larger hope. One day the entire planet will be the Promised Land. As the prophet Isaiah foretold, 'he will make her deserts like Eden' and 'wastelands like the garden of the LORD' (51:3). When David established the city of Jerusalem and Solomon built the temple, these were not isolated building projects but visions of a new world. One day, a vast population will come down like a New Jerusalem to inhabit a space more sacred than the Holy of Holies.

Centuries later in Bethlehem, Herod's slaughter of the innocent (Matthew 2:16–18) turned out to be a desperate satanic attempt to stop God's rescue plan at source. In Revelation 12, John revisits the birth of Christ from an apocalyptic perspective. A woman is in labour (Mary) and a terrifying dragon stands poised, ready to snatch her baby away. Try sending Christmas cards depicting that nativity scene! The vision captures the gravity of the situation. Through Mary's womb, the divine author has entered his own story to take on our enemies himself. Though the Messiah got nailed to a Roman cross, a tragic end soon became a new beginning. The risen Jesus won the decisive victory right in the middle of history. The Son of God hung on a Roman *tree of death*, so that we might return to the *tree of life*.

The whole Bible turns out to be a beautifully crafted narrative. The Great Author had the end worked out from the beginning. Even the knotty parts and apparent tragedies are woven into the tapestry he's making. At present, we are on the wrong side to appreciate it all but, one day, we will. In the meantime, the Bible reassures us that life is not a pointless tragedy or a random comedy. Life is a divine story full of meaning. Hope is not wishful thinking; it's a reflection of reality itself, when viewed from the end. As Archbishop Desmond Tutu therefore put it: 'I am not optimistic but I am a prisoner of hope!'[9]

In the light of the visions we have glimpsed together, begin to imagine all that lies ahead: *environmental renewal* so that the entire cosmos will be as innocent as a newborn baby; *bodily resurrection* with no more pain, brokenness or loss; an *emotional reunion* as loved ones embrace again in the presence of Jesus. Recently, I spent an hour at the arrivals hall at Heathrow airport waiting for friends to emerge. Extraordinary human emotions were on display. As a couple emerged from customs through the sliding doors, several people shrieked with abandon; they then broke through the barrier and practically mugged them with hugs and tears, suitcases tumbling in all directions. Can you begin to imagine the joyful carnage when we exiles finally emerge through the ultimate arrivals gate; embracing loved ones, worshipping Jesus, setting up home together? No wonder the Bible finishes with an emotive cry: 'Come, Lord Jesus' (Revelation 22:20).

With the ultimate outcome secured, hope shines back from the far horizon and provides two vital resources here and now. First, hope gives *confidence* in the face of uncertainty. So much anxiety, stress and anger derive from the fact that the future is out of our control. However, the risen Jesus guarantees our ultimate destiny and promises to be with us all the way home. So we can live with a deep sense of certainty, come what may. Whether we get the grades or miss out on the place, whether the boss wants to discuss promotion or redundancy, whether the test results are benign or malignant, our ultimate hope is unmoved. As the New Testament puts it:

> We have this hope as an anchor for the soul, firm and secure.
>
> *Hebrews 6:19*

I love to go sailing each year with friends, even though I am not particularly confident at sea. One year we sailed off the coast of south-west England to the Isles of Scilly. The next day we dropped anchor off shore. But in the night, the wind picked up, the waves rose and I couldn't sleep. After pacing the boat for a while I woke my friend the captain and expressed my concerns. Having assessed the situation, he looked me in the eye and said: 'Have you seen the size of our anchor? Go back to bed and sleep!' Hope is an anchor for the soul through the storms of life. We may feel fragile and vulnerable but we are secured to Jesus Christ and he will not give way. Have you seen the size of our anchor?

Second, hope gives us *courage* to make a difference. Throughout history, Christians who have made the greatest impact in this life were those most confident about the next – caring for plague victims, fighting against slavery, championing civil rights. Hope is an unstoppable force for good.[10] However, when we think this life is all we've got, our horizons shrink. The fear of missing out holds us back and self-preservation becomes our biggest priority: 'Alas, for those that never sing, but die with all their music still in them.'[11] Hope liberates us from self-centred living and gives a bigger vision for life, shaped by eternity. As the Apostle Paul put it: 'Since we have such a *hope*, we are very *bold*' (2 Corinthians 3:12).

On a visit to Hong Kong, I visited a lady called Jackie Pullinger. Called by God, she left the UK aged nineteen, boarded a ship and got off with no money or provisions. There she began to serve in the Walled City, a notorious ghetto run by Triad gangs and rife with drugs and prostitution. For decades, Jackie refused to give up or back down, despite relentless challenges. Slowly she gained the trust of gang leaders and the Walled City began to experience the sort of transformation that only Jesus can bring. When I met with Jackie, I asked a perfectly reasonable question: 'What made you so brave?' But she retorted, 'Brave? I wasn't brave! I just believed what every Christian should believe. We're heading for glory, so let's make a difference on the way!'[12] If we really grasp how secure our hope is, then Jackie's reaction is right. What might seem radical is actually perfectly reasonable. Looking back from eternity, we won't regret any of the risks we take or sacrifices we make to share hope with a broken world in Jesus' name.

In my rugby-playing days, towards the end of a match we often asked the referee: 'How long left?' If the game was nearly over, he would reply: 'The next whistle you hear will be the final whistle.' That realisation gave a surge of energy. No point holding back and playing it safe. Time to leave everything on the pitch. In the grand scheme of things, the Bible story is nearly over. Major prophecies have been fulfilled – the Messiah has come, the Spirit has been poured out. We are living in the last days. The next whistle we hear will be the final whistle. Jesus Christ will dramatically appear to usher in our full and glorious hope. So in the meantime, let's leave everything on the pitch. In the light of our eternal hope, let's live with *confidence* – have you seen the size of our anchor? And with *courage* – what have we got to lose?

READ: 2 Corinthians 4:16–5:10.

REFLECT: In the light of eternity, ask God what difference he wants you to make on the way home. Pray for greater confidence and courage to live this out.

# Epilogue

So our journey through the Bible has now come to an end. I wonder how you have found it? What have you seen in a new light? What made sense and what still feels confusing?

As you've probably picked up by now, I love mountaineering. A few years ago, I went to Scotland with friends to enjoy some winter climbing. The snow conditions were perfect, so we hired a guide for a couple of days to help us take on a challenging route. After training us in some new techniques, he led us on a mountain traverse that was one of the best days of my life. Initially, it felt quite scary; we had to scale a dark, threatening gully, which we would never have attempted on our own. But the guide helped us navigate the difficult sections and reach the summit ridge. Suddenly our heads popped out into glorious sunshine – we had made it. Exhausted but elated, we gazed over a patchwork of lochs and glens beneath us. The beautiful vista made all the effort worthwhile.

The Bible is a big, rugged and at times intimidating landscape. But I hope this book has been a helpful guide for you along the way. It's taken some effort but together we have seen the big picture. The journey has also given us a mental map that we can use to navigate the Bible storyline from now on:

Back to the highlands of Scotland . . . Once we were up on the summit ridge, our guide turned to us and said: 'Right. I'm off to take some photos. Head on up in that direction. You should be fine from here.' Initially, it felt a bit disconcerting, but we went for it! We now had confidence to explore for ourselves. That's the aim of a good guide and that's been my desire for you. After all, the Bible offers endless adventure if you want to explore further. In the process of researching and writing this book, I've discovered new things myself . . . and I'm supposed to be the guide!

So where will you go from here? What will you explore next? As you think about that, let me share three principles that have helped me:

## Practice makes perfect

Little-and-often is the best way to learn a language or master a new skill. It's the same with the Bible. I occasionally *binge* read large sections. But for me the most effective approach is *bite-size*. First thing in the morning I listen to a short passage from the Bible with a mug of tea. Our family also reads the Bible together over breakfast. It's a great set-up for the day. There are plenty of good resources that can help (see p.327). But the most important resource we have is the author himself. The Spirit who inspired the Bible is with us. The author happens to be our roommate. So before reading the Bible, make a point of praying and asking for help.

A busy friend recently summarised the challenge of making time for the Bible: 'I read the Bible almost every day. Almost on Monday, almost on Tuesday, almost on Wednesday . . .' If we want to become people who grow with the Bible, we need to develop what James Clear calls an 'atomic habit' – a small practice, which over the long haul makes a big difference:

> Every action you take is a vote for the type of person you wish to become. No single instance will transform your beliefs, but as the votes build up, so does the evidence of your new identity.[1]

So how can you build the Bible into your daily routine? Is there a particular book or character that has sparked your interest, which you could explore next? Put one foot in front of the other and soon small steps will take you to some great places.

## Participate in the story

I confess that sometimes reading the Bible is still a struggle for me. There are many reasons for this. Some sections are just plain hard going, especially Israel's laws and history. So don't expect every page to rock your world or change your life. A couple of years ago, my eight-year-old son scribbled a note to me which I have kept since. He decided to read the whole Bible for himself but part way through he got stuck. The note simply said: 'I'm finding it confusing in 1 Chronicles.' You and me both, son! At times like this, it's important to keep the big picture in mind. Any puzzle piece lacks meaning in isolation. We need to frame each book, character and story in the light of the big picture to appreciate its significance. I recently developed an eight-session resource called *The Bible Course* (Bible Society) to help with this.[2] Perhaps you could give it a try?

However, for me the biggest key has been to immerse myself in the Bible story and to read it as though I am part of it . . . because I am! Through Jesus, I have been co-opted into an epic drama that centres on him. Unlike a visit to a theatre, I am not a spectator in the crowd but an actor on the stage. So I read the Bible to hear the heart of the director and to learn the lines of truth, in order that I might play my part. The Bible is not an academic exercise. As this book has shown, when we make sense of the Bible, the Bible makes sense of us. Israel's story is just like Russian dolls; inside their experience we discover our reality. Now we are invited to experience Exodus freedom through Jesus. Now we are exiles called to bring hope to a broken world. The director has a part for me to play. That's why I read the Bible.

## Persevere to the end

I imagine you're still wondering: So *did he make it?* Did my son get past 1 Chronicles? Indeed he did. On 2 December 2019, he read the last page of the Bible and crossed the finishing line, now age ten-and-a-half! It took some guts but he persevered to the end. Reading the Bible is not easy. But it's worth it. Not so you can say, 'I've read it.' There's a much more important reason than that. Let me put it simply: *if you keep going with the Bible, the Bible will keep you going.*

Life is punctuated with tough experiences that are enough to break us. So where does the strength come from to persevere? I believe the Bible has what we need. When we face tragic suffering, it can pick us up off the floor. When we face important decisions, it gives wisdom and guidance. When we start down the wrong path, it can turn us round. When uncertainties loom, it can make us brave. When we are prone to despair, it helps us struggle on in hope. The Bible will not save us from trouble or tragedy but it will help us through them.

One Saturday morning, I was playing rugby and my father was on the touchline as a vocal supporter. Towards the end of the match, it became clear that we were going to lose. So we'd all but given up. Suddenly a voice roared from the touchline: 'Ollerton!' (You know it's serious when they use your surname.) 'It's OK to lose, but don't quit!' That truth spurred me on to play to the final whistle. In life we will sometimes feel like we are losing. But through the pages of Scripture the voice of a heavenly Father roars us on . . . until that day when he will welcome us home.

So I encourage you to *keep going with the Bible* because *the Bible will keep you going*:

> For everything that was written in the past was written to teach us, so that through the *endurance* taught in the Scriptures and the *encouragement* they provide we might have hope.
>
> *Romans 15:4*

# Discussion questions

*These questions provide a useful resource for small group discussions.*

## Introducing the Bible

At the end of *Introducing the Bible*, take a moment to review the ground we have covered:

- What experiences have you had of reading the Bible? What are some of the challenges you've faced with it?
- This section introduced the Bible in three ways:

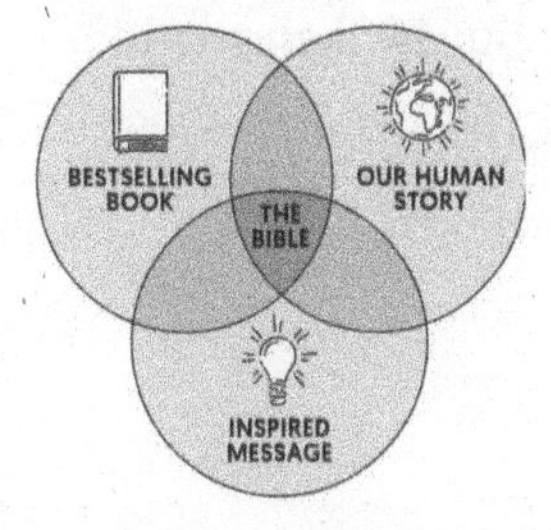


- If the Bible is the world's bestselling book, why can it be difficult to read? How can we become more confident with this ancient library and its different styles of writing?
- Does it surprise you that the Bible is one big story? What are the threads linking it all together?

- 'Something mysterious happens when people engage with the Bible' (p. 21). What do you make of this claim? Have you ever experienced this?

## Part 1: Origins

At the end of *Origins*, take a moment to review what we've learned and how it makes sense of life:

- Why is tracing ancestry and family history so popular today?
- How would you respond to the objection that we can't take Genesis seriously because it contradicts modern science?
- Based on the world we see around us, what can we deduce about what God is like?
- Read Genesis 1:26–8 again. What might it mean to be made in the image of God? How should this affect the way we see ourselves and treat others?
- How does the story of Adam and Eve being tempted by the serpent in Genesis 3 still resonate with our experiences today?
- Read the promise in Genesis 3:15 and consider the flood story and the rainbow. How do these point forwards and declare hope over our broken world?
- Overall, how has the origins story in Genesis helped you make sense of life today?

## Part 2: Exodus

At the end of *Exodus*, take a moment to review what we've learned and how it makes sense of life:

- How does Western culture define freedom? Why does this not seem to work in the end?

- What feels like your 'Egypt' or Pharaoh-like challenges at the moment?
- How has Jesus fulfilled the story of Exodus in the ultimate sense?
- In what ways do we experience increased freedom when we choose to live God's way?
- How can the story of Exodus inspire us to work for justice and freedom today?
- Overall, how has the story of Exodus helped you make sense of life today?

## Part 3: Exile

At the end of *Exile*, take a moment to review what we've learned and how it makes sense of life:

- How does the Bible's concept of *shalom* help us appreciate what true peace really means?
- In what sense are we all living away from home, in a state of exile? How do we experience the sharp end of this in everyday realities?
- During the era of the Judges and Kings, Israel got stuck in negative cycles. What patterns of behaviour in our lives rob us of peace? How can we end these negative cycles?
- In the sixth century BC, the Israelites experienced the darkness of exile. When have you faced seasons of suffering and pain? How have you, or people you know, experienced God's peace in and through the storms of life?
- Despite exile, Daniel shows that God's people can 'win away from home'. What specific practices can help us stand strong in a hostile culture?
- Overall, how has the Bible's story of exile and peace helped make sense of life today?

## Part 4: Messiah

At the end of *Messiah*, take a moment to review what we've learned and how it makes sense of life:

- What are some of the main differences between the way our culture defines love and the way God's love is revealed through Jesus?
- 'Messiah' means 'the anointed king'. What is God's kingdom like if Jesus is the one who rules it? Think about the way he treated people, his teaching and his healing ministry.
- How would you respond to the question: 'If Jesus was so good, why did he die like a criminal?'
- The cross has become the globally recognised logo for the Christian faith. How does this symbol of torture and execution reveal the extent of God's love for us?
- What piece of evidence for the resurrection do you find most compelling and why? What difference does it make if Jesus really rose again?
- Overall, how has this section on the Messiah helped make sense of life?

## Part 5: Spirit

At the end of *Spirit*, take a moment to review what we've learned and how it makes sense of life:

- In what ways is true community a challenge in our modern culture? Why do so many of us experience loneliness in a hyperconnected age?
- What has been your experience of the Holy Spirit? How can you open up your life more to his empowering presence?

- The book of Acts tells the story of the early church. What made their community life so radical and attractive (e.g. Acts 2:42–7; Galatians 3:28)?
- What do you think of when you hear the word 'church'? How has the book of Acts helped you reimagine what Christian community can be like?
- The mission of Acts continues today. Now we are called to faithful 'impro!'. In what practical ways can you play your part and make a difference where you are?
- Overall, how has this section on the Spirit and community helped you make sense of life today?

## Part 6: Hope

At the end of *Hope*, take a moment to review what we've learned and how it makes sense of life:

- What is true hope and why is it such a vital energy for humans? What false hopes do we put our trust in as society?
- How does the resurrection of Jesus reveal the nature of our future hope?
- Dramatic visions at the end of Revelation reveal our ultimate destination. What surprised you about the physical and sociable nature of our ultimate hope?
- Read Revelation 22:1–4. What are you most looking forward to about our future home and why?
- How can this hope on the far horizon inspire us today? How does it change the way we approach bereavement and death? How does it shape our priorities in life?
- Overall, how has this section on the theme of hope helped make sense of your life today?

# Further Resources

## To download or watch

*The Bible Course: Explore the BIG Story* (Andrew Ollerton, Bible Society)
An eight-session course, showing visually how the whole Bible fits together. It includes video teaching, discussion time, personal reflections and daily readings.

*The Bible Project* (Tim Mackie and Jon Collins, bibleproject.com)
Videos that introduce each book and major Bible themes in a visual way.

*The Bible App (YouVersion)*
Bible-reading plans that include devotional reflections, Bible passages and video content.

*Bible in One Year (BioY) App* (Nicky and Pippa Gumbel, Alpha)
Journey through the Bible with daily applications and prayers linked to Old and New Testament readings.

## To read or listen to

*NIV Study Bible* (Hodder & Stoughton)

*The Drama of Scripture: Finding Our Place in the Biblical Story* (Craig Bartholomew and Michael Goheen, Baker, 2004)

*All Things New: Joining God's Story of Recreation* (Pete Hughes, David C. Cook, 2020)

*Why Trust the Bible? Answers to Ten Tough Questions* (Amy Orr-Ewing, IVP, revised edition 2020)

*How to Read the Bible for All Its Worth* (Gordan Fee and Douglas Stuart, Zondervan, 2014)

*Read the Bible for Life* (George Guthrie, Broadman & Holman, 2011)

*The Art of Reading Scripture* (Ellen Davis & Richard Mays, Eerdmans, 2003)

# Notes

## Prologue

1 G. K. Chesterton, *Orthodoxy* (New York: Como Classics, 2007), p. 41.
2 'On Fairy Stories' in *Essays Presented to Charles Williams* (Grand Rapids: Eerdmans, 1966), pp. 62–3 (emphasis added). He went on to say of the Christian story: 'There is no tale ever told that men would rather find was true.'
3 Quoted in 'Humans are more than their bodies', Ruth Jackson Ravenscroft, *Church Times*, https://churchtimes.co.uk/articles/2019/26-July/features/humans-are-more-than-their-bodies.
4 Bear Grylls, *Soul Fuel: A Daily Devotional* (London: Hodder & Stoughton, 2019), p. 3.
5 From their song 'The Cave'.
6 This quotation is taken from Gregory's Latin commentary on the book of Job in the Bible. I have used the translation provided by Andy Naselli's blog post: 'On Swimming Elephants'. http://andynaselli.com/on-swimming-elephants.

## Introducing the Bible

1 See http://chinachristiandaily.com/news/church_ministry/2019-11-15/amity-printing-celebrates-production-of-200-million-bibles-8659.
2 The Bible doesn't actually appear in the *New York Times* or *Sunday Times* lists but, on aggregate, worldwide, it continues to top the charts. See https://www.guinnessworldrecords.com/world-records/best-selling-book-of-non-fiction.
3 See https://www.nytimes.com/1982/04/11/books/imaginative-proclamation.html.
4 In an online interview debate with Susan Blackmore, hosted by Justin Brierley on Premier Christian Radio, Saturday, 9 June 2018.
5 https://www.bbc.co.uk/programmes/b03bpxxq.
6 Quoted in Cynthia Inniss, *Escaping Obscurity: Napoleon Encounters Jesus* (Cynmar Enterprises, 2014), p. 6.

## Part 1: Origins

1 Studies by clinical psychologists have demonstrated that a deep-rooted sense of heritage increases our emotional stability so that we can flourish in the world. See, for example, https://www.nytimes.com/2013/03/17/fashion/the-family-stories-that-bind-us-this-life.html. As parents, my wife and I have noticed how much our kids benefit from looking through family photo albums and rehearsing memories. Try it sometime, if you have children.
2 Like many books of the Bible, the title 'Genesis' is derived from the first word that opens the book.
3 Neil Postman, 'Science and the Story that We Need', an

online article for *First Things* (January 1997): https://www.firstthings.com/article/1997/01/science-and-the-story-that-we-need.

4 *The Blind Watchmaker* (New York: W. W. Norton, 1986), p. 136.

5 Ernest's book is well worth a read: *Can We Believe Genesis Today?* (London: IVP, 2005).

6 *The Language of God: A Scientist Presents Evidence for Belief* (London: Simon & Schuster, 2007).

7 *Miracles: A Preliminary Study* (London: Collins, 1947), p. 110.

8 See *God's Undertaker: Has Science Buried God?* (Oxford: Lion, 2009).

9 I picked up this helpful distinction ('to us' versus 'for us') from the work of John Walton, though I have applied it differently. See *The Lost World of Genesis One* (Downers Grove: IVP, 2009).

10 See Chapters 2, 3 and 4 in Justin's book *Unbelievable?* (SPCK, 2017).

11 Brian Cox and Andrew Cohen, *Human Universe* (London: Collins, 2014), p. 4.

12 From *Aurora Leigh*, 1856.

13 Cox and Cohen, *Human Universe*, Introduction.

14 Yoko Ono, 'Spec of Dust' in *New York Rock* (Capitol, 1994).

15 *On Ecclesiastes* (4.1). In this sermon, Gregory attacked slavery in a manner that was unparalleled in ancient literature.

16 In a sermon entitled 'The American Dream' (4 July 1965).

17 *Dominion: The Making of the Western Mind* (London: Little, Brown, 2019), XXV.

18 'The Weight of Glory', a sermon first preached in Oxford

on 8 June 1941. See *The Weight of Glory* (San Francisco: HarperOne, 2015), p. 46.

19 https://www.dailymail.co.uk/femail/article-477573/Did-Mother-Teresa-believe-God.html.

20 The *Independent* reported this bizarre incident at the time: https://www.independent.co.uk/sport/olympics/shot-at-wrong-target-costs-rifleman-gold-587595.html. Sadly Emmons also missed out on gold in the final of the Beijing Olympics in 2008. He was ahead with one shot to go when his gun went off accidentally while still lining up.

21 *Confessions* (1.1.1).

22 Desmond Tutu, *God Has a Dream: A Vision of Hope for Our Times* (London: Ebury Publishing, 2005), p. 25.

23 This alludes to a quote by Randy Alcorn in his book, *Heaven* (Carol Stream: Tyndale House Publishing, 2007). We will return to it in Part 6.

24 W. B. Yeats, 'The Second Coming'.

25 https://www.nationalgeographic.co.uk/environment-and-conservation/2018/05/plastic-bag-found-bottom-worlds-deepest-ocean-trench.

26 *Being Human: Bodies, Minds, Persons* (London: SPCK, 2018).

27 Cited in Beena Rammohan, *Letters Beneath the Willow Tree*, 'Epilogue'.

## Part 2: Exodus

1 See Robert Bellah (ed.), *Habits of the Heart: Individualism and Commitment in American Life* (California: University of California Press, 1985).

2 *Not in God's Name: Confronting Religious Violence* (London: Hodder & Stoughton, 2015), p. 13.

3 *Reappearing Church* (Chicago: Moody Publishers), p. 139.

4 *The Big Ego Trip: Finding True Significance in a Culture of Self-esteem* (London: IVP), p. 20.

5 In the New Testament, the birth of Jesus is framed this way and Mary's famous song, the Magnificat, delights in the way God exalts the oppressed. See Luke 1:46-55.

6 This observation comes from Craig Bartholomew and Michael Goheen in *The Drama of Scripture: Finding Our Place in the Biblical Story* (Grand Rapids: Baker, 2004), p. 53.

7 *Against Heresies* (4.20.7).

8 Quoted in Robert Edward Luccock,*If God Be For Us: Sermons on the Gifts of the Gospel* (New York: Harper, 1954), p. 38.

9 This illustration is taken from the *Bible in One Year* resource by Nicky Gumbel (Day 44).

10 *Counterfeit Gods* (London: Hodder & Stoughton, 2009), p. xviii.

11 C. S. Lewis, *The Weight of Glory* (San Francisco: HarperOne, 2015). We will develop this idea in more detail in the *Exile* section.

12 *Counterfeit Gods*, pp.171–2.

13 An article in *The Times* newspaper entitled 'Having God in a squad is no longer mocked' (Matt Dickinson), Friday 22 May 2020, p. 58.

14 Bob Dylan, 'Gotta Serve Somebody'. Copyright © 1979 by Special Rider Music.

15 From their song 'Sigh No More'.

16 In Wilberforce's journal.

17 Joyce Meyer, *I Dare You: Embrace Life with Passion* (London: Hodder & Stoughton, 2009), p. 115.

## Part 3: Exile

1 *Shalom* appears over 250 times in the Old Testament. The Greek equivalent in the New Testament is *eirene* ('peace').
2 See https://www.statnews.com/2017/03/15/anxiety-rich-country-poor-country/.
3 This idea goes all the way back to a book by W. H. Auden, *The Age of Anxiety* (New York: Random House, 1947).
4 *The Weight of Glory* (San Francisco: HarperOne, 2015).
5 For a helpful approach to this knotty issue see: Joshua Ryan Butler, *The Skeletons in God's Closet: The Mercy of Hell, the Surprise of Judgment, the Hope of Holy War* (Nashville: Thomas Nelson, 2014).
6 Theologian Cornelius Plantinga refers to sin and its consequences as the vandalism of *shalom*. See *Not the Way It's Supposed to Be: A Breviary of Sin* (Grand Rapids: Eerdmans, 1995).
7 In *Clippings from my Notebook* (London: Triangle, 1983), p. 129.
8 Some of my favourite Proverbs capture this practical wisdom: 'Above all else, guard your heart, for everything you do flows from it' (Proverbs 4:23); 'Start children off on the way they should go, and even when they are old they will not turn from it' (Proverbs 22:6); 'As a dog returns to its vomit, so fools repeat their folly' (Proverbs 26:11).
9 See Philip Sheldrake, *The Business of Influence: Reframing Marketing and PR for the Digital Age* (Chichester: Wiley, 2011), p. 153.
10 Cited in the Alpha Course, Session 1.
11 *River Out of Eden: A Darwinian View of Life* (London: Weidenfeld & Nicolson), p. 132.
12 In this sense, exile traces back to a principle that Moses

had spelt out long before Israel entered the Promised Land: 'See, I set before you today life and prosperity, death and destruction . . . if your heart turns away and you are not obedient . . . You will not live long in the land you are [about] to enter' (Deuteronomy 30:15, 17, 18).

13 C. S. Lewis, *The Problem of Pain* (New York: HarperCollins, 2001), p. 91.

14 Again, it's not as simple as good versus bad. Babylon had a lot going for it. It rose out of the Mesopotamian desert in a spectacular way, with hanging gardens that were a wonder of the ancient world.

15 As David Kinnaman puts it: 'We are on the front end of a digital revolution that is tinkering with what it means to be human . . . we are all residents of digital Babylon. We are all exiles now.' See *Faith for Exiles* (Grand Rapids: Baker Books, 2019), p. 20.

16 *Twelve Rules for Life* (Toronto: Random House, 2018), pp. 147–9.

17 'On Fairy Stories' in *Essays Presented to Charles Williams* (Grand Rapids: Eerdmans, 1966), p. 63.

18 Lewis, *The Weight of Glory*.

## Interlude

1 This eighteenth-century hymn was composed in Latin (*Veni, Veni Emmanuel*). It traces back to medieval Advent antiphons. This is an English translation of two of the verses by John Mason Neale from *Hymns Ancient and Modern*. The verses capture deep longings that surface throughout Israel's story.

## Part 4: Messiah

1 *As You Like It*, Act 5, Scene 2.
2 C. S. Lewis' book, *The Four Loves* (New York: HarperCollins, 2002), provides a helpful overview of four Greek words commonly used for 'love' in the ancient world.
3 *The Denial of Death* (New York: Simon & Schuster, 1973), pp. 166–7.
4 *Soul Fuel: A Daily Devotional* (London: Hodder & Stoughton, 2019), p. 9.
5 Cited in *Soul Fuel*, p. 9.
6 'On Fairy Stories' in *Essays Presented to Charles Williams* (Grand Rapids: Eerdmans, 1966). p. 63.
7 Bill Johnson, *Jesus Christ is Perfect Theology* (Destiny Image, 2017).
8 For a helpful summary of the reliability of the Gospels, see Peter Williams, *Can we Trust the Gospels?* (Wheaton: Crossway, 2018).
9 *Mere Christianity* (Glasgow: Fontana Books, 1952), pp. 52–3.
10 A point I once saw made in an edition of the *Jesus Army* 'Street Paper' publication.
11 For an overview of the 'minimal facts' approach to the evidence for the resurrection, see Gary Habermas, *The Case for the Resurrection of Christ* (Grand Rapids: Kregel Publications, 2004).
12 N. T. Wright, 'The New Unimproved Jesus', *Christianity Today*, 13 September 1993.
13 Aquinas wrote about this in his epic work: *Summa Theologica*, III, q. 54, a.4.
14 I have drawn some of the ideas for this illustration from a blog by Barbie Swihart called 'Life in the Spacious Place'.

See https://lifeinthespaciousplace.wordpress.com/2017/01/23/kintsugi-beauty-in-the-broken-places/.

## Part 5: Spirit

1 https://www.nytimes.com/2016/12/22/upshot/how-social-isolation-is-killing-us.html.
2 *The Connected Generation*, Barna: https://theconnectedgeneration.com/key-findings/.
3 C. S. Lewis, 'The Inner Ring', Memorial Lecture, King's College London, 1944.
4 'As Kingfishers Catch Fire'.
5 For a helpful TED talk on this subject see Brene Brown, 'The Power of Vulnerability', https://www.ted.com/talks/brene_brown_the_power_of_vulnerability?language=en.
6 Eugene Peterson, *Christ Plays in Ten Thousand Places: A Conversation in Spiritual Theology* (Grand Rapids: Eerdmans, 2008).
7 *The Purpose Driven Life: What On Earth Am I Here For?* (Grand Rapids: Zondervan, 2002), p. 121.
8 Tertullian made this point in *Apologeticus*, which he addressed directly to the Roman Empire and which gave a forceful defence of Christian belief and practice.
9 In Acts 13:1 there is a beautiful window into the diversity of the early church: 'Now in the church at Antioch there were prophets and teachers: Barnabas [a Jew from Cyprus], Simeon called Niger [an African], Lucius of Cyrene [from Syria], Manaen (who had been brought up with Herod the tetrarch) [from a privileged background] and Saul [the former persecutor].'
10 An article in the *Telegraph* newspaper captured the headline: 'China on course to become world's most Christian nation within 15 years' (19 April 2014): https://www.

telegraph.co.uk/news/worldnews/asia/china/10776023/China-on-course-to-become-worlds-most-Christian-nation-within-15-years.html.

11 See Kyle Harper, *From Shame to Sin: The Christian Transformation of Sexual Morality in Late Antiquity* (Cambridge, MA: Harvard University Press, 2013); Tom Holland, *Dominion: The Making of the Western Mind* (London: Little, Brown, 2019).

12 N. T. Wright, *New Testament and the People of God* (London: SPCK, 1992), pp. 139-43. I have adapted the illustration slightly for the purposes of this book.

13 Eusebius, 'Festival Letters' in Rodney Stark, *The Rise of Early Christianity* (New York: HarperCollins, 1997), p. 82.

14 This is the title of an important book by Neil Postman.

15 In *Culture Making: Recovering our Creative Calling* (Downers Grove: IVP, 2008), p. 263.

## Part 6: Hope

1 *Heaven* (Carol Stream: Tyndale House Publishers, 2007), p. 442.

2 I owe the essence of this illustration to Tom Wright who said something similar in an interview on Premier Christian Radio.

3 *Paul: A Biography* (San Francisco: HarperOne, 2018), p. 158.

4 In *The Weight of Glory* (San Francisco: HarperOne, 2015), pp. 42–3.

5 *The Great Divorce* (Glasgow: Fontana Books, 1972), p. 28.

6 *Surprised by Hope* (London: SPCK, 2007), p. 154.

7 *The Last Battle* (London: William Collins, 1989), p. 161.

8 This quote may originally have come from D. L. Moody.

See https://www.christianitytoday.com/ct/2018/february-web-only/billy-graham-viral-quote-on-death-not-his-d-l-moody.html.

9 In an interview with *Sojourners Magazine*, 24 December 1984. See https://sojo.net/magazine/february-1985/prisoner-hope.

10 C. S. Lewis develops this observation brilliantly in his book *Mere Christianity* (London: Collins, 2012).

11 Attributed to Oliver Wendell Homes.

12 Jackie tells the gripping story in her book, *Chasing the Dragon* (London: Hodder & Stoughton, 2006).

## Epilogue

1 James Clear, *Atomic Habits: Tiny Changes, Remarkable Results* (New York: Random House, 2018), Chapter 2.

2 To find out more about this resource search: 'The Bible Course, Bible Society' or visit https://www.biblesociety.org.uk/explore-the-bible/the-bible-course/

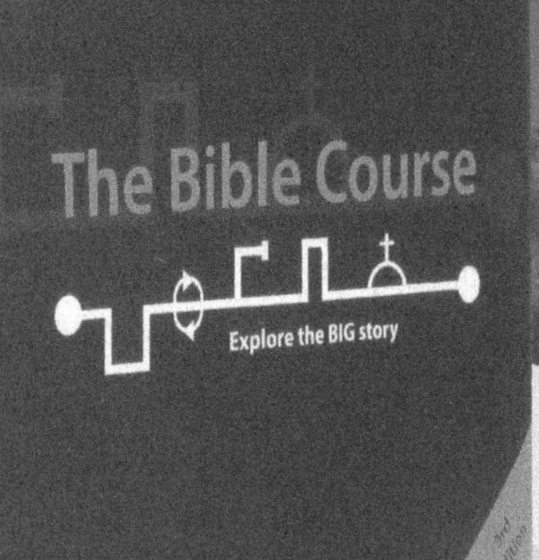

## The Bible Course

Although the Bible is the world's bestselling book, there are still many of us who find it to be big and intimidating.

**But it needn't be that way.**

Using a unique storyline, this eight-session course shows how the key events, books and characters all fit together.

You'll get to see the BIG picture and discover how the Bible applies to your life.

**Visit biblesociety.org.uk/thebiblecourse**